Schmoker has lit a fire in this book to make clear that there are right ways, across all curricula domains, to promote the acquisition of knowledge, deeper understanding, greater curiosity, and fun in learning.

—John Hattie, Laureate Professor at
Melbourne Graduate School of Education

One of those books **every educator needs to read.**

—Dick Allington, educator and author of
What Really Matters for Struggling Readers

Once again, Mike Schmoker takes a wide array of complex concepts and initiatives and weaves them into **a framework that is not only easily understood but translates into immediate action.**

—Robert J. Marzano, C.E.O. of Marzano Research Laboratory
and author of *The Art and Science of Teaching*

Mike Schmoker's FOCUS is clear, concise and authoritative. It will be valuable for teachers, and—dare I say it?—also for those who teach them.

—E.D. Hirsch

This is a book to which many teachers will say "Hallelujah." It challenges educators and policymakers alike to focus on what's most important and not become distracted by numerous "fads." **If we can get our schools focused on the elements Schmoker identifies, more teachers will be achieving dramatic results in their classrooms.**

—David T. Conley, director of the Center
for Educational Policy Research, University of Oregon

Finally, a book that cuts through the noise and helps us return to sensible, authentic teaching. *Focus: Elevating the Essentials to Radically Improve Student Learning* is insightful, practical, and, above all else, inspiring—**a must read** for all teachers, administrators, board members, and policymakers.

—Kelly Gallagher, educator and author of *Readicide:
How Schools Are Killing Reading and What You Can Do About It*

This is a brave, powerful book, brimming with good ideas and plain-spoken common sense. Forswearing the fads of the day, Schmoker reminds us of what the sales force of "new and improved" professional development wants us to forget: We already *know* what good teaching looks like—and we've known it for a while. The real question is: Do we have the will to make it happen? This powerful book shows us the way.

—Sam Wineburg, Margaret Jacks Professor of Education,
Stanford University

If you admired Schmoker's earlier writings, **you won't be able to put this newest entry down.** Once again, he provides a simple way to do a complex thing while supplying a roadmap for real classroom and school improvement. Just think how we might impact student learning if we all put his ideas to work.

—Greg Netzer, principal of Van Horn High School, Independence, Missouri

Mike Schmoker's new book is **brimming with ideas that I immediately want to pass along to the principals, teachers, and district leaders** I work with. [It] is learned, accessible, packed with specific examples, and powerfully convincing.

If you read one book this year, read this one!

—Kim Marshall, author, educator, and editor of *The Marshall Memo*

Mike Schmoker nails it again. His guidelines for clarifying what we teach and how we teach should bear positive results across this great land.

—Carol Jago, president of the National Council of Teachers of English

In his most ambitious book to date, Mike Schmoker moves beyond generalities about education in the United States to offer *very* specific advice on how to improve schools. Any educator who is willing to consider thoughtful critiques of traditional practices and the thinking behind those practices will be intrigued (and challenged) by Schmoker's ideas.

—Richard DuFour, educator and coauthor of *Learning by Doing: A Handbook for Professional Learning Communities at Work*

This book will help new teachers focus on the essentials of curriculum and lessons, and will help veterans, weary of the perpetual hail of silver bullets, to rediscover the joy of teaching with purpose. Most importantly, this book will help students who are depending on leaders and policymakers to **listen to the evidence, give up the fad of the day, and focus on learning.**

—Douglas B. Reeves, author and founder of Creative Leadership Solutions

Mike Schmoker gets it right in this trenchant diagnosis of why American schools are failing: Even when the teachers are all good, the school curriculum is a poorly organized clutter that diffuses students' attention rather than focusing it on the essentials they need to learn to be college-ready. Schmoker's book itself is **a model of how to cut through the curricular clutter** in precisely the way schools need to do.

—Gerald Graff, 2008 president of the Modern Language Association and author of *Clueless in Academe: How Schooling Obscures the Life of the Mind*

FOCUS

2nd Edition

Other Books by Mike Schmoker

*Results Now: How We Can Achieve Unprecedented Improvements
in Teaching and Learning*

*Leading with Focus: Elevating the Essentials for School
and District Improvement*

ASCD MEMBER BOOK

Many ASCD members received this book as a
member benefit upon its initial release.

Learn more at: **www.ascd.org/memberbooks**

MIKE SCHMOKER

FOCUS

ELEVATING
THE ESSENTIALS
to Radically Improve
Student Learning

2nd Edition

ASCD

Alexandria, Virginia USA

1703 N. Beauregard St. • Alexandria, VA 22311-1714 USA
Phone: 800-933-2723 or 703-578-9600 • Fax: 703-575-5400
Website: www.ascd.org • E-mail: member@ascd.org
Author guidelines: www.ascd.org/write

Deborah S. Delisle, *Executive Director;* Stefani Roth, *Publisher;* Genny Ostertag, *Director, Content Acquisitions;* Julie Houtz, *Director, Book Editing & Production;* Joy Scott Ressler, *Editor;* Judi Connelly, *Associate Art Director;* Georgia Park, *Senior Graphic Designer;* Valerie Younkin, *Production Designer;* Mike Kalyan, *Director, Production Services;* Trinay Blake, *E-Publishing Specialist;* Kelly Marshall, *Production Specialist.*

PAPERBACK ISBN: 978-1-4166-2634-3   ASCD product #118044

PDF E-BOOK ISBN: 978-1-4166-2636-7; see Books in Print for other formats.

Quantity discounts are available: e-mail programteam@ascd.org or call 800-933-2723, ext. 5773, or 703-575-5773. For desk copies, go to www.ascd.org/deskcopy.

ASCD Member Book No. FY18-8A (Jul. 2018 PSI+). ASCD Member Books mail to Premium (P), Select (S), and Institutional Plus (I+) members on this schedule: Jan, PSI+; Feb, P; Apr, PSI+; May, P; Jul, PSI+; Aug, P; Sep, PSI+; Nov, PSI+; Dec, P. For current details on membership, see www.ascd.org/membership.

Library of Congress Cataloging-in-Publication Data
Names: Schmoker, Michael J. author.
Title: Focus : elevating the essentials to radically improve student learning / by Mike Schmoker.
Description: Second Edition. | Alexandria, Virginia : ASCD, [2018] | Previous edition: 2011. |
    Includes bibliographical references and index.
Identifiers: LCCN 2018012384 (print) | LCCN 2018013520 (ebook) | ISBN 9781416626367 (PDF)
    | ISBN 9781416626343 (paperback)
Subjects: LCSH: Effective teaching.
Classification: LCC LB1025.3 (ebook) | LCC LB1025.3 .S384 2018 (print) | DDC 371.102--dc23
LC record available at https://lccn.loc.gov/2018012384

26 25 24 23 22 21 20 19 18   1 2 3 4 5 6 7 8 9 10 11 12

For my 5th grade teacher,
Karen Redpath, who inspired me.

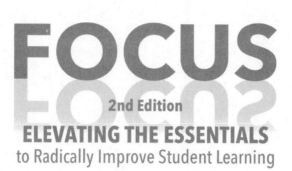

FOCUS

2nd Edition

ELEVATING THE ESSENTIALS

to Radically Improve Student Learning

Foreword to the Second Edition:
The Importance of Evidence

Education is not just another issue. It is the most powerful force for accelerating economic growth, reducing poverty and lifting middle-class living standards. Well-educated adults earn much more, live longer and are happier than poorly educated adults.

—David Leonhardt, *The New York Times*

If David Leonhardt is even half right, educators face a moral obligation: to act on the best evidence-based practices that will ensure that record proportions of students receive a quality education. But we have yet to act on those practices.

Why? Because we continue to be more enamored with "innovation" than with evidence. In the main, educational initiatives are rarely selected on an empirical basis; they are chosen on the basis of "whims, fads, opportunism, and ideology" (Corcoran, Fuhrman, & Belcher, 2001; Sawchuk, 2015). For decades, we have preferred the easier work of adopting new, unproven initiatives to the harder work of *mastering and implementing* proven practices. It is within our power to change this—to enable unprecedented numbers of students to live longer, happier, more productive lives.

In the years since the first edition of this book was published, the case for the evidence-based elements advocated here has grown prodigiously: our best researchers now agree that their effect—if implemented—would be both rapid and dramatic.

That may sound intemperate. It is not. The notion that schools can improve both swiftly and significantly is not new and continues to gain support (Ripley, 2013). Michael Fullan, among our most eminent educational researchers, doesn't hedge: if we actually implemented the most "high-leverage" practices, they would result in "stunningly powerful consequences" for students (Fullan, 2010). And as researcher Bruce Joyce discovered, the best evidence-based practices are (1) virtually *always* effective and (2) they work "*rapidly*"—within the first year of implementation (in D. Sparks, 1998, p. 34). The schools described in these pages affirm this.

In my own effort to promote such "stunningly powerful consequences," I have updated every chapter to help educators navigate recent educational developments and mandates; to share the upsurge in evidence that supports the core elements advocated here; and to add more detailed guidance on how to implement them.

To that end, I have added:

• Late-breaking research and school evidence for the importance of **simplicity**—ensuring that improvement efforts are focused on an exceedingly *clear, minimal* set of essential actions.

• New evidence of the surging concurrence among researchers about the critical role of **coherent, content-rich curriculum** for improving both reading ability and educational quality. Because of this, I have clarified the process for building coherent, literacy-rich curriculum in any discipline.

• A detailed **analysis of the Common Core standards**, which emerged just as the first edition of *Focus* went to press. Since then, we have learned vital information about their best and worst features—and how to implement them successfully.

• An update on the growing acknowledgment of the **power of explicit instruction**—and how it is the friend, not the enemy, of the best open-ended, inquiry-based lessons, projects, and activities.

• A section, in Chapter 3, on the **"obstacles to effective instruction"**—the popular but unproven pedagogic fads and mandates that prevent us from focusing on the most high-leverage, evidence-based practices.

• **Samples of learning objectives** and stems at the end of each of the subject-area chapters, as these critical components of effective teaching continue to be a challenge for many educators.

• Updated treatment of the most **straightforward ways to integrate literacy** into the subject areas that includes a succinct set of **"essential moves of writing instruction"** that any teacher could adapt and implement routinely—*without having to spend excessive time grading papers.*

• Recent information about the **Next Generation Science Standards** (NGSS), which also emerged after the first edition. There is explicit guidance on how to capitalize on the new, reduced "Progressions" (a positive development) while simplifying teachers' use of the (unfortunately) complex ancillary documents. I've also expanded the sections on science inquiry, investigations, and activities.

• Numerous **new tasks, prompts, and questions;** these can form the basis of ready-made, literacy-intensive lessons in each subject area.

• Expanded treatment of how we can create **authentic, high-quality *local* assessments** in every subject area. The effects of such changes would be transformative.

• Enhanced guidance on **how we can significantly increase success rates in mathematics**—in which failure rates are highest. We'll also look (for those interested) at the emerging consensus that math education is still in need of revision—well beyond the Common Core math guidelines.

• **New evidence, from multiple schools**, that reinforces the case that *improvement can occur quite swiftly*—within a single school year of focusing intensively on the best-known practices.

I hope these updates and additions will make this second edition clearer and more helpful to readers as they seek to achieve "stunningly powerful" results in their own schools.

Introduction

The real path to greatness, it turns out, requires simplicity and diligence.... It demands each of us to focus on what is vital—and to eliminate all of the extraneous distractions.

—Jim Collins

*Hedgehogs see what is essential and **ignore the rest.***

—Jim Collins

The argument of this book is fairly simple: that if we focus our efforts on certain amply proven, essential actions, schools will improve dramatically. Numerous studies have demonstrated that such a focus could appreciably decrease most of the achievement gap within five to seven years (Garnaut, 2007; Kane & Hanushek in Haycock, 2005; Marzano, 2003).

But the price for such swift improvement is steep: most schools would have to stop doing almost everything they now do in the name of school improvement. Instead, they would have to focus almost exclusively on implementing "what is essential." Hardest of all, they would have to heed Jim Collins's exhortation to "ignore the rest"—the fads, programs, and innovations that directly prevent our best methods from being consistently employed in classrooms (Collins, 2001a, p. 91). I will address these popular "Obstacles to Effective Instruction" in Chapter 3.

But what is truly "essential" for schools? The evidence points hard to three fundamental elements: reasonably coherent curriculum (*what* we teach); soundly structured lessons (*how* we teach); and large amounts of purposeful reading and writing in every discipline (*authentic literacy*—integral to both what and how we teach). Unfortunately, every credible study confirms that all three are still pushed aside by various initiatives, every year, in the great majority of schools (as we'll see in Chapters 2 and 3).

If we want to improve schooling by large margins, this has to change. We insult and frustrate our teachers and leaders when we keep asking them to adopt complex, unproven methods and initiatives that can't possibly succeed in the absence of sound curriculum, lessons, and literacy practices. These constitute the indisputable—if age-old—core of effective practice of education itself.

In the past few years, I have found that educators yearn to be told something like this:

> We are declaring a moratorium on new initiatives—at least for a time. Instead, we will focus *only* on what will have the most immediate and dramatic effect on learning in your classrooms: ensuring the implementation of just three indisputably proven elements. Moreover, we will not expect you to commit to these strategies until we have fully clarified the evidence base for their unrivaled effectiveness.

If we can maintain such a focus, our schools will make unprecedented progress. Best of all, none of these essential methods need be implemented perfectly. Throughout this book, I'll cite schools and teachers who implement them in ordinary, imperfect ways—and still achieve exceptional results within one or two school years.

The success of such schools points to an exciting prospect: that current levels of educational attainment reflect a system that *isn't operating at even a fraction of its power or potential*. If we can clear away the clutter and focus instead on the best, empirically proven classroom practices, our best days are just ahead of us.

About This Book

Section I, Chapters 1–3, focuses on the power of simplicity—applied to the best evidence on *what* and *how* we should teach. It is intended for all educators.

Chapter 1 is about the need to embrace simplicity—and focuses on the three elements described in the chapter. Indeed, any initiative we adopt *before these three primary elements are implemented* only postpones their implementation and their enormous effects on student learning.

Chapter 2 clarifies the powerful, evidence-based case for coherent curriculum—of *what* we should teach, inclusive of *literacy:* the reading, writing, and discussion that must pervade the disciplines. Such an education is not new, but it has been under siege for decades, the victim of various fads, programs, and ill-conceived state and national standards. The last section of Chapter 2 provides a simple process for how to optimize our use of standards documents as we build a clear, "viable" curriculum for every course.

In **Chapter 3**, I clarify *how* we should teach, inclusive of literacy instruction, in every subject. We'll examine the age-old fundamentals of *effective teaching:* their pedigree and some exciting new findings on their impact. I have also added an essential section on the most popular—but unproven—innovations that are the primary "Obstacles to Effective Instruction." Chapter 3 ends with two simple, straightforward templates for incorporating best practice—which could immediately be used or adapted for most of the instruction we provide, in every subject area.

Section II, Chapters 4–7, is designed to allow secondary teachers or elementary subject-area specialists to read—if they wish—only those subject-area chapters that pertain to their respective discipline.

In **Chapters 4 through 7,** I describe both *what* and *how* we can effectively teach in the four core subject areas—with special emphasis on the following:

- How to navigate the challenges of the new standards documents
  - How to incorporate literacy into each discipline

We've complicated teachers' lives for long enough. It is time to simplify their work in ways that make them *more* effective, but with *less* effort and frustration.

Let's begin by looking at the concepts that make these aspirations possible: *simplicity, clarity,* and *priority.*

SECTION I

First Things First: *What* We Teach,
How We Teach—and Literacy

The Importance of Simplicity, Clarity, and Priority

The Key to Success? Doing Less.

—*The Wall Street Journal*, 2018

The first principle of simplicity is: reduce.

—John Maeda, 2006

As odd as it sounds, organizational health and improvement are largely the result of simple, well-known strategies and structures (Pfeffer & Sutton, 2000). In education, this means that the general underperformance of schools is directly attributable to a failure to implement three simple, well-known elements: coherent curriculum, soundly structured lessons, and adequate amounts of fairly traditional literacy activities. We love to talk about these elements, but they are rarely implemented.

As Allan Odden writes, our failure to improve schools isn't because we lack funding or know-how. What we lack are the "will and persistence" to maintain a focus on the best practices *that we already know but that are grossly underutilized* (Odden, 2009, p. 22). As Jim Collins writes, the key to success is not innovation; it is a combination of "simplicity and diligence" applied with fierce, exclusive devotion to what is truly most effective (Collins, 2001b, p. 104).

According to Michael Fullan, decades of studies have demonstrated that the key to success is neither innovation nor technology. Rather, it is an abiding commitment to the "smallest number of high-leverage, easy-to-understand actions that unleash *stunningly powerful consequences*" (Fullan, 2010; emphasis added).

This book argues that for the majority of schools, the three elements addressed here meet Fullan's criteria better than all other initiatives combined; they are indeed few in number, exceedingly high-leverage, and easy to understand. You'll find evidence for these claims in every chapter. For that reason, these actions all but guarantee "stunningly powerful consequences."

First Things First—The Three Elements

We'll begin with a brief description of the three elements, which will be fully clarified in the next two chapters (and for the subject areas outlined in Chapters 4 through 7). As these elements are so potent, they need not be implemented perfectly or with any special skill. Their impact will be largely realized when most teachers simply apply them reasonably well and consistently.

The elements are:

1. *What we teach.* This refers to the actual implementation of a coherent, user-friendly curriculum, with topics and standards collectively selected by a team of teachers from the school or district. The number of essential skills and topics must not be excessive; it should reflect a deliberate reduction of the standards contained in our typically verbose standards documents (Marzano, 2003). As we'll see, this especially applies to English language arts (ELA) standards, even in the Common Core era. Such "guaranteed and viable curriculum" (Marzano, 2003, p. 22) is perhaps the most significant school factor that affects learning. But it is found in exceedingly few schools (Berliner, 1984; DuFour & Marzano, 2011; Hirsch, 2016; Marzano, 2003; Schmidt, 2008).

2. *How we teach.* Think of this as ordinary, structurally sound instruction that consists of just a few elements that educators have

known about for decades but that few educators are ever given time and opportunity to master. As we'll see in Chapter 3, these elements were formally codified in the 1960s (but are essentially thousands of years old). The pivotal feature of such instruction is the conscientious effort, *throughout the lesson,* to ensure that all students are learning each step or segment *before the teacher moves on* to the next one. If such instruction is implemented with any consistency, its impact would be as powerful as any action schools would take (Black & Wiliam, 1998; Wiliam, 2007).

3. *Authentic literacy.* This is integral to both what and how we teach. It is, in the words of Phillips and Wong, the "spine" that "holds everything together" in all subject areas (2010, p. 41). In this book, "literacy" or "authentic literacy" simply means purposeful—and usually expository, argumentative, or interpretive—reading, discussion, and writing (Lunsford & Ruszkiewicz, 2009). Authentic literacy embraces the best aspects and emphases of the Common Core, but (as will be explained) it rejects the bulk of the grade-by-grade minutiae found in the standards documents. Genuine literacy is still the unrivaled key to learning both content *and* thinking skills. But it is categorically different from the so-called "reading skills" and pseudo-standards that continue to wreak havoc in language arts. We'll examine the case for very different kinds of literacy standards—and skills—in Chapter 4.

Implementation of the elements just described will benefit immeasurably when teachers work in teams—that is, in true "professional learning communities" in which curriculum, units, and lessons are continuously developed and refined on the basis of assessment results (DuFour & Marzano, 2011; Schmoker, 2006).

A focus on these three elements would have more impact than all other initiatives combined. In the majority of our schools, they will ensure that record numbers of students are prepared for college, careers, and citizenship. They would wholly redefine what schools can accomplish with children from every socioeconomic stratum. Because of this, their implementation should be our most morally urgent, jealously guarded priority: the ongoing focus of every team meeting, every professional development session, and every faculty and central office meeting. *Until these elements are reasonably well implemented,* it makes little sense to chase after new programs, technology, or other innovations.

Once these elements are implemented, any evidence-based innovation is fair game, as long as it does not dilute or distract us from these always-vulnerable priorities.

Does this sound too "simplistic"? Can such simplicity really be the elusive key to better schools? To get some perspective, let's step outside our own profession for a moment.

The Power of Simplicity, Clarity, and Priority

Consider a football team that loses about half of its games, year after year. (This is a bit autobiographical; I coached football for a short time.) Each week, the coaches scour the Internet to find new, complex plays. This confuses the players, who never mastered the last set of plays. All the while, the coaches never take note of something boring but important: the performance of their offensive line. If they paid closer attention to what every coach knows, they would see that their linemen have never mastered the timeless fundamentals of effective blocking, such as footwork and body position. These fundamentals make a literal "game-changing" difference. Therefore, the solution to this team's mediocre performance is quite simple: stop introducing new plays and start focusing strenuously on the most mundane but hugely effective blocking techniques *until they are mastered by all of the lineman.* The results would be immediate and significant.

Now imagine a hospital in which infection rates are high. (This is a true story.) Internal research reveals this to be the number one cause of illness and mortality at that location. All of the staff know the small handful of procedures that inhibit infection. According to one doctor, these "are no-brainers; they have been known and taught for years." But, alas, doctors and staff don't implement them consistently, even as they continue to attend various conferences and training sessions in complex, cutting-edge practices and procedures. In fact, the hospital (like the football coaches) seldom acquaints the staff with the ironclad case *that these simple, well-known hygienic procedures are directly linked to life, death, and infection rates.* The solution to this hospital's problem is simple, not complex: the powerful evidence for these practices is shared with staff, and then a short checklist is generated, followed by training in each of the procedures. In addition, the use of the checklist is monitored to ensure that all medical staff implement these practices consistently.

The result? In two years, the infection rate plummets from 11 percent to 0 percent. These simple, easy-to-implement measures also prevent eight deaths during that period and save the hospital approximately $2 million in malpractice lawsuits (Henig, 2009).

If we educators can't see ourselves in these two examples, I fear for us. They clarify why so many schools fall short of their potential: because we have yet to focus our time and attention on the mastery of simple, familiar practices that would have the swiftest and most significant impact on achievement (i.e., the implementation of common curriculum, effective lessons, and authentic literacy). We don't even share the evidence for why these deserve to be our highest priority.

Our failure to be clear and focused prevails even as we continue to attend conferences, workshops, and book studies; as we adopt complex programs and initiatives; and as we largely ignore these elements in the overwhelming majority of American classrooms (DuFour & Marzano, 2011; Hirsch, 2016; Pianta, Belsky, Houts, & Morrison, 2007; Schmoker, 2006).

In subsequent chapters, we'll see detailed evidence for why these elements should be our highest priority—implemented *before* we adopt any other initiative. To ensure this, perhaps we should require a warning label like this one on all notices of upcoming workshops, trainings, conferences, or book studies:

If you or your staff do not already implement a reasonably sound, common curriculum that (1) *is taught with the use of the most essential, well-known elements of effective lessons, and* (2) *includes ample amounts of meaningful reading and writing, then please don't sign up for this training. It will have no effect on learning in your classroom or school. Master the above fundamental practices first. Then, if you still need this workshop (and you might not), we look forward to seeing you. Have a nice day.*

Three Books That Reinforce the Power of Simplicity

Priority is itself a function of simplicity. It dictates that we select, clarify, and then focus on only a few things at a time: what is most likely to help us achieve our goals. Education has never been so beholden to complexity, the enemy of clarity and priority. This is especially apparent in our complex teacher evaluation templates (Dreilinger, 2013; TNTP, 2013) and our inanely-phrased standards documents (Garner, 2010; Ravitch, 2013; Schmoker & Graff, 2011). Three books can help us to correct this.

The Art of "Ignoring": *Good to Great*, by Jim Collins

Jim Collins's book *Good to Great* (2001a) is the best-selling organizational improvement book of the last generation. Collins found that "the essence of profound insight" into organizational improvement "is simplicity" (p. 91). That's why he reveres the hedgehog of Aesop's fables, who does one thing well (rolls into a ball to protect itself), as opposed to the fox, who plans and plots as he "pursues many ends at the same time." Foxes aren't simple; they are "scattered and diffused, moving on many levels" (p. 91). That's why they fail. In contrast, hedgehogs focus only on "what is essential and ignore the rest" (p. 91).

On some level, the educational community knows "what is essential." But it has never clarified or reinforced its priorities assiduously. In addition, it is especially difficult for us to "ignore the rest":

the endless parade of new programs or innovations that distract us from those few, powerful actions and structures that are the soul of good schooling.

An ironclad law is at work here: we will never master or implement what is most important for kids if we continue to pursue new initiatives *before* we implement our highest priority strategies and structures. Collins (2005) had schools in mind when he wrote that "social-sector organizations" must overcome their addiction to doing too many things. To succeed, they must "attain piercing clarity" about what is truly most effective and "then exercise the relentless discipline to say, 'No thank you' to opportunities that fail the hedge-hog test" (p. 17).

It's All About Implementation: *The Knowing–Doing Gap*, by Jeffrey Pfeffer and Robert Sutton

Simplicity, clarity, and priority are intimately linked. For an organization to maintain a focus on its highest priorities, it must routinely clarify them so that everyone in the organization knows implicitly what to do and *what not to do*. Priorities are fragile. If they aren't regularly clarified, practiced, and refined, they are always at the mercy of our natural forgetfulness, and a failure to protect them from the encroachment of new, but far less effective, practices or programs.

According to Jeffrey Pfeffer and Robert Sutton in *The Knowing–Doing Gap*, leaders resist simplicity but are enamored with novelty and complexity. This tendency prevents them from implementing their core priorities (Pfeffer & Sutton, 2000, p. 33). The result is stagnation or decline. "Complexity," the authors warn, is the enemy of effective action and implementation.

Worse still, leaders have a bias against "old ideas and simple prescriptions," even though these old, simple ideas are the key to better results (p. 53). Many leaders would rather launch new initiatives because it excuses them from the harder work of ensuring that their highest, simplest priorities are implemented—that is, are "actually done" (p. 54).

In contrast, the most successful leaders are those who know that "success depends largely on *implementing what is already known*" (p. 14; emphasis added). They know that "simple prescriptions" conveyed with "clarity and simplicity" are the hallmarks of effective action and leadership (p. 55). At the successful companies profiled by Pfeffer and Sutton, the primary driver of improvement was "the implementation of simple knowledge" (p. 15).

It is critical that schools learn that "best practice" is rarely *new* practice. On the contrary, the most effective actions are "well-known practices, with the extra dimension that they [are] *reinforced and carried out reliably*" (p. 14). Are the most effective, evidence-based practices "reinforced and carried out reliably" in our schools? Usually not, according to every credible study going back to the 1970s (Darling-Hammond, 2010; DuFour & Marzano, 2011; Hirsch, 2016; Schmoker, 2006). To ensure that they are, we must make continuous efforts to *clarify, reinforce, and reward* their mastery and implementation by teams and teachers.

Which brings us to the findings of Marcus Buckingham.

"Lopsided Focus": *The One Thing You Need to Know*, by Marcus Buckingham

In *The One Thing You Need to Know,* Marcus Buckingham (2005) reinforces the principle that we accomplish more when we focus on less. He found that successful organizations carefully determine their focus and then make every effort to clarify and simplify those priorities.

According to Buckingham, survey data reveal that employees crave clarity; they want to know precisely what they must do to be most effective—and not be distracted from that. Their highest priorities must be clarified incessantly. "Clarity," writes Buckingham, "is the antidote to anxiety... if you do nothing else as a leader, be clear" (2005, p. 146). In his interviews with employees in multiple organizations, he found that "everywhere, the wish was the same: 'Get me to the core'" (p. 3); that is, "relentlessly clarify our primary focus— and then let us concentrate on it alone." And protect us, as DuFour

(2007), in reviewing Buckingham's book, writes, from new initiatives that wash upon school employees "in waves" (p. 69).

To protect the core, leaders must "sift through the clutter" in order to "apply disproportionate pressure in a few selected areas" (Buckingham, 2005, p. 188). This "lopsided focus" fuels people's productivity, creativity, and morale (p. 26). Less is more.

Leaders must be seen as clarifiers, focusers, "keepers of the core" who incessantly "cut through the clutter... to distinguish between what is merely important and what is *imperative... those few things you must never forget*" (Buckingham, 2005, p. 26; emphasis added). And the core must be monitored obsessively: as Buckingham writes, "you get what you inspect" (p. 176).

Let's now look at how these principles play out in some of the organizations Buckingham describes. Their implications for schooling will be obvious.

Carefully protected focus at Best Buy. Research revealed that the "core" for Best Buy's sales force was the ability to master and then confidently explain the different features of the products they sold. That's it. Since making this discovery, Best Buy reduced their product line by 50 percent so that salespeople could fully master their core inventory. To preserve the core, they try to discard an existing product every time they add a new one. This is the secret to the company's success (Buckingham, 2005, p. 155).

Apple Computer and one thing. Apple Computer was constantly invited to embark on new initiatives and partnerships. But Steve Jobs strenuously resisted heavy lobbying from those within and outside of the company and stayed true to one thing: "figuring out how to invent cool technology but making it wonderfully easy to use." Jobs was as proud, he said, "of the things we have not done as I am of the ones we have done" (Buckingham, 2005, p. 165).

Borax: safety at the core. The Borax mine is north of Edwards Air Force Base in California. The company's in-house research revealed that its simple core was safety: if it could keep its employees safe from on-the-job accidents, then morale, efficiency, and profitability would take care of themselves. And they did—on every metric (Buckingham, 2005, pp. 167–174).

Borax officials knew that the key to protecting the core focus was communication. Leaders constantly reminded, trained, and told stories to make sure that people understood the outsize importance of safety procedures. Every meeting began with an anecdote about how injuries were averted by employees. Leaders displayed and celebrated measurable benchmarks, such as the number of days without an accident, and progress toward monthly and annual accident-reduction goals. Profits soared commensurately.

Simplicity, Clarity, and Priority in Education

In schools, leaders should collect, share, and celebrate analogous data (e.g., on the percentage of classrooms in which common curriculum, sound lessons, and authentic literacy are being consistently implemented). We should celebrate progress in these areas as we guide and advise teachers at faculty meetings. And we should celebrate gains made each grading period on common assessments that themselves reflect the level of implementation of these three areas.

What happens when an individual teacher or a whole school focuses on the most effective, high-priority practices? The following cases are instructive.

Simplicity, Clarity, and Priority in the Classroom

Some might remember a teacher I described in *Results Now* (Schmoker, 2006). His teaching consisted of the oldest, best-known practices. His only "technology" was an overhead projector. I observed him a few times during his second year at the lowest-achieving high school in our community. I noted that all he did was *actually teach* a sound English curriculum, rich in reading and writing, using ordinary, structurally sound lessons. I will elaborate on such lessons in later chapters, but in essence, his whole-class lessons started with a clear learning objective. He then taught in short instructional "chunks," punctuated by multiple cycles of guided practice; brief, purposeful pair-share opportunities; and "checks for understanding," followed by reteaching, when necessary. None of his teaching reflected *any recent innovations whatsoever.*

The result? The success rate in his classes alone was so high that his *entire school* made the largest writing gains in the state (85 percent of students passed the high school exit exam, up from 59 percent). Moreover, his school outperformed the other two schools in the city, despite their overwhelming demographic advantages. His simple, effective teaching and curriculum obliterated the socioeconomic factor for his students—in *a single school year* (a phenomenon we'll find in multiple schools described in this book).

Simplicity, Clarity, and Priority in One School and One District

Years ago, I was fortunate enough to teach at a middle school in which both curriculum and instructional priorities were made crystal clear. They were clarified in the interview process and reinforced at every faculty and department meeting. For those of us teaching English, priorities included the expectation that we taught structurally sound lessons (in which we had extensive training and follow-up) and that students would learn to write effectively by completing two substantive, career-/college-preparatory writing assignments per grading period. These priorities were reinforced and clarified at faculty and department meetings. In addition, leaders routinely monitored to ensure their implementation. Professional development was focused exclusively on these priorities, and it was *internal,* provided largely by department heads. In addition to classroom observations, school leaders met with teams briefly, each quarter, to discuss end-of-quarter evidence of student performance for improvement purposes (e.g., grade book data, the number of books read and papers written). If these conferences or observations revealed that we needed help implementing the curriculum or sound instruction, we were mentored by an effective teacher until we had improved our performance.

As a result of such simple, focused efforts, virtually every teacher in that school *actually taught* the curriculum and *consistently provided* sound lessons, almost every day. At this school, there was no test preparation whatsoever, but our test scores were among the very highest in the state—sometimes *the* highest. Of more importance, *all students* in that school read and wrote more—and vastly better—than students in typical schools.

Simpler still: administrative advancement was based on the aspiring administrator's demonstrated proficiency in teaching the curriculum effectively. There were no annual initiatives, no new innovative programs or "strategic plans" to get in the way of our simple core: a year-to-year insistence on sound curriculum, sound instruction, and authentic literacy.

• • •

Until these core practices become common practice, schools need to focus almost exclusively on them alone. We must be sure that *what we want* from our schools is precisely *what we communicate*—simply, clearly, and persistently.

If we wish to educate unprecedented numbers of students, the ball is in our court: we need to be as obsessive about our "core" as Best Buy, Apple Computer, Borax, and the schools discussed in this chapter are about theirs. we need, as Collins tells us, to define our priorities with "piercing clarity" and then say, "no, thank you" to anything that would divert us from successfully implementing them.

In the next two chapters, I will clarify the features of the three elements, which I believe should be our core priorities. I will also provide their unrivaled evidence base, which we have a moral and professional obligation to honor—because good-faith efforts here would indeed result in "stunningly powerful consequences" for our students.

2

What We Teach

21st century learning is not new but represents what our best educators have been teaching us for several centuries.

—Jay Mathews

Despite a two-decade-long focus on standards, American schools still are not delivering a content-rich curriculum for all students.

—Andrew Rotherham, founder, 21st Century Schools Project

What we teach—the actual, taught curriculum—matters immensely. An in-depth, meta-analytic study revealed that the implementation of a coherent curriculum may have more effect on achievement levels than any other factor (Marzano, 2003). That said, the assumption that most schools currently implement anything resembling a coherent curriculum is "a gravely misleading myth" (Hirsch in DuFour & Marzano, 2011, p. 90). Robert Marzano's definition is helpful here: what he calls a "guaranteed and viable curriculum" simply means that the school can "guarantee" any parent or community member that an agreed-upon body of content and skills is indeed being taught by every teacher. Of importance is that this agreed-upon curriculum must be "viable": it can't contain more content than can be effectively taught within the time constraints of a nine-month school year (2003). If it exceeds those constraints, it will be ignored—and instruction will devolve into "curricular chaos" (Schmoker & Marzano, 1999).

In this chapter, we will look at the case for curriculum, at the importance of its being rich in literacy—though not, as we'll see, in lockstep with the English Language Arts (ELA) Common Core: we'll take an unblinking look at the best and worst aspects of these new standards. We'll finish with simple procedures for building curriculum around a carefully selected, "viable" set of standards.

Because of its centrality, the case for curriculum should be made forcefully and revisited frequently by preservice teachers and professional development providers.

The Urgent, Ironclad Case for Coherent, Literacy-Rich Curriculum

The case for curriculum cannot be overstated. For Linda Darling-Hammond, a clear, teacher-friendly schedule of what to teach and when to teach it is the essential precondition for effective teaching. A quality curriculum alters a student's academic trajectory; it is a more powerful determinant of eventual achievement than their academic readiness when they enter school (Darling-Hammond, 2010–2011, p. 23). The effect of curriculum is almost 40 times as cost effective as class-size reductions (Wiener & Pimentel, 2017).

Recent evidence from school networks, states, and whole nations affirms the "stunningly powerful" effects of curriculum on levels of learning. Charles Sahm points to a "mountain" of such "real-world evidence." According to the National Assessment of Educational Progress (NAEP), achievement has soared in schools in which "a coherent, content-rich, multi-year curriculum" has been employed. Both France and Germany provide sobering lessons in what happens when we abandon coherent curriculum—and in the case of Germany, how achievement levels rebound when we reinstitute such curriculum. A network of Catholic schools replaced their "hodge-podge" of offerings with a common curriculum—and then ensured that it was taught. In two years, twice as many students achieved proficiency in English, and almost three times as many in math (Sahm, 2017, p. 2).

In the highest-scoring countries, educators have always known that a content-rich curriculum—*not* skills-based test preparation—is the key to achievement levels and intellectual development. As Lynne Munson (2011) writes, "No nation that scores competitively on the PISA [Programme for International Student Assessment] exam puts skills before content or focuses chiefly on reading and math" (p. 13). And for those who embrace the concept of team-based "professional learning communities," common curriculum is the essential prerequisite to effective PLCs (DuFour & Marzano, 2011, pp. 93–94). As Lisa Hansel (2013) points out, the ability to learn from peers "is minimal when everyone is teaching different things."

In a landmark issue of *American Educator,* the editors write that the benefits of coherent curriculum are prodigious: without it there can be "no educational equity" and no meaningful teacher collaboration. It instills confidence, reduces teachers' anxiety, and rescues them from having to guess haphazardly about what is most important—that is, about what will be on assessments (*American Educator,* 2010–2011, p. 2). It has become increasingly certain that knowledge—acquired from a content-rich curriculum—is the key to reading ability, that what we know determines how well we can comprehend text (Hansel, 2013; Hirsch, 2016; Munson, 2011; Willingham, 2009b).

Common curriculum can have a swift and enormous effect on learning in real schools. Not long ago, math achievement soared at the high school where my wife taught. Their gains were a result of simply (1) selecting a common, "viable" set of essential standards for each math course and establishing a sensible schedule for teaching them, by grading period, and (2) identifying the best *selected* pages and activities from their common textbook from which to teach each topic. In a two-year period, they made the third-highest math gains in the state. Something similar happened at Mather Elementary School in Boston. After years of low achievement, the school created a coherent, literacy-rich curriculum and ensured that it was implemented throughout the school. As former principal Kim Marshall

(2003) described it, the improvements came "with amazing speed"; in one year, Mather rose from the bottom to the top third in citywide standings—with the largest gains in the city (p. 112).

Coherent, content-rich curriculum isn't just important: it is indisputably essential to the educational enterprise, to all we aspire to accomplish for students. Meta-analytic evidence now affirms that curriculum may be the single largest factor that affects school achievement levels (Marzano, 2003). For the editors of the *American Educator*, Core Curriculum "guides and brings coherence to the whole educational endeavor" (*American Educator*, 2010–2011, p. 2). If we truly care about education for all, we must ensure that every school owns and operates a common, content-rich curriculum.

• • •

Because of curriculum's outsize effect, my aim in this chapter (and Chapters 4–7, on the subject areas) is to simplify and clarify its use and its most essential features. In advocating for what might seem "old school," I occasionally refer to the most enlightened advocates of 21st century education. Please don't confuse them with some of their high-profile, commercially driven counterparts, whose "inchoate" notions of education have been rightly ravaged (Maranto, Ritter, & Levine, 2010, p. 25). The advocates of 21st century education that I cite in this chapter are not urging us to rashly reinvent curriculum around technology or innovation (although there is room for both— once we have implemented our highest priorities). I'll cite those who urge us to go back to the future, to embrace—at long last—a combination of the following curricular components for *all* students:

• Adequate amounts of essential subject-area content, concepts, and topics
• Intellectual/thinking skills (e.g., argument, problem solving, reconciling opposing views, drawing one's own conclusions; these are not to be confused with insipid test-prep skills such as "inferring" or "finding the main idea")

• Authentic literacy—purposeful reading, writing, and discussion as the primary modes of learning both content and thinking skills

None of this is unique to this century (Mathews, 2010). What *is* new is the recognition that all students need—and deserve—such curriculum. The demands of 21st century careers and citizenship necessitate it—and are increasingly similar to what students need to be prepared for college, whether they decide to attend or not. It is also a grim, indisputable fact that a major reason why students aren't ready for college is that the default curriculum is startlingly short on opportunities for students to read, discuss, and write thoughtfully (Allington, 2001; Conley, 2005; Goodlad, 1984; Hirsch, 2009; Rotherham, 2008; Schmoker, 2006; Sizer, 1992).

Withal, what is glibly referred to as "the curriculum" obscures the enormous differences in what individual teachers in the same school or district actually teach; in most schools, there is a "huge gap" between the taught and written curriculum (DuFour & Marzano, 2011, p. 89). The net result is what Robert Marzano and I have referred to as "curricular chaos" (Schmoker & Marzano, 1999). Until we address this, too many students will be deprived of a quality education—and will struggle to succeed at postsecondary studies.

Preparation for College, Careers, and Citizenship—for All

For too long, we have indulged in errant, offensive notions about who we deem to be—or not to be—"college material." We are realizing that (1) preparation for college, careers, *and* citizenship overlaps considerably and is needed by all students, and (2) such an education is within the reach of almost any student who learns from a reasonably coherent, literacy-rich curriculum. According to one study, "all high school students should experience a common academic core that prepares them for both college and workforce training, *regardless of their future plans*" (Olson, 2008, p. 19). Another study, by the

American Diploma Project, revealed that the needs of the workplace are "increasingly indistinguishable" from the knowledge and skills needed for college success. The U.S. Chamber of Commerce calls the findings of these studies "right on target" (Olson, 2008, p. 19).

A *reasonably good* K–12 education can provide virtually all students with what they need to be active, informed citizens, effective workers, and—if they choose—successful college students. What holds us back is an institutional failure to fully acknowledge that the fundamental elements of our so-called "curriculum" are largely missing.

Needed: A Moment of Candor

Common sense should tell us that any curriculum worthy of the name should contain a "common academic core"—adequate amounts of essential content and critical thinking skills, with sufficient opportunities to read, write, and speak. Anything less than this is a sham—a pretense of "curriculum." Nonetheless, according to every study, literacy-rich curriculum is exceedingly rare in our schools, even in the "honors" track (DuFour & Marzano, 2011; Hirsch, 2016; Schmoker, 2006).

In their widely read book *The Manufactured Crisis: Myths, Fraud, and the Attack on America's Public Schools,* David Berliner and Bruce Biddle (1995) make an incisive call to 21st century education. The book contains a bracing critique of typical schooling, with regard to both *what* and *how* we teach. The authors emphatically call for a curriculum rich in content, advanced literacy, and thinking skills. And they lament their manifest absence in most schools.

In a section titled "Skills for the 21st Century," the authors report that we have never provided an intellectually demanding, content-rich curriculum for most students. Their observations were prescient: even then, the authors could see us lurching toward technology in the hope that it would fix education, even before we attended to the much higher priorities of curriculum and improved instruction.

Despite years of lip service, schools have never made the "cultivation of thoughtfulness" (p. 298) a priority. Like John Goodlad (1984) before them and many others since, Berliner and Biddle (1995) found that students are seldom asked to read, write, and discuss as they seek to resolve "conflicting views," to exercise judgment, or to engage in "critical thinking" (pp. 298–299). In the 21st century, however, students will benefit greatly from opportunities to connect literature to their lives, to "create meaning from related readings," and to do their own research (p. 319).

Berliner and Biddle's (1995) book contains a ringing endorsement of a shared body of subject-area content. "Let there be no mistake," they write, students need to learn and acquire a common "knowledge base that constitutes our cultural heritage... our country badly needs a citizenry that shares such a heritage" (p. 302).

Content matters. And educators need to be very clear about the relationship between content and our ability to think and reason.

Content *and* Intellectual Skills—More of Both

Any credible curriculum has to reflect the link between knowledge and critical thinking (usually done as we read, talk, or write). Andrew Rotherham is the former head of the Progressive Policy Institute's 21st Century Schools Project. He too laments our failure to provide a content-rich curriculum to students, because

> content undergirds critical thinking, analysis, and broader information literacy skills. To critically analyze various documents requires engagement with content and a framework within which to place the information. It's impossible, for instance, to critically analyze the American Revolution without understanding the facts and context surrounding that event. (Rotherham, 2008, p. 1)

E. D. Hirsch (2008) argues similarly that the abilities to argue, evaluate, and reason are "attained by studying a rich curriculum in math, literature, science, history, geography, music and art and *learning higher-level skills in context....* There is a scientific consensus that academic skill is highly dependent on specific relevant knowledge" (p. 40; emphasis added). This knowledge can, however, be acquired through disarmingly simple, age-old teaching methods that can be captured in two simple, versatile templates (described in Chapter 3).

More recently, Hirsch (2016) has written that "the achievement gap is chiefly a knowledge gap and a language gap" (p. 2). The ability to perform well on tests of "higher order" reading skills—such as making inferences or identifying the main idea in a text—is largely a function of knowledge attained—of how much the students know about the topic they are reading about. That means we must ensure that students acquire a sufficient vocabulary and knowledge base through content-rich curriculum and extensive reading (Hirsch, 2016, Chapter 1).

To make his point, Hirsch cites the curious case of the French school system. In the 1980s, all French students learned the French national curriculum, with impressive results for every demographic category. But in 1989, a radical new education law required schools to abandon the curriculum; they were now charged to provide content on the basis of each student's individual abilities, culture, and interests. The French, writes Hirsch, "completely Americanized their school system overnight."

What was the result of France's experiment with individualized, differentiated education? Researchers in the French Ministry of Education discovered an "astonishingly steep decline in achievement in each demographic group." There were "massive declines" in every socioeconomic subgroup, from rich to poor. All students were "academically harmed by the new system, [and such harm] became greater as one went down the economic scale . . . inequality increased dramatically" (Hirsch, 2016, pp. 3–4).

French educators should have read the work of Daniel Willingham, the prominent cognitive scientist. Like Hirsch and Rotherham, he found that reading, learning, and critical thinking depend enormously on the acquisition of content knowledge. He also is dismayed by the tacit disparagement of subject matter by certain "21st century" educators. As Willingham (2008) points out, critical thinking is, in fact, highly dependent on content knowledge. We can't understand, much less critically evaluate, the ideas in a textbook, newspaper, or magazine *if they contain too much unfamiliar information*. And by the time we're actually reading, it's too late to Google every unfamiliar word and concept: if we don't already know enough about the subject we're reading about, we become bogged down and confused.

As of this writing, a legion of researchers, including the architects of the ELA Common Core, have come around to Hirsch's long-held view: that once we can decode simple text, growth in reading comprehension—and critical thinking—has little to do with practicing "reading skills" or standards (Heitin, 2016). Reading growth depends, more than anything, on our ability to build up students' knowledge base and vocabulary. This can be achieved only by ensuring the delivery of an organized, content-rich curriculum—matched with abundant opportunities to read increasingly complex fiction and information-rich text. There is no other way (Lemov, 2015; Pinker in Hirsch, 2016; Shanahan, 2011, 2014).

Again, however, the acquisition of knowledge need not be divorced from critical thinking. As we'll see in subsequent chapters, we have always learned content best through thinking skills and activities, even as small children—that is, "ideally *beginning in preschool and even before*" (Willingham, 2009a, p. 19; emphasis added). Or as Elena Silva (2008) notes, "there is no reason to separate the acquisition of learning core content… from more advanced analytical and thinking skills, *even in the earliest grades*" (emphasis added).

The best means by which to exploit this connection between content and intellectual engagement is through fairly simple, higher-order literacy activities—with a redoubled emphasis on books, textbooks, newspapers, and magazines in all disciplines. In subsequent chapters, I describe simple formats for how we can teach students to read, discuss, and write about such texts in the subject areas.

Let's now look more closely at what the wisest advocates of 21st century education have to say about the need for advanced levels of literacy, long assumed to be the province of the college-bound. Advanced literacy can be acquired by all, using variations on simple, repeatable literacy activities.

All-Pervasive Literacy

Think of literacy as a spine; it holds everything together. The branches of learning connect to it, meaning that all core content teachers have a responsibility to teach literacy.

—Vicki Phillips and Carina Wong (2010)

As we've seen, there is compelling evidence that all students will benefit from a curriculum that embraces a "common academic core" (that leaves adequate space for teachers to supplement the curriculum with some of their own content and creativity). What is less recognized is that to optimize and enliven learning, our curriculum must be liberally infused with frequent opportunities for students to read, discuss, argue, and write about what they are learning.

Literacy—and Destiny

How important is literacy? Let's listen again to E. D. Hirsch (2010; his "verbal competence" is a close synonym for literacy):

To impart adequate verbal competence is the *most important single goal of schooling* in any nation. Verbal scores are reliable indexes to general competence, life chances and civic participation.... Decades of data show that the earnings gap between racial and ethnic groups in the United States largely disappear when language competence in Standard English is factored in. (p. 31)

Or consider the words of Vince Ferrandino and Gerald Tirozzi (2004), the former presidents, respectively, of the National Association of Elementary School Principals and the National Association of Secondary School Principals:

Under-developed literacy skills are the number one reason why students are retained, assigned to special education, [and] given long-term remedial services and why they fail to graduate from high school. (p. 29)

It is impossible to overstate the importance of literacy. Yet nothing so begs for clarity in K–12 education. Because literacy is foundational to learning in every subject, we must be crystal clear about *what it is* and what it *is not*. Alas, the ELA Common Core (and its close cousins in non–Common Core states) has lent both clarity and confusion to literacy. We'll see how we can navigate these new standards in a moment.

First, however, let's listen to some people whose work helps us to achieve clarity about literacy in its simplest and most liberating forms.

"Plain Old Reading and Writing" Versus Literacy Standards

When he was growing up, Frederick Douglass learned to read—on the sly—by sharing his lunch with his fellow dock boys. I don't imagine those kids made much use of state standards or taught him to find the "main idea" or determine where the "rising action" occurred in a story. No. They simply taught him the code—in about the same way I taught my own children to read and write. Once Douglass had that code, he read everything he could get his hands on, thus becoming a remarkably eloquent writer, speaker, and courageous force for abolition.

In the heartbreaking *New York Times* bestseller *When Breath Becomes Air,* the late Paul Kalanithi (2016) describes how his parents moved him to a rural community with an "impoverished school system" (p. 26). But this didn't prevent him from attending Stanford, Yale, and Cambridge—or from becoming an award-winning neurosurgeon.

What gave him an edge, enough to overcome the effects of a subpar education? Books. From the age of 10, his mother began to furnish him with books that she thought would compensate for what he did not receive from the school. He read voraciously, and that made all the difference.

I'm reminded of Thomas Friedman's (2005) observation in his bestseller *The World Is Flat: A Brief History of the 21st Century.* For him, the most successful people in this century will be those who acquire a facility with "plain old reading and writing"—who learn, that is, to use knowledge to develop and communicate creative combinations of ideas, applications, and strategies to solve problems (p. 353). As we'll see, a focus on individual language art "standards" often interferes with the acquisition of authentic literacy—with "plain old reading and writing."

Friedman cites Marc Tucker, the president of the National Center on Education and the Economy (who we'll be hearing more from). Tucker recommends a broad liberal arts curriculum for every student that includes "a very high level of preparation in reading, writing, and speaking" (Friedman, 2005, p. 319). But as Friedman observes, these skills have taken an enormous hit. Fewer students than ever can read the kinds of "lengthy, complex texts" that nourish our ability to learn and innovate (pp. 353–354). The reason for this is simple: our schools don't require students to read texts of increasing length and complexity—such as textbooks. This pattern begins in the earliest grades, and it persists right up through high school graduation (Duke, 2010; Gomez & Gomez, 2007).

Textbooks? Yes

Although it may sound unfashionable, textbooks (as we'll see in later chapters) are an underestimated resource for learning essential content and acquiring literacy skills. By "textbook," *I do not mean elementary grade basal readers,* whose endless activities and exercises only divert students from meaningful reading, discussion, and writing.

In "Reading for Learning: Literacy Supports for 21st Century Learning," Louis and Kimberly Gomez (2007) write that the new century will routinely require students to "critically analyze and synthesize information" gleaned from the kind of dense, complex prose found in science and social studies textbooks. Our current failure to make them a prominent part of schooling may be the primary reason for "poor student performance in the content areas" (p. 225).

This does not mean we should read entire textbooks; most aren't worthy of being read cover to cover. But we should make selected readings from textbooks a regular part of students' reading material in science, social studies, and the arts.

In an incisive *Educational Leadership* article, Kathleen Cushman (2007) describes the "culture shock" most students experience when they arrive at college. Having rarely read and never been taught to read textbooks, they lack the "deeper reading, writing and inquiry that college requires" (p. 47).

So how should practitioners utilize the array of available texts—the increasingly complex textbook material, literature, poems, or op-ed pieces—that are integral to curriculum? *With questions* (or higher-order "prompts," which are questions in another form).

Questions and texts: an essential combination. There's nothing complicated here. The better part of a quality education has always consisted of this straightforward combination of a quality text matched with an arresting question. As we'll see, a single question—with perhaps a few related follow-up questions—can be very powerful; one question can inform our reading, discussion, and writing about an entire text.

Once students understand the question (or the higher-order prompt), we then simply teach them how to read deeply and purposefully to answer such questions—by routinely modeling our own reading and thinking. We would then discuss the text as a class and have students write (if even briefly) about what they learned from it. This is the essence of both learning and literacy in just about any subject.

It is especially important for teams of teachers in every discipline to make the development and refinement of effective, text-based questions among their highest priorities. In this way, teams can benefit from each other's collective intelligence as they share the load of developing interesting lines of inquiry for the various texts in a course. We'll be looking at versatile, common questions and question stems that ensure high-quality inquiry for any text.

Such content-based, inquiry-driven learning, reading, and discussion should periodically culminate in more formal or extended writing and, for certain assignments, in public presentations—which have become, as Arnold Packer (2007) points out, "essential in the 21st century job market" (p. 2).

Papers and presentations. The New York Performance Standards Consortium is a network of 28 schools, mostly in New York City. They have received awards for being models of (once again) 21st century education (see their website at http://performanceassessment.org). The consortium's focus is on authentic literacy: close reading, discussion, and writing in every course. All students write substantive, complex, end-of-course essays, research papers, and graduation projects in each discipline. Students write papers with titles like "Why Do They Have to Die? An Analysis of the Protagonists' Deaths in *Dr. Jekyll and Mr. Hyde, Metamorphosis,* and *Of Mice and Men.*" In addition, all seniors must deliver a presentation based on one of their research papers to a panel of judges from the school and community. The consortium uses data on the strength and weakness of these papers and performances to promote continuous improvement.

Students love it. Ann Cook, the consortium's director, told me that students who left other schools thrive in the consortium schools and do better in college than their counterparts. And *teachers love working in these schools;* there is very little turnover (Schmoker, 2008–2009).

Let's hope such clear, literacy-driven requirements—much truer forms of "standards," in my view—are the wave of the future. I advocate that we require a research paper and a presentation from students in certain subjects, at certain grade levels (e.g., at the end of 5th, 8th, and 12th grades). *Their performance on these or on end-of-course papers should be among the primary data we use for purposes of accountability and continuous improvement. Such assessments would tell us vastly more than standardized tests do and would have a profound effect on the quality of both instruction and classroom assessments—as they do in the highest-achieving countries* (Darling-Hammond, 2010; Ripley, 2013, p. 16). I will expand on this topic in Chapter 4, on English language arts.

Literacy is integral to both what and how we teach—the "spine" that holds content together in every subject. Implementing authentic literacy depends primarily on this simple combination of a good question matched to a good text—in every subject. If such work seems daunting or complicated, fear not: as we'll see in the next chapter, literacy is best integrated into the content areas when variations on fairly simple, age-old templates are used (and reused) in every course.

In light of this discussion, what are we to make of the ELA Common Core, or its close counterparts in states where it hasn't been adopted (but where the Common Core has plainly had an influence)? It turns out to have been a very mixed blessing: it will benefit us only if we embrace its best aspects—and reject its worst.

The English Language Arts Common Core: At Odds With Itself

Many readers know Carol Jago, the respected author, teacher, and former president of NCTE (National Council of Teachers of English). As she and I have written, the best aspects of the Common Core had "the potential to right the ship of literacy" and to "rescue us from the fads and pseudo-literacies of recent decades." The new standards (which were published just as the first edition of this book went to press) were initially intended to liberate us from the corrupting, atomized minutiae of state ELA standards. For Carol and me, these goals were fairly well met in the introduction and appendixes of the Common Core documents. They were an eloquent call for the inclusion of far more substantive reading, writing, and speaking in every discipline, all with a focus on argument, evidence, and inquiry. This is the quintessence of both academic and real-world literacy (Schmoker & Jago, 2013).

But then the educationists got hold of the project—and inanity won the day. The anchor standards gave way to the grade-by-grade standards, an exhaustive taxonomy of jargon-laced skills and descriptors. Anyone who knows teachers could have guessed that these standards—not the good introductory materials—were bound to become the default guide to instruction in most schools; we've been bred to work from (or *pretend* to work from) such lists for decades.

And that's where the trouble begins. One expert on standards characterized them as "pretentious gibberish" (Garner, 2010, p. 8); another expert referred to them as "blithering, poorly thought-out abstractions" (Ravitch, 2013).

The new ELA standards are almost as prone to encourage the kinds of test preparation and worksheet exercises as their state-level predecessors. They are also a clear departure from the spirit of the introductory materials and appendixes to the ELA Common Core. Mentioned in that introduction is Gerald Graff, a prolific author, professor, and former president of the Modern Language Association. In Appendix A of the ELA Common Core, Graff's work is liberally cited by its architects in support of what they regard as the most important standard of all: argument and argument literacy (English Language Arts Standards/Common Core Standards, 2017, Appendix A, pp. 24–25). This was a good thing.

But what are we to make of the hundreds of actual grade-by-grade standards? Just after these long grade-by-grade standards were vetted and published, Graff and I read them carefully. In a commentary for *Education Week,* we wrote that there are still far too many standards, that most of them were unnecessary, and that we simply couldn't understand many of them; Gerald referred to them at one point as "word salad" (Schmoker & Graff, 2011). We discovered, for instance, that 8th grade teachers were supposed to teach students how to do the following:

> Analyze different points of view of the characters and the audience or reader (e.g., created through the use of dramatic irony) creating such effects as suspense or humor.

Compare and contrast the structure of two or more texts and analyze how the differing structure of each text contributes to its
meaning and style.

For Graff and me, such standards have too many potential
meanings—or none at all. We found many others just as mystifying.

To compound such ambiguity, the authors of the standards made
many tortured attempts to write each standard at a higher level of
sophistication than its counterpart at the previous grade level. For
instance, students at one grade level must learn to "find the main
idea" in a selection (a mindless standard at best; see Hirsch, 2016, p.
21; Pondiscio, 2014a; Shanahan, 2014). In the next grade, teachers
are asked (I'm not making this up) to instruct their students in how
to "find two main ideas."

Who vetted these documents?

Similarly, students at one grade level must be taught to "introduce" a topic—and then develop it. At the next grade, they are to
"examine" the topic—and then develop it. Is there a meaningful distinction here? Could the writers possibly have had a precise sense
of that distinction when they wrote it? Or was this standard written (as is more likely) in haste, because "examine" just sounds more
advanced than "introduce"?

In the same way, the standard for one grade would have students
"supply reasons" for their opinion pieces, but at the next grade level,
students must "supply reasons that *support a point of view.*" What is
the difference? Or does this pseudo-distinction simply set in motion
(as I've seen in several schools) a series of vapid, worksheet-driven
exercises on "point of view" (which itself has multiple meanings).
Make no mistake: the prevalence of such exercises explains precisely
why students do less actual reading and writing in school than ever.

The late Rick DuFour (2015) understood this. With charming
understatement, he remarked on the folly of asking teachers to
address the "less-than-informative distinction" between "relevant
descriptive details" at one grade level and "well-chosen details" at

a subsequent grade level (p. 146). Think of all the rabbit holes such thoughtlessly wrought standards could take us down.

Alas, many good-hearted teachers feel obligated to plan individual lessons for each of the standards on these long, ambiguous lists. As Willingham (2009b) writes, developing such lessons would be the most unfortunate possible outcome of the ELA Common Core.

He is not alone. Before we look at a much simpler, more effective way to promote real-world literacy *and* higher test scores, let's listen to the views of some highly respected but disillusioned commentators on the new ELA standards. Their analysis helps explain why they have had such a disappointing, if not negative, effect on both literacy instruction and outcomes (Hirsch, 2016; Lee & Wu, 2017; Shanahan & Duffet, 2013). (For those interested, I will explore this in more detail in Chapter 4.)

Separating the Wheat from the Chaff: ELA Common Core Critics and the Way Forward

[The ELA Common Core is] "just another set of blithering, poorly thought out abstractions."

—Robert Shepherd in Ravitch (2013)

While well-intended and certainly a step in the right direction, the Common Core standards have not solved the problem for the classroom teacher of developing standards that truly represent a viable curriculum.

—Rick DuFour and Robert Marzano (2011)

E. D. Hirsch was among those who initially embraced the ELA Common Core and then retreated from his endorsement. Every educator should read the first chapter of Hirsch's (2016) latest book, *Why Knowledge Matters*. He now realizes that despite the positive emphases expressed in the introduction and ancillary materials, the grade-by-grade standards "automatically force schools to focus on strategies and skill drills" at the expense of reading, writing, and learning across the disciplines (p. 21).

Years after its rollout, research findings now confirm that the ELA Common Core has made hardly a dent, even in ELA, in which worksheets and skills instruction continue to predominate (Lee & Wu, 2017; Shanahan & Duffet, 2013).

I can relate to curriculum expert Robert Pondiscio (2014a). In "A Missed Opportunity for Common Core," he describes a segment about a Common Core lesson on National Public Radio. At first, he excitedly anticipates what the narrator describes as an "exemplary" 9th grade lesson. "This is gonna be *great!*" he thinks to himself. But as he listens, the instruction devolves into a "mechanistic, skills-driven lesson." As the broadcast continues, his initial anticipation morphs into despair: "Please, no," he writes, "This can't be happening." And then, "Shoot me now." At the end of the segment, he finds out that the source of this "exemplary" lesson is a *53-lesson skills-based module*—presumably based on the ELA Common Core—in which no complete works of literature would be read (p. 2).

Timothy Shanahan, one of my favorite literacy experts, is equally disturbed by the malpractice issuing from an adherence to the grade-by-grade standards of the Common Core. In "How and How Not to Prepare Students for the New [Common Core and related] Tests," Shanahan (2014) describes a troubling day in the field. At a certain point in his presentation, he notices that the curriculum director is regarding him with "skeptical abhorrence." Why? Because she had presumed that he would show her teachers how to conduct "item analysis of standardized tests," followed by targeted remedial instruction (p. 1). Even now, several years into the Common Core launch, he still sees such "data-driven school reform... played out in thousands of schools around the country."

But it doesn't work. Such test-preparation exertions sometimes have a slight upward effect on scores, but then the scores plateau. The reason, as Shanahan points out, is that in the real world, "Readers do not work their way through texts trying to apply a set of skills analogous to question types." Instead, all of these supposedly "discrete skills" must be employed simultaneously—and almost never consciously. That's why well-read students do so well on such tests—even if they are never taught such discrete "reading skills" (Shanahan, 2014, p. 2).

There is one feature of schooling that will always produce more effective readers and higher reading scores: a far more generous diet of increasingly complex, vocabulary-rich text (Shanahan, 2011, 2014). Shanahan cites an ACT study of over half a million students that demonstrated that good readers perform almost uniformly on every kind of test item—from recall to "cause and effect" to "inferential" items. That's because students' ability to comprehend and make inferences about what they read is not a function of how much practice they've had with such skills. It is instead a function of *"knowledge and vocabulary, acquired from wide, deep reading across the curriculum"* (Shanahan, 2011, p. 1).

The new breed of state reading assessments confirms this: the passages in both the Partnership for Assessment of Readiness for College and Careers (PARCC) and Smarter Balanced tests contain more general knowledge and challenging vocabulary than their state-level predecessors (Wattenberg, 2016). More than ever, wide, deep reading is the key to success on these and other new state assessments.

For the previously stated reasons, the Common Core hasn't had anything like the effect its architects hoped for. But how, right now, can we properly appropriate the best of the ELA Common Core for curricular and instructional purposes? Let's look at two simple alternatives to the grade-by-grade standards. First, we'll learn about the landmark work of David Conley on the kind of curriculum and literacy required for success in college or post–high school studies. Then we'll look at an important recent amendment to the Common Core—added by the Common Core architects themselves. Their simple, concise postscript to the Common Core may just rescue it from the shoals of yet another educational failure.

Alternatives to the Grade-by-Grade ELA Common Core Standards

Less Is More: Conley's "Standards for Success"

David Conley and his colleagues at the University of Oregon conducted an in-depth study of the skills and content that students need to succeed in college. In doing so, they reviewed hundreds of college syllabi, interviewed hundreds of students, and met with professors from every discipline. The findings appear in Conley's (2005) book *College Knowledge: What It Really Takes for Students to Succeed and What We Can Do to Get Them Ready.*

First, Conley lays out a fairly concise outline of the knowledge most essential to college success for each discipline. Second, however, in a triumph of concision, the book provides a short, simple list of the primary *intellectual skills* we should impart to K–12 students. These four intellectual "standards for success" form the basis for both content area studies and literacy instruction: for the analytical reading, discussion, and writing that students must do in college—or in any postsecondary studies. These short, simple standards would replace the majority of our (so-called) literacy standards:

1. Read to infer/interpret/draw conclusions.
2. Support arguments with evidence.
3. Resolve conflicting views encountered in source documents.
4. Solve complex problems with no obvious answer.

These four simple "habits of mind" (as Conley sometimes refers to them) are a patently superior basis for student reading, writing, and talking in every discipline.

I'm convinced that something like these four standards (coupled with the most obvious criteria for effective writing, discussion, and speaking) would provide teachers with much greater clarity and focus than do our bloated, imprecise language arts documents.

But there is one more imperative piece in his scheme. If the purpose of "standards" is to *more precisely clarify what is essential to an education,* then this "standard" may be the most important: the inclusion of explicit, minimum parameters *for the amount and kind of reading and writing students should do* in every course (Conley, 2005, pp. 82–83). In my view, these parameters are far more essential to student success than most of the inane verbiage now found in our long, atomized state standards documents.

Quantity Counts: A New Kind of Standard

Why—when so much depends on it—are we hesitant to set minimum parameters for the number of books and articles students should read and the length and number of papers they should write? These too are "standards"—but are of far greater consequence than conventional ELA standards. In the great majority of schools, we've never been explicit about what may be the most "high leverage" factor that contributes to an education and to closing the achievement gap: the *amount of purposeful reading and writing that students do in school.*

To exploit this factor, Conley (2005) would define the following for every course in the curriculum:

• Minimum number of pages to be read [or approximate number of fiction/nonfiction books]

• Minimum number of pages to be written [e.g., per week or per grading period]

• Minimum number of papers to be completed [and approximate length of major writing assignments]

• Common scoring guides for written work (pp. 82–83; bracketed material added)

Imagine the effect such "standards" would have—and the crippling deficiencies they would address. Among the most dismaying, consequential shortcomings of modern schooling is the paltry amount of reading and writing assignments that students complete each year. This fact is seldom brought to light, even as we divert ourselves with new literacy programs, reforms, and standards documents.

Reading and writing are central to good schooling—and they influence each other reciprocally. Writing reveals how much and how well we read—even as it makes us better readers and thinkers. Until we require and specify far greater amounts of reading and writing in school, however, students—from highest- to lowest-achieving—won't approach their potential in terms of reading, writing, and intellectual ability (Schmoker, 2006).

Conley (2005) goes so far as to urge us to assign three- to five-page writing assignments as soon as students are capable of accomplishing them. If my audience surveys mean anything, students could be producing two-page papers by 3rd grade and a reasonable number of three-page papers in multiple courses by upper elementary school. The requirement for such writing, however, is so rare that when students reach college, most are unprepared for college writing (I know this firsthand from teaching college English courses). In this vein, Conley's research team came to this conclusion:

> If we could institute *only one change* to make students more college ready, it should be to increase the *amount and quality of writing* students are expected to produce. (Conley, 2007, p. 27; emphasis added)

Sheryl Sandberg is the best-selling author of *Lean In.* In describing her high school years, she laments the fact that in the four years she spent at her affluent, high-scoring high school, she only had to write one five-page paper. This left her ill-prepared for college, where she suddenly "had to write five-page papers overnight" (Alter, 2014, p. 72). Sandberg's story exemplifies Gerald Graff's troubling estimate: that only 20 percent of students arrive at college with the kind of basic writing ability needed to survive there (Graff, 2003, p. 3).

With regard to literacy, quantity counts. We'll look at how to integrate this new "standard" in Chapters 4 through 7, the subject-area chapters.

Let's now look at an equally succinct list of ELA standards that complement Conley's work and would similarly replace most of what we find in our grade-by-grade lists of state ELA standards. Like Conley's work, they apply across the curriculum.

The "Three Shifts": The Soul of the ELA Common Core

As mentioned, Carol Jago and I have written that, for the larger ELA Common Core project to succeed, teachers need permission to ignore the great majority of the grade-by-grade standards. Instead, they should focus on the best parts of the introductory and ancillary materials (e.g., pp. 1–3 and 24–25 in Appendix A of English Language Arts Standards/Common Core Standards, 2017).

But we also wrote to bring attention to a little-known development in the evolution of the ELA Common Core: the "three shifts" that lend needed clarity and concision to how we should teach reading, writing, and speaking across the disciplines (again, written by the Common Core architects themselves [Coleman, Pimentel, & Zimba, 2012]):

- Building knowledge through content-rich nonfiction
- Reading and writing grounded in evidence from text, both literary and informational
- Regular practice with complex text and its academic vocabulary

That's it, although the authors then expound briefly on the need for "careful analyses" of texts that lead to "well-defended claims" in the service of "argumentative literacy" (Coleman et al., 2012, p. 2). These shifts urge teachers to focus on what matters most: that students are to read far more complex, vocabulary-rich text and to "ground" their written and spoken arguments and interpretations in evidence from both fiction and nonfiction.

There is a profound, if tacit, admission here that these shifts are a critical corrective to the grade-by-grade standards—indeed, to any state ELA standards. These, not the grade-level lists, are intended to "clarify expectations for teaching and learning" in order to "deliver on the promise of the Common Core."

Better late than never. In their clarity and brevity, these simple shifts represent a return to sanity and a retreat from the excesses of list-based literacy instruction. Like Conley's "Standards for Success" (Conley, 2005, p. 171), these shifts constitute a *return* to traditional literacy (Schmoker & Jago, 2013). They are precisely what was emphasized by the best teachers I had in K–12 and college. In that sense, they are a call to the kind of literacy that preceded the standards movement itself and that once informed high-quality studies in English, history, and other courses.

Let's now look briefly at some schools whose success demonstrates what might happen in every subject area if we adopted practices more consistent with Conley's work, or the "three shifts." In each case, teachers conspicuously avoided the use of ELA standards.

Successful Schools—That Shun English Language Arts Common Core Standards

View Park Preparatory High School is in South Los Angeles. For several years, the language arts curriculum at View Park consisted almost exclusively of having students read documents closely and then write argumentative papers that were based on their interpretations. A typical reading and writing assignment would be built around a question like this: "In *One Flew over the Cuckoo's Nest*, does McMurphy liberate or further imprison his fellow inmates?" (Hernandez, Kaplan, & Schwartz, 2006, p. 51).

What were the results of this minimalist curriculum that virtually ignored the state's language arts standards? View Park, whose student body is 97 percent African American, became the highest-achieving majority-minority school in the state of California (Hernandez et al., 2006).

Tempe Preparatory Academy is a grade 7–12 charter school in the Phoenix area. In every area of the curriculum, students read and write far more books and challenging texts than do most public school students; their list of common, required reading assignments is available to anyone on their website. In their daily, two-hour English/social studies block, students engage in extended "Socratic discussions" about complex texts as they learn to analyze and then articulate and defend their answers to meaningful questions. Each month, students complete a substantial, multipage writing assignment—"grounded" in one or more texts read that month. Teachers pay no attention whatsoever to ELA standards—students would never be asked to "find the main idea" or be taught "inferencing" or "cause and effect." They are too busy analyzing and discussing characters and themes, too busy writing—and being taught to write—their arguments and interpretations of literature, history, and primary resources. This hasn't hurt their test scores; since the inception of this curriculum, Tempe Prep has been among the highest-scoring schools in the state.

I know personally of students with only the most meager academic background whose verbal and writing abilities soared within months of entering this school. We'll hear more about Tempe Prep and the network of schools they spawned in subsequent chapters.

Brockton High School is the largest high school in Massachusetts. At one time, it was also the lowest achieving. Embarrassed, the faculty rallied around a plan to raise achievement under the leadership of the Social Studies Department head (and eventual principal), Susan Szachowicz. They implemented a simple plan that started with curriculum: a clear schedule of what to teach, and when, for every course. Into that curriculum, they integrated what became their mantra in every course: "reading, writing, speaking, and reasoning" every day, for every student. That meant that there were explicit weekly expectations for what and how much students would read, discuss, and write in every course.

And they didn't just write these teacher-generated expectations into the curriculum; school leaders *monitored regularly* to ensure that students were indeed benefitting from common curriculum and from a tremendous increase in the amount of reading and writing.

They didn't have to wait long for improvement. As Susan told me in her office in Brockton, she received a call during the summer after the first year of implementation: it was the state education commissioner calling to tell her that Brockton had made the highest gains in the state. It didn't stop there. Over the next 10 years, Brockton rose from rock-bottom to the top 10 percent in the state—where it remains. We'll be hearing more about Brockton in subsequent chapters.

I hope such examples (and we'll be hearing about others) demonstrate that most ELA standards—unlike their more legitimate counterparts in other subjects—are both problematic and largely unnecessary. We are wise to avoid the bulk of them as we create curriculum for English language arts courses and as we seek to integrate literacy into all of the subject areas—which I'll explicate in Chapters 4–7. We'll specifically address the unique characteristics of ELA curriculum—and how to build it—in Chapter 4.

But what of the rest of the curriculum? What of the standards documents in all remaining subjects? They too are fraught with imperfections: many are poorly written and ambiguous—like "Rorschach inkblots," according to assessment expert Rick Stiggins (2017, p. 55). Many curricula contain more standards than can be meaningfully taught in a 180-day school year (Marzano, 2003).

Nonetheless, the best of them are still useful in a way that ELA standards are not. A review of standards in the content areas can provide a starting point; once the standards are reduced and revised, any willing team of teachers can produce a curriculum that is superior to what prevails in the majority of schools.

Let's examine how we can use these still-imperfect subject-area standards documents to build the kind of "guaranteed and viable curriculum" that may have more effect on achievement than any other factor (Marzano, 2003). We'll see some additional specifics in the subject-area chapters (5–7) that build on this simple scheme.

• • •

A Brief Guide to Building Subject-Area Curricula

To provide clear, teacher-friendly curricula in the subject areas, we must make discriminating use of state and national standards documents. That means we must employ simple processes for selecting and clarifying a reduced set of the most essential standards. Then we must establish "standards"—minimum parameters for the number and length of written assignments—or at least for major written assignments.

The aim here is to create documents that are so clear, useful, and reasonable that teachers will *want* to use them and will know precisely when or whether they are deviating from that curriculum.

The process isn't complicated. As with language arts standards, it begins with an awareness of the peculiar verbiage of the standards themselves.

Topics, not Verbiage

I have pored over state and national standards documents for decades. Many have received high ratings from prestigious agencies. I'm bewildered by these ratings: the documents read as if they were never proofread, never tested for clarity and ease of use on real teachers. We know they are never field-tested at even a single school. As Marzano and others have found, these standards aren't even "viable": it would be impossible to teach them, in adequate depth, within a nine-month school year (Marzano, 2003; Marzano & Kendall, 1998).

But there is another problem: the verbs that accompany the topics. Words such as "analyze," "identify," "understand," "evaluate," "discuss," and "explain" seem to have been assigned almost randomly to their various topics.

These standards and their verbiage not only mislead teachers and create anxiety; they are also plainly a bluff: as Fuhrman, Resnick, and Shepard (2009) point out, state assessments consist of "a grab bag of items only loosely matched to state standards" (p. 28). There is a very tenuous connection between actual state tests and these large, particularized lists of standards.

So ignore most of the verbiage surrounding the topics, as Hirsch (2009) and others recommend. Look primarily at the content topics. Then, once your team has determined which topics you agree on, establish your own higher-order purposes for teaching them.

Now we're ready for the next simple step—selecting only the most essential topics and standards to include in your curriculum.

The Case for Drastically Reducing Content Standards

It stands to reason that if we reduce the number of standards we teach and clarify each remaining standard for our teachers, we greatly increase the odds that teachers will actually teach them. Reducing the number of standards also allows us to teach them *in adequate intellectual depth*, and so subsequently students will learn more, retain more, and have more opportunities to discuss and write about what they are learning.

How much risk is involved in taking this bold but essential step? Not much—and the payoff could be unprecedented. As we've been seeing, reducing our standards to a realistic, "viable" amount invariably contributes to gains in achievement (Marzano, 2003).

We've known for decades that on international assessments, the highest-achieving countries teach fewer than half of the standards we teach (Schmidt, 2008). Singapore, Japan, and China teach to about a third as many math and science standards—about 15 per grade level, in comparison with our 50 (Leinwand & Ginsburg, 2007).

Oregon reduced the number of its math standards by more than two thirds, which allowed teachers to teach them in more depth. As a result, students from "every racial, ethnic, and income group" achieved significant math gains. Math achievement in the 8th grade in Oregon nearly rose to the same level as that of an average high school sophomore (Hammond, 2009, p. 1).

In Los Angeles, a Title I school adopted Singapore's in-depth approach to math, with its "greatly reduced number of standards… a fraction of a conventional American text." The very first year of implementation, the school's scores on the California math exam rose from 45 to 76 percent—a 31 percent increase (Landsberg, 2008a).

Adlai Stevenson's (Chapter 3) rise to prominence began with specific directives for teams to make significant reductions in the number of standards and topics in each course (DuFour, DuFour, Eaker, & Many, 2006).

So how do we achieve "viable" curriculum? How do we select the most essential standards—and then use them to build course curriculum?

How to Create "Viable" Curriculum in the Content Areas

Initiating the following procedures is certainly not the only way to select essential standards and build curriculum. But these procedures demonstrate how any school can create coherent, easy-to-understand curricula. This work can be done, for every course, by grade-level or course-alike teams at the school or district level: if a *district* team completes the work, it is imperative that their curricula be sent out for review to all district teachers, whose collective input or suggestions should be reflected in the final version (although, of course, no curriculum is ever wholly "final"; it is a living document, always subject to improvements).

The first important step is to determine the approximate number of days you have to *actually instruct,* after subtracting for days devoted to assemblies or to taking state or local assessments. You might determine, for instance, that you have only about 150 instructional days to teach your curriculum. The next question is how many of those days should be devoted to the common curriculum—and how many should be left to teacher discretion. I like Rick DuFour's (2007) suggestion that we leave teachers two to three weeks per semester to teach their own preferred topics or units.

The next step, once you know how many days you have to spend on teaching your common curriculum, is quite logical: the team should review state or national documents, or both, and estimate, in writing, the approximate number of days it would take to teach each one. Again, I would focus on topics and content, and ignore most of the verbiage (e.g., "analyze," "identify"). I would calculate these time-per-standard estimates somewhat quickly, with a time limit—maybe 30–45 minutes—to avoid becoming bogged down in minutiae and digressions. I would also use pencils; this allows for some adjustment along the way.

When this is done, add up the number of days. If it exceeds the number you have to teach (and it often will), you will need to thoughtfully subtract topics and standards until you achieve "viability"—a match between the most essential standards you want to teach and the number of days you have to teach them. Keep in mind that your curriculum has to make room for what is typically missing in our (so-called) curricula: time and days devoted to purposeful reading, discussion, and writing.

Once this rough, preliminary list is completed, don't be surprised if the team feels a sense of relief—and confidence—in this work: even a crude list—which can now be discussed and adjusted—will exude what most curriculums lack: coherence and economy. Without the "clutter" of the less-essential standards, it will reveal the opportunity for in-depth instruction of a potent core of agreed-upon topics.

Apportion the standards by grading period, in a logical progression of units, topics, or skills. For this work, I suggest teams simply create a four-period grid on a large whiteboard or screen. As you apportion the standards, be sure not to cram too many into a single grading period. Once this is completed, you can proceed to the next step.

Match topics to texts or to teaching resources as appropriate. Not every topic must be taught with a text. On the other hand, texts must play a much larger role in our curricula; they must be liberally infused with purposeful, topic-specific reading, discussion, and writing assignments. Social studies, science, and many elective curricula should include far more texts than has been typical; music and art should include some amount of reading about artists, composers, artistic and musical periods, and so forth. In math, reading assignments should be alternated with—perhaps dominated by—carefully selected textbook or other pages or materials chosen for their ability to effectively teach essential standards.

In all of this work, avoid providing an unfocused array of "optional" readings or resources that adds clutter to your curriculum; that can be as confusing and unhelpful as no resources at all.

The next step is to add focus/guiding questions that provide direction for the reading, lecture, or learning activities that activate the knowledge or skills to be learned. We'll be seeing examples of such questions in Chapters 4 through 7.

In math and many electives, such questions may not always be suitable or essential. As I mentioned earlier, math achievement at my wife's high school soared when teachers selected common standards and then matched them to the best pages in their textbooks for teaching them.

One last, critical step remains, and it may be the most important: we must establish expectations for major or benchmark writing assignments—*prominently and in writing.* The curriculum document itself should clarify expectations for a certain minimum number of common benchmark assessments that include a description of the approximate length and nature of these assignments (Conley, 2005). Without this, we will continue to have what we've had for decades: minimal amounts of writing and tremendous variation in writing expectations among teachers of the same course in the same school or district.

Ideally, our curriculum documents would be reviewed and discussed "vertically" at some point: to make final adjustments that reduce unnecessary redundancy, build on previous-grade learning, and prepare students for essential learning at the next grade level. But even grade-level work of this kind will profoundly increase coherence and thus produce equally profound results.

During the first year of implementation especially, expect some of the contents of these documents to be discarded or replaced. For all of this work, simple curriculum templates can be very helpful.

These can be found in Schmoker (2016) and online at http://www.ascd.org/ASCD/pdf/books/SchmokerAppendixB.pdf.

Once this work is finished, course-alike teams or departments can begin to work together to create lessons, units, and common assessments, beginning with unit or quarterly assessments. The results of these common curriculum-based assessments inform the all-important team discussions among same-course peers and with leaders—principals, assistant principals, department heads, or teacher leaders—at quarterly meetings. These are at the heart of effective leadership in the professional learning community. As DuFour (in Schmoker, 2006) points out, *such meetings are among the best means of ensuring that the essential curriculum is actually being taught.* They were enormously effective at the school where I experienced these curricular and leadership practices firsthand (for additional material on leadership and implementation, see Schmoker, 2016).

I'll end this chapter with a plea to state-level or regional educators: it is high time we realized, as experts such as Lisa Hansel (2013) recommend, that the most effective step we could take to ensure the creation of clear, coherent curricula would be for states or regions to develop and distribute samples of full-year curricula. Even pacing guides, with essential topics or texts, or both, with standards laid out by grading period, would demystify the process of establishing coherent curricula and embolden schools and districts to undertake this task with much greater confidence.

These would be merely state-sponsored or approved samples—subject to local adoption or adjustment—to help schools establish this critical foundation for learning in every course, with all the immense educational and social benefits it would have for teachers and students.

Such efforts could lead, as Hansel (2013) points out, to truly *curriculum-based state tests* that would surpass our still-generic state assessments. The new tests reflect some progress: they help assess more general knowledge and challenging vocabulary than their predecessors, which explains why scores have plummeted on the new assessments (Wattenberg, 2016). But we could devise much richer, curriculum-based assessments that would be more clearly aligned with some amount of core content defined by the state or state consortia—while still leaving plenty of room for local priorities (Hansel, 2013).

We need to do this. Right now.

That's enough, for now, on *what* we teach; we'll look at additional details in Chapters 4 through 7 (which, once again, **are written to allow practitioners, if they wish, to read only those chapters that pertain to their respective subject areas**).

Let's now look at the other factor that, coupled with good curriculum, is equally deserving of our intense and immediate focus: *how* we teach, inclusive of literacy.

3

How We Teach

Improved classroom instruction is the prime factor to improve student achievement gains.

—Allan Odden and Marc Wallace

Finland's most popular methods aren't exactly 'cutting edge'... [Finland's] teachers typically employ **traditional, teacher-directed classroom instruction** *(emphasis added).*

—Timothy Walker, American/Finnish teacher

Perhaps the most salient characteristic of a great teacher is her ability to recognize the difference between "I taught it" and "They learned it."

—Doug Lemov

In this chapter, I describe the well-known, evidence-based elements of *how* we should teach the curriculum—inclusive of authentic literacy practices. The case for these practices has never been stronger. The same could be said for the case *against* the "enemies of effective practice"—the host of popular, feckless pedagogic fads, which I will also describe in detail. This chapter also contains two simple, versatile lesson templates that simplify—and thus facilitate—the employment of the best teaching practices.

Decades of research reveal that teaching matters enormously. Linda Darling-Hammond (Goldberg, 2001) argues that "the single most important determinant of success for students is the knowledge and skills of that child's teacher" (p. 689). Allan Odden and Marc Wallace (2003) observe that "improved classroom instruction is the prime factor to improve student achievement gains" (p. 64). Evidence has compelled us to acknowledge that instructional quality is indisputably "the most important school factor in how much children learn" (Colvin & Johnson, 2007). John Hattie has analyzed hundreds of meta-analyses that themselves represent thousands of studies. As he puts it, the "variability in student outcomes" is largely "the consequence of the variability in teacher effectiveness" (Hattie, 2015).

Effective teaching can alter the academic trajectory of low-achieving students—vaulting them from the lowest to the highest quartile in *three years* (Bracey, 2004; DuFour & Marzano, 2011, Sanders & Horn, 1994). Teaching quality—the what and how of instruction—is the most important factor that affects student learning (DuFour & Marzano, 2011). Or as Katie Haycock (DuFour & Marzano, 2011) sums it up: "In the hands of our best teachers, the effects of poverty and institutional racism melt away" (p. 65).

These facts have caught the attention of the popular press. Writing for *The Atlantic*, journalist Amanda Ripley (2010) has reported on educational practices around the world. She discovered that even in the most challenging schools, certain teaching strategies overcome nonschool factors by large margins. For her, this constitutes "the most stunning finding to come out of education research in the past decade" (p. 2). More recently, she found that the most popular instructional fads and technologies have played no role in the success of the world's best and most improved school systems (Ripley, 2013). As we'll see, they are the primary obstacles to effective, evidence-based practice.

These findings are doubly interesting in light of the discovery that "effective teaching" does not consist of some rare or complex combination of skills unique to each teacher or their circumstances. As Harvard's Richard Elmore (2000) avers, good teaching is not a "mysterious process that varies with each teacher" (p. 16). On the contrary, the most effective teaching is often banal—characterized by seemingly mundane whole-class practices that can be success-fully performed by any conscientious instructor; the practices found in the highest-performing schools are "as plain vanilla as could be imagined" (Goodwin, 2015, p. 135). The most effective teaching methods are "mundane, unremarkable" and even "disappointing" to those who expect them to be complex or "innovative" (Lemov, 2015, p. 10). And they're usually *old*: we've known about these practices for decades.

The evidence for these strategies is now indisputable—so well established that for Robert Marzano (2007), they ought to be "rou-tine components of every lesson" we teach, regardless of grade, topic, or subject area (p. 180). But if, in light of the evidence, we want these practices to *move to the head of the line,* we need to make and reinforce this case ardently and persistently. Our profession has never been driven by evidence, but instead by "whims, fads, opportunism and ideology" (Corcoran et al., 2001). The requirements of the Every Stu-dent Succeeds Act (ESSA) of 2015 may be fortuitous here, with their directive that teacher training be based on evidence of effectiveness.

If the educational impact of these "routine components" is this significant, then we dare not overcomplicate them. To that end, I will attempt to simplify and clarify these elements. Then I will describe two highly effective (and fairly unoriginal) teaching templates that are based on these elements—to make them as "easy to understand" and implement as possible. In combination, these overlapping tem-plates could be used by any teacher, new or veteran, to deliver the majority of the curriculum in any course or grade level.

Effective Lessons: A Refresher Course

Sometimes the first duty of intelligent men is the restatement of the obvious.

—George Orwell,

*[We must resist] the default mechanism that directs us to study and learn more rather than to take action **using what we already know*** (emphasis added).

—Peter Block

Despite their limitless variations, effective lessons share the same, widely recognized structure. It is arguably thousands of years old— as old as teaching itself (e.g., Popham, 2008). When we violate this structure, students underperform by an order of magnitude (Fisher & Frey, 2007; Wiliam, 2007). Although terms may differ, this structure consists of something like the following (which represents my preferred rendering of this basic structure): a clear learning objective or target, accompanied (usually) by an attempt to create interest in the topic (think "anticipatory set"); teaching and modeling in small, "scaffolded" steps, each of which is followed by practice or "guided practice" for each step; checks for understanding ("formative assessment") during and after each practice attempt; and, finally, independent practice/assessment (which can be one and the same). All of these must occur in a classroom in which steps are taken to ensure that students are attentive and engaged.

These terms are not new; they are anything but innovative. Most of us are familiar with them, even if a full understanding—and mastery—of these elements still eludes us. They were formalized in the 1960s, but their essence is as old as teaching itself. And as we'll see, these components apply to the entire range of learning, including the most intellectually challenging, higher-order knowledge, skills, and *projects*.

Let's begin with a look at student attentiveness and engagement.

Student Attentiveness and Engagement

During instruction, the goal should be for all students—not some, not most, but *all* —to be attentive, with eyes on the teacher, listening and responding to directions. There are simple ways to achieve this; for example, the teacher can establish a word or signal—or a brief countdown—that conveys unambiguously that students need to be sitting and looking forward at the teacher. If some students aren't visibly attentive, the teacher might then inform the class that he is still waiting for "some students" or "three [or two] students" to get their eyes on the teacher. When this fails, the teacher can employ eye contact or can move toward the inattentive student (using "proximity"). Done consistently, these steps are enormously effective. I use them, my wife uses them, and every effective teacher I know uses variations on these methods to good effect. That said, when I teach, I carefully avoid having students listen to instructions for unreasonable periods of time. Good teaching should represent sensible proportions of listening, collaborating (usually in pairs), and working independently.

Clear Learning Objectives/Targets

The learning objective should focus on a topic, skill, or concept selected from the agreed-upon curriculum. It must clarify, in student-friendly language, what will be learned and *how the lesson will be assessed.* Some examples:

- **Solve/complete** problems using ratios.
- **Write** an effective **introductory paragraph** for an argument.
- Evaluate a (literary/historical/living) character **in writing.**
- Compare and contrast meiosis and mitosis and represent your work in a **Venn diagram.**

Please note how the words in boldface let learners know *how the lesson will be assessed*—how they will demonstrate their learning of the intended outcome. In Hattie's (2009) lexicon, the learning objective or target should describe how learning will be made "visible" to both the teacher and the students (more on this later in this chapter).

Good learning objectives (or "targets") are very different from the pseudo-objectives I observe in typical classrooms, such as:

- "Vocabulary"
- "Fill out worksheet on *The Call of the Wild.*"
- "Answer the questions at the end of Chapter 4."

These objectives do not describe legitimate, curriculum-based learning; hence they can't describe a legitimate assessment aligned to a worthy learning goal. These are merely assignments or activities, which too often pass for learning targets.

I have provided some versatile, representative learning targets and stems in or at the end of each of the subject-area chapters; these are adapted from learning targets I've seen in effective classrooms. In Chapter 4, you'll also find a list of samples and stems for language arts objectives that can be selectively applied to reading, discussion, and writing lessons in any subject whatsoever. These sample objectives, or variations on them, could cover the majority of the curriculum in most subjects.

But how, then, do we teach sound, curriculum-based objectives—so that the maximum number of students will succeed on each lesson? Like this:

- *Teaching/modeling/demonstrating.* **Effective instruction typically begins with some form of** explicit teaching—explaining, demonstrating, showing students *what to do, what actions to perform,* one at a time, in order for them to acquire knowledge or skills. Such instruction must be conducted in small, incremental steps or chunks.

This doesn't guarantee that students—even very attentive students—will learn every step or increment. Two more elements are critical and often simultaneous: guided practice and checks for understanding (a near-synonym for the most common kinds of "formative assessment").

• *Guided practice.* After each small, manageable chunk of instruction, the teacher must immediately provide an opportunity for students to practice, mimic, or apply what the teacher just taught or modeled. This practice/application step should be brief—and students should be given a **time limit** to complete the step; this conveys urgency and ensures that they don't waste time. I often give students two to four minutes to practice or complete a typical step (it's amazing how much they can accomplish within that time). Guided practice can often include or alternate with opportunities for students to work in pairs and *occasionally* in groups, as students are often each other's best translators of what has been taught.

• *Check for understanding/formative assessment.* This often occurs while students are engaged in guided practice. Although I use the terms "check for understanding" and "formative assessment" almost synonymously, I prefer "check for understanding" because it is the older term, referring to the simplest kinds of formative assessment. This element is especially crucial for the success of the lesson. Both during and after each guided practice attempt, the teacher should be checking—formatively assessing—a sample of students to determine whether students seem to have mastered that particular step and are ready to move on to the next one.

As I discuss later, almost any attempt to "check for understanding" during lessons will immediately increase the proportion of students who will succeed on that day's lesson (as it did for me at a critical stage in my teaching). Here are some simple, common forms of checking for understanding:

—Circulating to observe student work, or listening to students as they work in pairs; even *one to two minutes* of circulating can give you an adequate idea of student progress.

—"Cold calling" on a random (or selective) sample of students or pairs *randomly* between each step (*instead of* calling every time on the same bright students, who typically raise their hands).

—Having students signal their understanding: for example, with thumbs up or down or with red, green, or yellow popsicle sticks.

—Having students hold up dry-erase boards with solutions/ responses.

Such ongoing checks for understanding must be conducted quickly and efficiently—in a minute or two; this is not a time to tutor individual students, which interrupts the important flow and pace of the lesson and isn't necessary if we properly carry out the next step (Rosenshine, 2012, p. 19). These quick checks allow the teacher to know whether and how they need to execute the next element: providing feedback and correctives in the form of adjustments to instruction.

Adjustments to Instruction

Once the teacher ascertains approximately how well students are succeeding on each instructional step, he or she can either move on to the next step (if students are keeping up) or make real-time, same-day adjustments to instruction (e.g., by precisely addressing student confusion, providing a different explanation or example, letting students help each other in pairs—or breaking a challenging step into smaller, easier-to-learn chunks). This additional instruction, or "reteaching," is followed, logically, by yet another cycle of guided practice and checks for understanding—until all students, or as many as possible, are ready for the next brief chunk of instruction.

When students have succeeded on each step of the lesson, they are ready for the final element: independent practice/assessment.

Independent Practice/Assessment

At this point, students should be ready to practice—and more fully demonstrate mastery of—what they have learned. Independent practice is tantamount to assessment; it should match the assessment as it was described in the learning objective. It can consist of a simple list; a diagram; a set of problems or exercises to complete; a solution to a complex problem; an explanatory or argumentative paragraph; notes, annotations, or underlinings that serve as evidence of a close or interpretive reading; and so forth (none of which must always be collected, formally graded, and recorded; much grading and recording can be done during the independent practice stage).

This is an excellent time for the teacher to work with students who still need additional assistance, and if some of the work is to be completed as homework, it allows the teacher to see whether students are truly capable of completing the assessment independently—without parental help (we should know by now that assigning students homework they can't complete is cruel and futile).

As most of you know, there's nothing new here (even if you take issue with my rendering of some of these basic teaching concepts). What *is* new is the mounting evidence that such teaching is not only effective but exceedingly so—perhaps as vital to school success as any other factor (we'll look at the evidence for this later in this chapter). If every teacher mastered and then consistently implemented these basic elements, in most of their lessons, our schools would make unprecedented progress toward the goal of "learning for all." I would estimate that I was able to reach half again as many students within two weeks of implementing these elements.

As mentioned earlier, routinely calling on students *who raise their hands* directly violates everything in this scheme. Even so, this unfortunate practice is still among the most ubiquitous features of schooling; it occurs in over 90 percent of the instruction we observe. Second, these elements *are not one-offs;* they must occur in a continuous cycle, several times, at a lively pace, *for each step in the lesson.* Some steps require several iterations of adjustment: reteaching, pair-share, or breaking one step into smaller chunks.

Our general failure to understand and implement the basic structure of an effective lesson accounts for a staggering amount of the failure we observe in schools.

The Consequences of Poorly Structured Lessons

Here are two true—and depressingly typical—scenarios that I see in many schools.

The first focuses on a veteran social studies teacher in an award-winning high school with better than average test scores (which hide the data indicating that fewer than half of the students are adequately prepared for college or careers). He has initiated inter-disciplinary teaching, employs the latest technology, and has students spend most of their time filling out worksheets or working in groups on multiple-day group projects, which are completed largely by the more capable students in each group. His students do almost no extended reading and even less writing. At no point, at this prize-winning school, has he or his colleagues ever been told that their lessons and projects are devoid of the most important elements of instruction—such as ongoing checks for understanding.

Many miles away, in one of the largest school districts in the United States, I have been invited to visit a subset of schools that have won an award for their modest test score gains (in a district where other schools are experiencing low or declining achievement). They are understandably proud of their gains, which are the result of massive expenditure and exceedingly tight supervision to ensure faithful implementation of a scripted reading program—and response to intervention (RTI). The program requires an army of additional personnel working from multicolored "data walls" to incessantly identify, test, track, and shuffle students to and from tutorials and small-group remediation in reading skills, all built around multiple-choice items like those on the state test.

But something goes wholly unnoticed: when we visit classrooms, *not a single lesson* is conducted appropriately. Throughout the school, these manifestly committed teachers make no attempt to ascertain *whether or how well students are succeeding* during the lesson. And as they implement the scripted program, they routinely call only on the students who raise their hands, while the majority sit idly or whisper quietly to friends. My inquiries reveal that the majority of students fail on daily assessments, the data from which are used to shuttle students to their respective tutorials. Moreover, the time spent on skills-based remediation ensures that students seldom *read or write for an extended time or ever read an entire book*. It never dawns on the program coordinators that this might account for the fact that despite the modest gains, reading comprehension scores have plateaued.

I can't stress enough how common these scenarios are, wherever I go. Educators continue to be diverted toward new methods and programs, toward an excessive, unwholesome obsession with "data," even as the most important aspects of curriculum, teaching, and literacy are mostly ignored.

. . .

To change these patterns, both the elements of good teaching and the case for them must be articulated, discussed, and revisited. Every undergraduate program, professional development department, and new teacher orientation should make these practices a high priority—until they are consistently implemented in our schools.

To that end, I have expanded this section to include late-breaking research that enhances the still-unheralded convergence of opinion about their power and primacy. Then I discuss research that confirms the unprecedented effect that such instruction is likely to have—if it becomes common practice.

Convergence: Research on the Elements of Effective Lessons

There is a remarkable convergence among our most credible researchers on the primacy and power of these fundamental elements of good instruction.

We begin with **Madeline Hunter,** whose seminal findings emerged in the late 1960s. More than anyone, Hunter helped formalize the essential parts of an effective lesson: "learning objective," "anticipatory set," "scaffolded" instruction, "guided practice," "check for understanding," and "independent practice." Even since writing the first edition of this book, I see her language used more than ever; for example, Shaun Killian (2015), writing for the Australian Society for Evidence-Based Teaching, puts the following at the top of his list of most effective teaching practices: "Clear lesson goals" followed by (the now ubiquitous) "Checking for understanding" between each small step in the lesson. An article about an enormously successful high school chemistry teacher attributes her dramatic one-year gains to her implementation of "clear objectives," "guided practice," and "checks for understanding" (Campbell, 2015).

As we've seen, Hunter's whole-class instructional methods are built around the pivotal element of "checking for understanding" that allows the teacher to make informed adjustments to their teaching *during* the lesson—so as to maximize student success at each stage of instruction.

Let's now look at some prominent researchers whose work confirms Hunter's basic model.

James Popham, an emeritus professor of education at the University of California, Los Angeles, is the former president of the American Educational Research Association (AERA). His research reinforces the same elements of effective lessons recommended here: a plan for delivering a "sequenced set of subskills… [in] step-by-step building blocks" (Popham, 2008, p. 24).

But he reserves special praise for formative assessment—or "checking for understanding," in Hunter's lexicon. Between each small "learning progression" (Popham's term) in the lesson, effective teaching requires that we collect formal or informal "assessment evidence" to make "informed adjustments." This ensures that the highest possible proportion of students will "master the target curricular aim" (p. 35). Indeed, the effects of such formative assessment on learning are "among *the largest ever reported*" (p. 2; emphasis added).

He is referring, in part, to research conducted by **Dylan Wiliam** (2007), whose work demonstrates the folly of our current priorities. Both Popham (2008) and Wiliam advocate for the same procedures we've been looking at, such as checking for understanding by using dry-erase boards or hand signals for students to let teachers know *whether they are or aren't ready to move on* to the next step, or "progression," in the lesson. Just as Pfeffer and Sutton (2000) found that old, simple principles are the real drivers of improvement, Wiliam (2007) believes these principles that inform effective lessons have been with us for thousands of years (p. 189).

More recently, **Doug Fisher and Nancy Frey** (2007) have built on Hunter's lesson structure in their book *Checking for Understanding*. They advocate for lessons taught according to the "gradual release of responsibility" model, which gives students increasing amounts of responsibility to complete an assignment independently on the basis of multiple iterations of "guided instruction" (their term) informed by checking for understanding and adjustments to instruction. As Fisher and Frey put it, "Knowing that six or seven students understand [e.g., those who raise their hands] is not the same as knowing that 32 do" (p. 37).

Marilyn Burns, a highly respected author and math educator, recommends that math lessons be taught in short, planned steps in which the teacher models learning and thinks aloud, followed by opportunities for students to practice. When checks for understanding of student practice reveal confusion from any student, the teacher should "stop, deal with the confusion and *move on only when all students are ready*" (Burns, 2007, p. 18; emphasis added). Echoing both Fisher and Frey (2007) and Hunter, Burns believes these methods ensure a "gradual release to independent work" as students demonstrate mastery (p. 20). She also insists, in keeping with Hunter's research, that lessons include frequent opportunities for *"think-pair-share"* (her emphasis) as the teacher notes students' progress and adjusts instruction accordingly (pp. 18–19).

Robert Marzano's meta-analyses have made a rich contribution to education. In his book *The Art and Science of Teaching* (2007), he gives generous credit to the influence of Madeline Hunter—as he makes the case for clear learning goals and the need to segment the lesson into small, manageable chunks of instruction, each one followed immediately by "guided practice"—wherein students process or apply new learning. Between each chunk—at what he calls "strategic stopping points"—the effective teacher gathers feedback on student progress—to determine whether additional explanation or practice is needed before the class moves on to the next chunk of instruction.

For Marzano (2007), these elements are so indispensable that they should be "routine components of every lesson" (pp. 176 and 180). They should be employed whether students are learning a science concept, learning how to write and edit a compare-and-contrast essay, listening to a lecture, or "reading a section of text" (p. 34).

The case for these practices continues to mount: since writing the first edition, I've met other prominent researchers who endorse this basic model. As we'll see—in this and in the remaining chapters—such instruction *does not preclude the proper kind and amount of project, problem-based, and independent student learning;* indeed, such instruction is essential for their success.

Barack Rosenshine, a professor at the University of Illinois, conducted a comprehensive study (Rosenshine, 2012) of "master teachers"—those whose students made the largest gains on achievement tests. He found that on the *most complex tasks and projects,* these teachers were careful to "scaffold" their instruction by teaching in "small steps with student practice after each step" followed by a "check for student understanding." When all students were ready, they could then engage in "independent practice," which the teacher had to continue monitoring. Rosenshine regards these as strategies that every teacher should know and use.

Rosenshine, like others I'll cite here, advises against the common but inefficient attempt to tutor individual students during the lesson: the *least* successful classrooms were those in which "the teachers had to stop at students' desks and provide a great deal of explanation during seatwork." The most successful were those who assessed and then addressed *common patterns of student confusion* for the whole class, followed by additional opportunities for "guided practice"; this saves enormous time and ensures that the greatest number of students will be ready, at the end of the formal lesson, to "engage productively in independent practice" (Rosenshine, 2012, p. 19).

I wish I had discovered the work of the eminent Australian researcher **John Hattie** before writing the first edition of this book. His much-celebrated compendium *Visible Learning* (2009) is based on

800 meta-analyses of over 50,000 studies, conducted with millions of students. It is based on "the largest ever collection of evidence-based research into what actually works in schools to improve learning" (Hattie, 2009, Preface). Researchers from around the world have praised the thoroughness and implications of his work.

Hattie makes many timely points: for example, that against all logic and evidence, we "enshrine" the notion that almost any kind of teaching can be effective and that teachers should be left alone to employ their own distinct teaching style. Educators, he writes, still work in an environment that uncritically adopts various innovations while *ignoring the evidence of what is most effective* (Hattie, 2009, pp. 1–2).

And what is most effective? The evidence points to the same basic foundation we've been describing, with particular attention to the need for most teaching to be explicit—and "visible." The most effective teaching is that in which the student knows precisely what is to be learned and how it is to be evaluated (learning objective); in which each phase of instruction makes the learning explicit and "visible" (modeling/demonstration); in which the teacher can then observe the students' "visible" efforts (check for understanding) as they attempt to mimic, practice, or apply the new learning; and in which the teacher intervenes and reteaches when necessary—until students are ready to complete the work on their own (Hattie, 2009, pp. 22–23). "It is critical," writes Hattie, "that the teaching and the learning are visible. There is no deep secret called 'teaching and learning'.... The teacher must know when learning is correct or incorrect—in order to provide additional instruction or guidance" (p. 25).

He then remarks on the damage done by those who advocate for less "teacher-centered" instruction. It is "stunning," he writes, "how active and involved the best teachers were in the classrooms—it was clear who was in control in those classrooms." Alas, the current rage for less explicit, so-called student-centered or discovery-based learning runs "almost directly opposite to the successful recipe for teaching and learning" for almost every subject, age, and context (Hattie, 2009, p. 31).

Doug Lemov's (2015) *Teach Like a Champion 2.0* is equally emphatic about the need for explicit instruction. But in reading the first edition (2011) of this excellent book, I was puzzled to find that it only contained a brief mention of "check for understanding," buried deep within the third chapter. It was refreshing to open the second edition (2015) to find that he had made an important discovery: that checking for understanding ("CFU," as he calls it) was the primary factor that accounted for the success of the highest-performing teachers in his network of charter schools. So central was CFU that it now occupies the first two long chapters of *Teach Like a Champion 2.0.*

As Lemov puts it, CFU is all about "'real-time' actions—things that teachers do 'before the final bell rings'" (2015, p. 24). Contrary to a common misperception, it is *not* primarily about quizzes, tests, or "exit tickets." His analogy is good drivers, who "check their mirrors every five seconds or so... seeking to identify and remedy misunderstandings on the road as quickly as possible." He likens the desultory results of typical lessons to a car accident that the driver could have prevented simply by doing quick, frequent checks (pp. 24–25).

Once again, CFU has to be done both frequently and quickly. In the middle of a lesson, we don't have several minutes to analyze student data; we must be able to do it in about two minutes (which precludes the frantic and inefficient practice of attempting to tutor individual children while others wait). When quick, efficient CFU reveals a pattern of weakness or misunderstanding, we must "act on the data" for the *entire class* by "immediately changing the course of the lesson to respond to the lack of mastery." Instruction itself must be conducted so as to make both success and errors *visible:* if we can't see students' work, we can't help them improve it (Lemov, 2015, p. 25). We must "have students actively show evidence of their understanding" (p. 27). He also prescribes cold calling, the use of whiteboards, and circulating to quickly assess a meaningful sample of students to determine whether we must reteach or can now move on to the next step of instruction (p. 27).

What kind of impact has CFU had on schools in his network? All of them outperform their counterparts by large margins. In one of them, Troy Preparatory School in New York, 96 percent of the population is eligible for free and reduced-price lunch. In 2011, 40 percent of such high-poverty schools passed the state math test. Not so at Troy—where 100 percent of its students passed the exam. During the first year of Common Core math testing, the passing rate for similar schools plummeted to 28 percent. But at Troy Preparatory, 74 percent passed—more than twice as many students. So much for the notion that explicit instruction succeeds only with lower-order tasks and assessments. Such evidence has convinced Lemov (2015) that CFU is "the most salient characteristic" of effective teaching—in any subject.

As mentioned, this convergence has found its way into the popular press. Journalist Elizabeth Green's (2014) widely read article "Building a Better Teacher" pulls back the curtain on what makes teachers effective. It consists of the same basic elements described in this chapter: showing students, in small steps, "one at a time... the exact processes they'll need to complete" in order to succeed on any lesson; adjusting or reteaching when necessary; and "cold calling," to determine whether all students are learning—not just the brighter ones (Green, 2014).

Amanda Ripley writes for *The Atlantic*. While writing about Teach for America, she stumbled onto what accounts for student success more than any other factor. The best teachers, she wrote,

> Frequently *check for understanding:* Are the kids—all the kids—following what you are saying? Asking "Does anyone have any questions?" does not work. (Ripley, 2010, p. 5; emphasis added)

For Ripley, this constitutes "the most stunning finding to come out of education research in the past decade" (p. 2).

With this much agreement among so many prominent researchers, it is time that our profession made the dissemination and discussion of this evidence one of its most urgent priorities. The big payoff will come if we *actually implement such lessons*. In quantitative terms, what would happen if we did?

"Stunningly Powerful Consequences" of Soundly Structured Lessons

We saw earlier that lessons built around same-day formative assessment or checks for understanding produce student learning effects that are "among *the largest ever reported*" (Popham, 2008, p. 2). Considerable evidence corroborates this observation. Paul Black and Dylan Wiliam (1998), whose research was based on more than 250 studies, found that lessons that include effective use of formative assessment or checks for understanding produced these results:

• They would have *20 to 30 times* as much positive effect on learning as the most popular current initiatives.

• They are about *10 times* as cost-effective as reducing class size.

• They would add between *6 and 9 months* of learning growth per school year, per student.

• They account for as much as 400 percent "speed of learning differences"; that is, in some classrooms, students would learn *four times as fast* as a result of its consistent use (Wiliam, 2007, p. 186).

• The results of such teaching would vault the *United States from approximately number 18 into the top 5 in international rankings in mathematics.*

• They could possibly have more upward effects on school out-comes than would any other instructional change.

Outcomes such as these help explain the findings cited earlier that seem too good to be true:

• Only *three years* of effective teaching will catapult students in the lowest quartiles into the second or even first/highest quartile (Bracey, 2004; Haycock, 2003; Marzano, 2007, p. 2; Sanders & Horn, 1994).

• Effective teaching could eliminate the achievement gap in about five years (Schmoker, 2006).

• The result of formative assessment is comparable with the results achieved through one-on-one tutoring (Stiggins, 2006).

• The highest-performing teachers ensure that students learn about twice as much material in the same amount of time as their peers do (Garnaut, 2007).

Even conservative extrapolations of the data just described would indicate that widespread implementation of such instruction would result in historic improvements: the lower-achieving half of students would make at least 8 to 10 percentile gains *per year*—as a group (this is actually much less than Marzano [2007, pp. 2–3] estimates). The poverty and ethnicity gap would shrink precipitously, even as high-achieving students would attain new heights of achievement. The number of students prepared for college or careers would increase at a rate that would redefine our assumptions about what ordinary schools can achieve with a broad spectrum of students. In short, the effects would be unprecedented.

And that's not all. Results of another study underline the larger cultural and economic benefits of effective schooling. According to the Brookings Institute, increases in levels of education have a larger than previously estimated effect on individual incomes, lifetime earnings, social mobility, health, and life expectancy—even the odds that children will be raised in stable, two-parent families (Greenstone et al., 2012).

This doesn't even take into account the two other "high-leverage" factors discussed here: coherent curriculum and improved literacy instruction. There is compelling evidence that this combination would indeed result in "stunningly powerful consequences" for our schools and students (Fullan, 2010).

None of these improvements will happen if these practices are already operative—or largely operative—in most schools. Are they? This next section points to a prodigious opportunity, the consequence of a profession that has put "whims, fads, opportunism, and ideology" (Corcoran et al., 2001) ahead of evidence for decades.

The Opportunity

> *You can't check for understanding* if you are sitting down. *Wherever I go as a consultant, it seems like* **90 percent of teachers** *are in the habit of spending too much time sitting during the period.*
>
> —Tim Kanold, author and former superintendent of
> Adlai Stevenson High School, Lincolnshire, Illinois

The most vital fact about these practices is that they are so terribly rare. That's not bad news. If they were implemented, the outcomes would be both swift and significant because of what might be called the "Fosbury effect" (described next), which occurs when any person or group adopts a practice that is (1) vastly superior to existing practices, and (2) absent or grossly under-implemented.

In the mid-1960s, an average high school high-jumper named Dick Fosbury discovered that he could jump higher by leaping backward—not forward—over the high bar. The result was immediate. Young Fosbury increased the height of his jump by a full 6 inches in a single afternoon—a massive increase. From then on, every high-jumper or track team had the opportunity to make similarly large, immediate gains—but only if they actually adopted what came to be known as the "Fosbury flop" (Burnton, 2012).

In education, we also made an analogous discovery in the 1960s: that if teachers build lessons like those described in this chapter, far more students will learn (and, I would add from personal experience, would enjoy and *be far more engaged* in each day's lesson). Unlike the high-jumping community, however, we chose to ignore the evidence. We are like coaches who have yet to discover—or implement—the Fosbury flop. As Brookhart and Moss (2013) found, school leaders are often confident that practices such as checks for understanding are indeed occurring in classrooms—even when they aren't, not even in the "best" teacher's classrooms.

Once again: this is not bad news. It means that we could be on the cusp of a historic breakthrough that would occur the moment our entire community turns its full attention to these powerful practices.

As with curriculum and literacy, our adoption of these strategies would be especially transformative *because they are now implemented in only a tiny fraction of our schools and classrooms.*

Numerous studies and testimonials affirm how rare these practices are in our schools and how they are merely introduced or ignored in our schools of education (Fisher and Frey, 2007; Hattie, 2009, p. 109; Marzano, 2007, p. 176). ASCD author Barry Beers gathered data from about 5,000 classrooms during a 10-year period. He found that fewer than 5 percent of the teachers he observed provided lessons with clear learning objectives or checks for understanding (2014, personal correspondence).

This confirms what I have observed in countless classrooms for more than two decades. In even the most recent work I have done with a handful of districts, the same patterns prevail: the overwhelming majority of district teachers did not implement clear learning objectives; they did not teach in small, manageable steps, provide guided practice, or check for understanding and adjust their pace or instruction accordingly. They had never been adequately taught how to do these things, nor urged to do so (we'll see why in a moment).

In every district, I was accompanied by central office personnel, teachers, and principals. After visiting only a few classrooms, they would become visibly uncomfortable as they saw how effective practice was almost wholly supplanted by worksheet-driven activities and almost always completed in groups (more on these patterns to be described). And the lessons themselves often took a back seat to inexplicably long "warm-ups" or "Do Nows," which ate up large portions of class time. In almost every classroom, teachers called on only the students who raised their hands, thus ignoring the needs of the silent, usually inattentive majority of students. These (mal)practices were common to both low- and high-scoring schools.

In one district, the central office team was so troubled that they had several of their reputedly most effective instructors provide a brief demonstration lesson. But not one made any attempt to teach in small chunks or to let us practice a step or procedure while they checked to ensure that we had successfully completed it. They didn't seem to know how—or to think this was important. It was an awkward morning.

Despite these revelations, not one of those districts made any changes to their professional development. Not one made any organized effort to train or mentor new teachers to master these elements (with the exception of one school in one district). When my contract ended, the central office simply moved on to other initiatives, comfortable in the above-average ratings they received from the state, still advertising in local outlets that they were "committed to excellence."

None of this should surprise us; such malpractice has prevailed at the expense of good teaching for decades (Elmore, 2000; Good & Brophy, 1997; Hirsch, 2016; Odden, 2009; Tyack & Cuban, 2003). Good and Brophy (1997) found that low-level worksheets dominate the school day and that instruction is still focused on "a small set of students"—the ones who raise their hands during instruction. They found that teacher training is so inadequate that teachers aren't even aware that the most common practices guarantee that our students are grossly shortchanged (pp. 24–25).

The point here is this: most schools are poised to experience swift, significant growth—once we choose to adopt practices that are vastly superior to the most common current methods. Let's now look at a possible future: at schools and teachers who shunned pedagogic fads and instead took up the gauntlet of effective instruction with a fierce and singular focus.

When Teachers Use Formative Assessment ("Checks for Understanding")

As you consider these brief profiles, keep in mind that not one of these educators used complicated new strategies or technology; none of them grouped students by "learning styles" or ability. Rather, they were all about effective, usually whole-class, teaching in classrooms whose students had a considerable range of academic abilities.

Elementary School Reading Teachers

I have been fortunate to know and observe several highly effective kindergarten and 1st grade teachers in high-poverty schools. Their students learn to master decoding skills two to three times as fast as their colleagues, often outperforming students from the affluent schools in their respective districts.

Their secret is that they spend far less time than their peers attempting to tutor multiple individuals or small groups while most of the students sit passively, waiting for their turn to learn (Ford & Opitz, 2002). From day 1, these teachers provide well-organized, whole-class reading lessons (which I'll detail in Chapter 4), replete with continuous checks for understanding. That's why virtually all of their students read and decode independently well before the end of the 1st grade.

Kristie Webster works at J. B. Sutton Elementary School in inner-city Phoenix. One hundred percent of this school's students receive free or reduced-price lunch. Sutton's students' scores soared in a two-year period when Sutton teachers began to provide whole-class lessons in which checks for understanding were consistently employed—and monitored by the principal. In Webster's 5th grade class, her inner-city charges write daily and read multiple chapter books each year. The year before I interviewed Webster, 92 percent of her students had passed the state reading exam; 100 percent passed the writing exam.

Middle School English Teachers

In a district where I worked, two middle school English teachers decided to radically revamp their teaching around a simple formula: effective whole-class instruction in reading, discussion, and writing. All students read the same books and documents, discussed them in depth, and then wrote argumentative papers about the *same readings. The teachers did not perform "differentiated" instruction; that is, they did not assign some or most students books that were below their grade level.* They did nothing innovative. On any given day, students were reading, analyzing text, discussing or writing about their common texts—or being taught explicitly to do so. These teachers' lessons were models of step-by-step instruction, guided practice, and checks for understanding. I saw, up close, that virtually every student succeeded on every major writing assignment (the most robust assessment of both skillful *reading* and writing). The first year these teachers implemented this approach, and despite the fact that 45 percent of their students qualified for free and reduced-price lunch, the students' achievement rose from average to first in the state (in a tie with two other schools, which had virtually no students living in poverty).

Two High School English Teachers

I knew an Advanced Placement (AP) social studies teacher who worked in a high-poverty high school across town from his district's affluent sister school. The majority of his lessons were models of "interactive lecture" (which we'll examine in a moment): whole-class lecture and note taking, punctuated by frequent opportunities for students to pair and to share and process their learning. He was always circulating, listening as students discussed, and checking for understanding to ensure that they were taking good notes as he adjusted his instruction on this basis. As a result, *almost twice as many* of his students took and passed the AP History exam as in his affluent sister school (curiously, none of the leaders from his school or the central office paid any attention to his accomplishments; they were too busy instituting multiple "innovations" and technology during those years).

Another high school teacher, of whom I've written elsewhere, is Sean Connors. It was a pleasure to watch him employ the very practices described here: he always "scanned" to ensure that *all of his students were attentive*—occasionally reminding them that all eyes needed to be on him as he modeled and explained each small step of his lessons. These were always followed, at a brisk, purposeful pace, by guided practice and very quick checks for understanding and similarly brief adjustments to instruction. No one was bored, and virtually every student—I'm not exaggerating—succeeded on each step.

The first time I observed Sean, we collected all of his students' introductory paragraphs (the focus of that day's learning objective). Every paragraph was at least competent; some were exceptional. There was no ability grouping in his class—he provided only sound, whole-class instruction that any conscientious teacher could emulate. After that first observation, his principal told me that the results Sean achieved—with his students alone—had increased the success rate on the state writing test *for his entire school* by 26 points. It was the largest gain in the state for a large, comprehensive high school (Schmoker, 2006).

Are we ready to redirect our time and leadership efforts away from the "initiative of the month" and toward the consistent implementation of such simple, evidence-based methods? One of the best ways to make that happen is for every school and district to create and employ a clear but versatile lesson template throughout the school and district. Adlai Stevenson High School benefited greatly from the implementation of such a template.

Adlai Stevenson High School: A Common Lesson Template

Adlai Stevenson High School in Lincolnshire, Illinois, is among the most successful and celebrated high schools in the United States. At Stevenson, there is a clear, written curriculum for every course, focused on a *judiciously reduced set of standards* determined by same-course instructors. For more than a decade, students made substantial, uninterrupted gains on every assessment administered—standardized tests, end-of-course and end-of-quarter assessments, and AP exams. And—once again—the success was almost immediate: some of the largest gains came in *the first and second years*. Over time, Stevenson increased its AP success rate by 800 percent (Schmoker, 2001). Stevenson is a model of effective team-based professional learning communities, in which teachers work in teams to ensure that common, coherent curriculum and effective, ever-improving lessons are consistently implemented.

Tim Kanold, referenced earlier, is the former superintendent and principal of Adlai Stevenson High School, as well as an award-winning teacher and distinguished author of multiple math textbooks. He succeeded Rick DuFour as superintendent in 2001. Over lunch, we talked about the simple elements of effective teaching that have made a powerful difference at his school.

To ensure consistency and to reinforce the fundamental elements of good lessons, teachers work from a common lesson format—one that contains the same basic elements described in this chapter. As Kanold explains, lessons are to be taught in *small steps*. For instance, each math teacher *models* only one or two problems in a math lesson and then *stops*—to let students *practice* only those one or two problems while the teacher *circulates*. There should, he insists, *be at least four or five such cycles* in any legitimate lesson.

For Kanold, "real-time, same-day" checks for understanding are the heart of an effective lesson. As he put it, checking for understanding is "one of the primary things we look for when we tour classrooms as a team.[1] Then we report back [to the faculty] on what we saw."

Brockton High School, as described in Chapter 2, made impressive gains under the leadership of Sue Szachowicz. I visited Brockton and interviewed Szachowicz in 2013. She told me that she had become "convinced that the key to improvement for a school was by improving instruction." Alas, as a new administrator who saw the importance of monitoring curriculum and instruction regularly, she found herself

> horrified by what I saw. At that moment, I knew that we had to work as a team on having a common system and vocabulary for observing teaching if we were going to improve instruction.

---

[1] As I've written elsewhere, I consider such classroom tours indispensable. After these tours, I think initial feedback to teachers can be collective: to the entire faculty, with a focus on the most common instructional concerns. This can be followed—when necessary—with feedback provided to individual teachers.

Fortunately, Sue had attended workshops by a knowledgeable local expert on such teaching, Jon Saphier. She "called Jon immediately and begged" him to train her coaches and administrators in his teaching and monitoring methods. Interestingly, Szachowicz told me in an email, "One of the first workshops we did was on 'checking for understanding.'" Fortunately for Brockton students, the faculty "loved his [Saphier's] strategies and constantly used them." Sue was emphatic that none of Brockton's achievements were the result of differentiated instruction: grouping students by ability and then frantically attempting to provide lessons to each group. Their success was a direct result of effective whole-class instruction using common, literacy-rich curriculum.

Brockton's focus on curriculum, literacy, and effective instruction was responsible—again, in the *first year* of implementation—for the largest gains in the state of Massachusetts. This was followed by their rapid rise into the top 10 percent in the state, where they remain. Harvard's Ronald Ferguson studied Brockton's storied achievement. He attributed their success to a deep understanding of effective instruction and to the "moral obligation" felt by the faculty of such schools to provide such teaching to every student (Ferguson, 2016).

• • •

As we've seen, the convergence of research, expert testimony, and school evidence is so compelling that these simple elements should be routine components of every lesson. So why is such instruction so rarely found in schools?

The following section is an attempt to answer that question. In it, I share evidence of some representative obstacles to effective instruction: widely implemented but unproven, ineffective practices that we accept unquestioningly, even as they prevent the very best practice from having a transformative effect on students. Parts of this section might offend some educators. I share it in the hope that it will help us to get past our addiction to the "whims, fads, opportunism and ideology" that have long plagued schooling and our efforts to improve it (Corcoran et al., 2001).

Obstacles to Effective Instruction

*[School improvement] takes recognition of and **moral outrage** at ineffective practices.*
>   —Roland Barth, Harvard Graduate School of Education

Every year, schools and districts adopt new initiatives that prevent us from maintaining a "hedgehog focus" on the best evidence-based practices. The research base for these new initiatives is typically weak to nonexistent. But best practice has other enemies as well: long-standing, destructive practices that are so entrenched that we barely notice and thus never question them.

All of the following both complicate improvement and divert precious time and attention away from that "smallest possible number of high-leverage practices" that could have a transformative effect on educational attainment (Fullan, 2010):

- Differentiated instruction and its close cousins: "personalized" or "individualized" learning
  - Ever-present worksheets
  - RTI (as often implemented)
- Project- or discovery-based learning (if improperly implemented)
  - Excessive group work
  - Complex teacher evaluation templates
  - Excessive dependence on technology
  - Teacher evaluation templates

All of them, as we'll see, intersect with each other's worst tendencies. Let's begin with an examination of differentiated instruction.

Differentiated instruction. There have always been those who advocate that each child needs and deserves a unique education, suited to their particular interests and abilities. The most radical and popular form of such "individualized" instruction is exemplified by the current rage for differentiated instruction.

Several hundred books have been written on this method, which explicitly advocates that students be grouped by ability. But it goes further, insisting that teachers customize both curricular materials and instruction around a number of other factors: the student's (often self-diagnosed and self-prescribed) "learning style," cultural background, interests, hobbies, and activities. Teachers are urged to take all of these factors into account as they develop and provide customized curricular materials and modes of instruction for groups and individuals (Tomlinson, 1999). Countless teachers have told me that this is a nearly impossible, anxiety-inducing expectation.

None of it is proven. All of it has been debunked in every aspect: barring the most exceptional cases, we know that ability grouping within the classroom suppresses expectations and achievement, especially for low achievers (Good & Brophy, 1997) and that the notion of "learning styles" is not only unfounded but also inimical to good instruction (Hirsch, 2016; Willingham, 2005, 2009a) and may "exacerbate achievement gaps" (Hattie, 2009, p. 194). Differentiated instruction makes effective, whole-class instruction difficult, if not impossible.

For more than a decade, experts have pointed out that there isn't any evidence supporting this approach (Goodwin, 2015; Finn, 2014; Schmoker, 2010; Willingham, 2005). As researcher Bryan Goodwin writes, there is "no empirical evidence" for the effectiveness of this popular pedagogic fad. Not even its advocates would claim that "differentiated instruction" is an "evidence-based practice." It is not listed anywhere, as one of the top 10, 100, or 200 proven practices. And yet somehow it became a requirement, built right into the most commonly used teacher evaluation frameworks (more on this later).

As John Hattie (2009) writes, the "highest effect was when the *same treatment was provided for all students* and not varying the instruction depending on learning preferences" (p. 197). His examples of successful or dramatically improved classrooms are never differentiated classrooms (Hattie, 2009, 2015).

As E. D. Hirsch (2016) tells us, "International studies have shown that a differentiated curriculum is harmful to achievement and equity." The idea that student success is "largely dependent upon the child's uniqueness is an idea unsupported by developmental psychology" (p. 11).

This doesn't mean we never provide extra tutoring or make accommodations for certain students—such as students for whom English is a second language or those receiving special education (as good instructors always have)—at certain times. It does mean that we must avoid the trap of routinely grouping students into specious, contrived categories that make effective whole-class instruction almost impossible. High-achieving countries (and the highest-achieving U.S. teachers) provide carefully structured whole-class lessons that work for all levels of students (DeWitt, 2016b; Stigler & Hiebert, 1999). They know the dangers of ability grouping (Allington in Good & Brophy, 1997; Oakes, 1992). And they know that mixed-ability pairs and groups are beneficial to *both low- and high-achieving* students. Stanford's Carol Dweck (in DeWitt, 2016a) found that high achievers benefit as much as or more than low achievers in mixed-ability settings, that "the act of explaining learning to others deepens... and strengthens what they know."

As Hirsch (2016) concludes, "our experiment in educational individualism" not only has failed; it also "has turned schools into soulless test-prep factories" (pp. 7–8). Because differentiated instruction requires different curricula for each group and level, it devolves predictably into a hastily assembled set of test-preparation activities and worksheets—one of the most pervasive and insidious features of American schooling. We need to take a moment to think about the catastrophic effect these features have had.

Ever-present worksheets. As described earlier, commercial worksheets have become a ubiquitous feature of American schooling. Both research studies and my focus groups confirm that students spend about half or more of their time in school completing these low-level, fill-in-the-blank commercial products that are seldom aligned with any coherent curriculum (Good & Brophy, 1997, p. 26). Because they are so pervasive and integral to so many popular programs and pedagogies, they may be the greatest obstacle to effective instruction—and to reading comprehension itself, inasmuch as they invariably consume time that should be spent reading.

There is a reason they have been called "shut-up sheets." They effectively pacify students—or groups of students—for alarmingly long periods of time. And their use is often accompanied by another extremely common phenomenon: their slow, passive completion by students. Well into the class period, we consistently observe that some students or groups have not even begun to fill out their worksheet, even as others are halfway through—or finished—with theirs. Teachers rarely assign sensible time limits for their completion. The time limit often appears to be: whenever the slowest student or group finishes the assignment.

Differentiated instruction has given new life and rationale to worksheet-centered practices. Because the teacher can be with only one "unique" group at a time, the remaining groups need something to occupy them while they are waiting for the teacher to give them the instruction specific to their "differentiated" assignment.

This brings us to the next popular obstacle to effective practice: response to intervention (RTI), which too often inadvertently encourages worksheet-driven, low-level instruction.

Response to Intervention: "more popular than proven." In the last few years, different versions of RTI have become a common feature of schooling. As one observer writes, RTI spread across the American educational landscape "like the latest diet fad" (Vanderheyden, Burns, Brown, & Tilley, 2016, p. 25). And like so many pedagogic fads, its benefits are largely unproven. The program is supposed to ensure that struggling students receive extra assistance on a timely, sometimes daily basis. This extra assistance is intended to reduce failure rates and increase the number of students who succeed. What's not to like?

Plenty, it turns out. The title of an *Education Week* report is telling: "RTI: More Popular Than Proven?" As Sarah Sparks (2011) writes in that report, "RTI's use is far outstripping its research base."

The most recent comprehensive federal evaluation of this ubiquitous program revealed that it is not only ineffective but also "may hold back some of the children it was originally designed to support." First graders in the program actually performed worse than their peers, and special education students "performed particularly poorly" when enrolled in RTI (Sparks, 2015, p. 1).

How can this be? Because RTI, like so many innovations, was never tested and refined before it went national. And so we failed to notice that it diverts our focus away from effective instruction—and may even encourage inferior instruction. Several studies confirm what I saw in Chicago: that RTI subtly diminishes a focus on the importance of good initial teaching—what the program calls "Tier 1" instruction. When teachers know that there is a large tutoring apparatus in place for students who fail on daily lessons, they are less prone to ensure the quality of those lessons. The program inadvertently conveys the notion that success depends primarily on *tutoring* that comes after (presumably effective) instruction. When we visited classrooms in which RTI was implemented, we observed teachers who took even less trouble than usual to assess student progress—and make critical adjustments—during the lesson. They flew through lessons while the less-capable and inattentive majority of students languished. That meant that the *majority* needed tutoring. But tutoring—as most teachers know—often consists of skills-based test prep, which robs students of what they really need time for: reading, writing, and the acquisition of knowledge and vocabulary.

Formal studies on RTI confirm this. According to one (Bryson, Maden, Mosty, & Schultz, 2010), the program encourages an insidious transfer of responsibility from the teacher to the cadre of tutors, who drill students in remedial exercises but deny them the benefits of a more robust grade-level curriculum. Another study (Lipson & Wixson, 2008) demonstrated that teachers of regular education believed that RTI absolved them of having to provide effective "Tier 1" instruction; if students didn't learn, RTI would take care of it. This study also confirmed that "Tier 2" tutoring typically consisted of multiple-choice, worksheet-driven remediation efforts.

The real issue for schools today is not that we don't have enough tutors or remediation (though sensible amounts are sometimes necessary). It is the need for all teachers to master and implement the basic moves of good teaching and to refine practice with their colleagues in collaborative teams. One of the reports on RTI makes it quite clear that

> When core instruction is strong, a majority of students perform in the "not at risk" range on screening. (Vanderheyden et al., 2016, p. 25)

That is, effective instruction greatly reduces or eliminates the need for most tutoring and remediation (Sean Connors did all of his own tutoring—when necessary—during the "independent practice" portion of his lessons). But RTI delays our reckoning with this central educational fact.

The interventions previously described either compete with or subordinate the importance of effective whole-class teaching focused on a rich, coherent curriculum. The same can be said of another popular—and misunderstood—approach: project-based learning, which often overlaps with another obstacle to effective instruction—excessive group work. Both can be effective, if implemented appropriately.

Project- or discovery-based learning. "Project-based" or "discovery-based" learning can be a powerful form of teaching. It allows students to independently acquire, explore, and apply knowledge to more extended, authentic tasks.

But there are risks; certain conditions are necessary to its success. Many of its advocates assume that independent, discovery-based assignments and projects should be the primary, dominant mode of instruction. They believe that if students are free to work alone or on group tasks, they will acquire essential skills and knowledge on their own. And they often assume that such "student-centered" or self-directed instruction is superior to explicit or teacher-led instruction.

These are not safe assumptions. In "The Perils and Promises of Discovery Learning," Robert Marzano (2011b) writes that research simply doesn't support unstructured instruction, which characterizes so much of "discovery-based learning." Similarly, as Anita

Archer and Charles Hughes (2011) point out, an endless list of skills and applications of knowledge cannot and will not be "discovered" independently or in groups by the majority of students (e.g., how to master and apply knowledge of ratio and proportions to a real-world problem; how to organize material for an argumentative essay). These require large initial amounts of explicit, intensive guidance from instructors—or they will be learned inadequately, inefficiently, or not at all (p. vii). And as John Hattie (Boss, 2014) informs us, project-based learning (as conventionally implemented) has an effect size of only 0.15—which doesn't even qualify as an "effective practice."

An example of this point: my niece enrolled in a new school. Until she arrived there, she had not been taught to write. At the new school, she learned, through explicit, carefully sequenced whole-class lessons, how to write an extended argumentative essay—a complex, open-ended project. She did not "discover" how to do this on her own or learn it by collaborating with her peers (although her instruction included such interaction). She learned the elements of composition from an expert teacher: how to carefully read, annotate, and take notes from a text; how to develop a clear argument or thesis; how to determine which portions of the text would best support her argument; how to integrate quotes and paraphrased material into her essay; and how to explain how this material supported and advanced her argument.

This project and limitless others could not be learned or successfully completed in the absence of large amounts of initial, explicit instruction (mindlessly derided by some as "teacher-driven"). She had to learn these skills before she could complete this and other written "projects" in all of her coursework, in every discipline. But having been taught these essential intellectual skills, she could now be given far more time to work independently on other discovery-based projects, even as she continued to receive explicit instruction on the finer points of writing.

Marzano, Hattie, and Rosenshine—all arch-advocates of explicit instruction—make plain that independent or collaborative projects *do belong in the curriculum*—but not until students have been explicitly taught the prerequisite skills and knowledge necessary to succeed on these tasks (Hattie in McDowell, 2017; Marzano, 2011b; Rosenshine, 2012, p. 13). And as Marzano points out, even such projects should be built around the elements of effective teaching (p. 87).

Under the right conditions, both independent and collaborative projects are not only permissible but also essential to a good education. The same might be said of one of its common components: group work, which carries similar risks unless implemented in proper proportion.

Excessive group work. The right amount of peer interaction is essential to learning, especially in pairs. And the right amount of *group* work can enhance students' social, intellectual, and communicative skills. That said, most educators agree with me when I hint that group work now consumes too much class time. They are even more apt to agree with this after I predict, before classroom tours, that (1) we probably won't see much actual teaching or instruction, but (2) we *will* see a heck of a lot of group work—much of it focused on the completion of worksheets. Once they are alerted to this pattern, they are often shocked by how excessive it is. They know this can't be optimal for students and their learning.

We are finally realizing the dangers of such an overemphasis. Researchers have been calling for us to scale back the amount of group work for years (Lemov, 2015; Marzano, Pickering, & Pollock, 2001). In *Classroom Instruction That Works*, Marzano, Pickering, and Pollock (2001) warn that group work is "frequently overused" at the expense of more productive modes of instruction (pp. 88–89). Good and Brophy (1997) found that active learning typically *declines* during group work, that certain students monopolize small group sessions, and that monitoring student learning is "much more complex" when students work in groups—and it is more difficult to know who's learning what (p. 29).

Most recently, researcher Tom Bennett (2015) has provided us with an eye-opening analysis of the research in a widely read article in *American Educator*. He is emphatically "not against group work" and makes judicious use of it with his own students (p. 8). But as he demonstrates, there simply isn't evidence that group work is superior to explicit whole-class instruction for teaching the bulk of the curriculum. There's even evidence that the most powerful form of "cooperative learning" is having students work in pairs—not groups (Berliner & Casanova, 1996).

This hasn't kept us from increasing the amount of time students spend in group work. Some authors estimate that group work now occupies about *70 percent of the school day* (DeWitt, 2016b). I have even worked with schools that have made this their primary innovation, with high but unfounded hopes that it will close the achievement gap. But as Bennett (2015), a still-practicing teacher, points out, such indiscriminate, excessive group work inevitably devolves into

> disguised inactivity... students are provided with an opportunity to put their backs into doing nothing, all hidden inside the smog of collaborative effort. (p. 8)

This echoes the findings of Shawn Killian (2017), who found that too much group work means a lot of "social loafing" but not much productive activity.

It might surprise many educators that there are tremendous benefits to, and advocates for, having students sit not in groups but *in rows, facing the instructor.* Timothy Walker (Stoltzfus, 2017), an American teacher who writes for *The Atlantic*, studied schools in high-performing Finland. He discovered that Finnish teachers have found that having students sit in rows is the most effective default arrangement. He also found that students in Finland are given more time to work silently or alone for extended periods (Stoltzfus, 2017).

Doug Lemov believes that group work can sometimes be effective but that the default arrangement should be for rows in which pairs of desks are joined side by side, with a space between pairs. This allows the teacher to circulate and check for understanding and is also ideal for students to easily and frequently "pair-share" (Lemov, 2015). Most critically, it means that *students are facing the teacher during instruction.* When I guest-teach, I request this arrangement beforehand: it facilitates frequent peer interaction, attentiveness, and eye contact between myself and the students as I teach.

Bennett (2015) also makes an arresting point: that teachers are often docked in their teaching evaluations for not including group work in their lessons. As with "differentiated instruction," we have allowed popularity to trump empiricism by building unproven pedagogic fads right into our teacher evaluations and then requiring teachers to abide by them. We've yet to grasp the absurdity of such requirements.

This brings us to teacher evaluation itself. If our success depends, in Fullan's (2010) words, on "the smallest number of high leverage, easy-to-understand" practices, then few things could wreak more havoc than the new complex frameworks for teacher evaluation. Let's look at them now.

Complex teacher evaluation templates. Our new frameworks for teacher evaluation violate everything we know about instructional quality and professional morale. Instead of helping teachers focus on the most vital practices, they contain an unproven profusion of criteria—all purportedly "research-based" (which they aren't). These new frameworks heighten anxiety even as they complicate improvement efforts.

As mentioned previously, Marcus Buckingham (2005) found that effective organizations made their greatest strides after reducing evaluation criteria to a bare minimum of crystal-clear priorities. In another study, Pulakos, Mueller-Hanson, O'Leary, & Meyrowitz (2012) found that both employees and managers perform best when evaluation criteria are reduced to

> *as few competencies as are necessary* to capture the job's critical requirements… as few as three or 4… there is no compelling, practical reason to rate a large number of competencies. (p. 11; original emphasis)

Educators didn't get the memo. *The New York Times* reports that one popular evaluation framework contains 116 separate categories (Anderson, 2012). The organization that first called attention to the inadequacies of teacher evaluation was TNTP (2009) in *The Widget Effect*. Ironically, they now regret that the new "observation rubrics are too long and complex to yield accurate ratings or useful feedback." It is time, they write, to put these rubrics "on a diet" (TNTP, 2013).

And guess who wrote the following? Charlotte Danielson (2015), the architect of the first and most widely used framework, now admits—to her credit—that it is

> just too big... there's just too much detail to permit [evaluators] to focus on the important ideas about teaching.... When observing a lesson, whether as part of a coaching relationship or for evaluation, it's too cumbersome for everyday use. (p. 9)

She advocates that her own framework be reduced *by at least 75 percent*—and perhaps even more in the future (Danielson, 2015). Her remarks, I believe, are just as true of the other major frameworks; Robert Marzano has performed a similarly draconian reduction of his evaluation framework (see The Marzano Focused Teacher Evaluation Model at www.learningsciences.com/wp/wp-content/uploads/2017/06/Focus-Eval-Model-Overview-20170321.pdf).

I find all these recent frameworks—even after their architects claim to have "streamlined" them—far too cumbersome, ambiguous, and unfocused. I had a personal encounter with the Teacher Advancement Program (TAP) evaluation rubric not long ago while working with university teacher evaluators. When I conducted a discussion with the group, all admitted deep frustration with the tool and a deep desire to make it clearer and much more concise. It was affirming to hear this, but I wasn't prepared for what they told me next: the lengthy, unwieldy version of the TAP rubric that was causing them such dissatisfaction *had already been cut in half.*

Not to mention the complex, mangled language in which the frameworks are written. Lessons are to be taught with "simultaneous multisensory representations" in one template. In another, instruction must "reflect understanding of prerequisite relationships among topics and concepts and a link to necessary cognitive structures." Another framework informs practitioners that its criteria "reflect the developmentally relevant construct of heterotypic continuity." You couldn't make this stuff up. Small wonder that superintendent Paul Vallas (in Dreilinger, 2013) remarked that the new frameworks "are so complex that... they'll just make you suicidal" (p. 2).

Moreover, none of these frameworks, despite their claims, are "research based" at all; they were never even pilot-tested. According to the centrist Brookings Institute, these new frameworks demonstrate, once again, education's uniquely "unwavering commitment to unproven approaches" (Anderson, 2012). Or as Michael Petrilli (2015) writes, "Nobody can say that teacher evaluation efforts are going well. This was an unforced error of enormous magnitude."

To the best of our ability, we should abandon these instruments or, if their use is mandated, creatively adapt them to ensure simplicity and clarity: for example, by operatively focusing on criteria similar to that found in Figure 3.1, "Basic Elements of Effective Teaching." In the age of ESSA, it should be easier for us to obtain permission to replace these failed templates with much clearer, simpler evaluation frameworks. The criteria in Figure 3.1 were the primary focus of evaluation in the most effective schools and districts I've known of— including the one where I learned to be an effective teacher.

Finally, a brief note on an equally perplexing criterion found in most evaluation templates: the requirement that teachers incorporate technology into their lessons.

Excessive dependence on technology. Laptops and Smartboards have their advantages; if you have them, keep them. But don't expect them to be a prominent force for academic improvement; they aren't. Also, realize that the time, money, and training we now devote to technology training supplants time that should be focused, for now, on training teachers to master the most powerful, evidence-based practices described in these pages.

FIGURE 3.1 | Basic Elements of Effective Teaching*

Element	Description	Look-Fors
Learning objective	A clear, concise description of **what will be learned and how it will be assessed**	Learning objective is **prominently displayed,** written in clear language, and based on grade-level curriculum.
		Objective clarifies how learning will be **demonstrated/assessed.**
		Teacher refers to the objective at strategic points during the lesson.
Anticipatory set	Explains purpose or relevance; captures student **interest** in the lesson	Teacher engages student interest by providing purpose, previewing learning, and/or linking to prior learning. *This should typically be no more than 3–5 minutes.*
Teach and model	A **demonstration or explanation** of a single brief step, procedure, or mental operation, delivered at a stimulating pace	Teacher clearly explains, models, or thinks aloud through each **brief, manageable step, one at a time.**
		Each lesson step *contributes directly* to success on that day's objective/assessment.
		Throughout instruction, teacher **"scans"** to ensure **all students—100 percent**—are on task and focused on learning.
Guided practice	Students immediately **imitating or practicing** each small, manageable step as teacher observes	After each **brief step**, students practice/process new skills/knowledge by attempting or demonstrating understanding or mastery of each **brief** step or topic (e.g., note taking; completing a single step in problem; writing).
Check understanding	**Quick** observation/assessment of each small step of lesson **during and after** *each* guided practice	Teacher *quickly* assesses student progress or (mis)understandings after each step (e.g., by circulating to observe student work; cold-calling a sample of students; having students hold up whiteboards).
		Teacher maintains pace by **limiting individual tutoring** during this time (it is best provided, if necessary, during independent practice).
Adjust/reteach	Adjustments to teaching made **on the basis of each "check for understanding"**	Teacher **reteaches**, clarifies instruction, or has students pair up to assist each other to ensure that students master each step **before moving on** to the next step in the lesson.
This cycle is repeated, sometimes **multiple times,** for **every brief step** in the lesson until all/almost all students are ready for independent practice (below)		
Independent learning/assessment	Students independently practicing/**completing assessment to demonstrate** mastery of learning objective	Teacher assigns independent work that allows students to further practice/**demonstrate mastery** of the larger learning objective.
		At this time, teacher may provide tutoring/small-group assistance to students still needing help.

*Essential for most instruction. Can be modified for certain lessons.

For decades, we've heard that digital literacy will usher in new possibilities and facilitate academic growth. But as Mark Bauerlein (2009) points out, digital natives are not more but *less* literate than ever. He makes clear that computers often compete directly with reading; but unlike reading, digital immersion does not result in increases in vocabulary, memory capacity, analytical skills, or erudition. We've had an entire generation to test this (pp. 107–109).

More than ever, U.S. schools are using computer-based games, tools, and instructional programs as the means by which we can raise levels of learning and narrow the achievement gap. Not one of the highest-achieving countries is doing this. Studies of the best educational systems in the world reveal that technology has played no role in their success (Goodwin, 2015; Ripley, 2013; Walker in Stoltzfus, 2017).

Noting this, the cofounder of Sun Microsystems remarked that other countries must take comfort in knowing that U.S. schools "are spending their time on this kind of crap" instead of truly educating our students (Bauerlein, 2009, p. 109).

I have known and observed many highly effective schools and teachers. I don't know a single case in which instructional technology played any significant role in their success whatsoever.

There is simply no proof that technology, in any of its manifestations, is a primary, proven boon to educational effectiveness. It should startle us, then, that the time, expense, and training sessions we now devote to technology *dwarfs* what we invest in evidence-based practices that would have an immediate and outsized effect on student learning and our persistent achievement gap. I can't count the number of districts in which technology initiatives and training consumed the lion's share of professional development—for teachers who had *never learned to implement effective lessons or a coherent curriculum.*

A well-known player in the emergence of educational technology once said the following:

> I used to think that technology could help education.... I've come to the inevitable conclusion that the problem is not one

that technology can hope to solve.... No amount of technology will make a dent.

The speaker was Steve Jobs (in Carmody, 2012). Until we have real evidence that technology supersedes the most game-changing (but low-tech) actions and practices, we have a moral obligation to ensure that our teachers master and implement practices that will have the largest payoff for students.

We've been looking at such practices. Their manifest superiority points up what Michael Fullan (2010) said about educational technology: that it is decidedly not a "driver" of school improvement. For the sake of students, we have no right to pretend it is.

• • •

At the least, I hope this discussion will stir reflection on our easy acceptance of weak or unproven practices and how they impede our efforts to ensure that students receive the life-changing benefits of effective instruction in our schools.

In the next section, I describe how the components of such effective instruction can be optimally and efficiently employed through the use of two simple, powerful templates.

Two Simple Templates for Lecture and Literacy Lessons

Here I will describe two unoriginal but versatile templates that optimize and operationalize the components of good teaching. These templates could be the basis for teaching a large portion of a coherent, literacy-rich curriculum. Because they can be widely applied, a facility with them would save teachers planning time (which is always at a premium). Both templates, by the way, are perfectly consistent with the three shifts of the Common Core and Conley's (2005) K–12 college-readiness standards, discussed in Chapter 2.

As you'll see, these (sometimes overlapping) templates are simple enough for teachers or teams to study and implement immediately with success, while refining their execution over time. I will refer to both of them throughout the four subject-area chapters.

The templates might be named and described as follows:

• *Interactive lecture and direct teaching,* in which the focus is on the teacher's words and directions, but the teaching is still both *intellectually active and interactive:* students frequently take notes, work in pairs, and complete problems and quick-writes throughout the lesson.

• *Literacy-based lessons,* **which are focused on analysis, discussion, and writing of any text. This template** requires a somewhat lengthier description.

If we implement our own version of such templates even reasonably well, in a fairly coherent common curriculum, we won't have to worry about changes in state standards or assessments. Our lessons will meet the demands of any standardized test (especially the new breed of assessments, which require more thoughtful reading and writing, despite their imperfections). Of more importance, they will ensure that students receive an education that prepares them for college, careers, and citizenship. Team-based professional learning communities should make the use and mastery of these templates—or something similar—a high priority.

Interactive Lecture and Direct Teaching

*Lecture proves to be a **marvel of efficiency**, allowing us to cover a lot of ground quickly. [But done improperly,] lecturing becomes a waste of precious classroom time.*

—Harvey Silver, Richard Strong, and Matthew Perini (2007)

*[Interactive lecture] **dramatically increases** students' understanding of new information across content areas and at every grade level.*

—Robert Marzano (2009)

Lecture, done wrong, is among the least effective forms of teaching. Done right, it is highly engaging and among the most effective ways to cover generous amounts of content.

Fortunately, the term "interactive lecture" has gained traction—even since the first edition of this book was published. To get a vivid sense of the power of "interactive lecture," let's look at some success stories from universities.

Formative assessment goes to college. At Ohio State University, physics professors began to conduct ongoing checks for understanding during their large-group lectures. This allowed them to stop and reteach difficult concepts before moving on to the next concept.

The results were immediate and dramatic. Students in the classes using formative assessment *performed a full letter grade better than those in classes without it.* In addition, the previously large gap between male and female achievement in physics was eliminated (Ohio State University, 2008).

Harvard physics professor Eric Mazur was accustomed to attributing student failure in his physics courses to indolence or inability—until, that is, he began to check for understanding by punctuating his lectures with opportunities for students to solve one or two short problems, alone or in pairs. He would then ask students for their answers, often by a simple show of hands. If not enough students understood the material, he would stop the lesson—and have them pair up to justify their answers for each other. As they talked, Mazur would circulate, listening for insights that allowed him to reteach the concept immediately, before moving on to the next chunk of his lesson.

His methods, like those at Ohio State, had an immediate effect on learning. This was not lost on Mazur's colleagues, who soon adopted his methods and realized the same kinds of gains. Success rates in physics at Harvard now hover around 95 percent, and the gap between the highest- and lowest-scoring subgroups has narrowed dramatically. One of the faculty's more promising findings was that these simple methods *work for anyone who employs them.* They increase achievement independent of the personality of the instructor (Mazur, 1997).

This is "interactive lecture." Let's look now at two especially helpful sources on how to execute it successfully in K–12 schools.

Interactive lecture in K–12. In their book *The Strategic Teacher,* Silver, Strong, and Perini (2007) provide a helpful description of "interactive lecture." Echoing Hunter, they recommend that the lecture begin with an "anticipatory" step—with a "hook," a question, or a link to previous learning (p. 25). They go on to describe two successful lectures they observed. One was focused on the topic of sectionalism in U.S. history; the other was a 2nd grade lesson on how to write effective sentences. In both cases, the teachers began the lesson with some background information, followed by questions to establish purpose and stimulate curiosity (note how both questions are forms of argument, making the lecture a higher-order activity):

- *Sectionalism.* How did we go from the Era of Good Feelings in the 1820s to a period of such deep division and disunity in the ensuing years?
- *Effective sentences.* Which of the following sentences is most effective?

After students responded to the question, by writing and then talking in pairs, the teacher called on a *random sample* of them to check for understanding—to see whether the students understood the task or if they needed additional instruction before moving to the next small step in the lecture.

Small steps and guided practice. Silver, Strong, and Perini (2007) then describe how the next few activities are delivered in *small, ordered steps,* between which students practice with new knowledge by talking, writing (often in the form of notes), or both. These "periodic thinking reviews" give students the chance to process their learning by drawing conclusions and making inferences as they listen, talk, and take notes. All the while, the teacher is observing and listening to ensure that all students are learning—before the teacher moves on to the next part of the lecture (Silver, Strong, & Perini, 2007, pp. 21–26). This is plainly a higher-order lesson.

These simple techniques are nearly indistinguishable from what Marzano (2009) recommends for lessons in which "the teacher intends to present content in the form of a lecture." As Marzano makes clear, this is a highly effective, versatile mode of teaching: "This process," he writes, "*dramatically* increases students' understanding of new information *across content areas and at every grade level*" (p. 86; emphasis added).

And as with any good lesson, the information in the lecture must be segmented into chunks or "small digestible bites" (Marzano, 2009, p. 87). Such teaching honors the limits of working memory and the average student attention spans; learners need the chance to process new information—*every few minutes.*

The five-minute limit. If we want all kids to learn and enjoy their learning, we simply can't lecture for long, uninterrupted periods of time. To this end, both Marzano (2009) and Silver, Strong, and Perini (2007) are emphatic about time limits between segments of a lecture. Silver, Strong, and Perini recommend that the teacher talk for *"no more than five minutes"* before giving students an opportunity to process the new information—by writing or by interacting with their peers about the stated learning goal (p. 23). Similarly, in Marzano's (2009) example, he suggests that after only a few minutes of lecture, students should be given the opportunity to digest or discuss what they've learned in the following ways:

• Reviewing their notes and adding any new insights or connections

• Summarizing what they learned at the end of each segment of the lecture

• Pairing up to compare or contrast notes, perceptions, and connections

Failure to give students these opportunities is what makes most lectures boring and ineffective. Without such breaks, lessons are long and dull, which we would never wish on ourselves. If we want all students to learn, they need frequent opportunities to write and share their thoughts with their partners.

These processes—taking notes, reviewing notes, and summarizing—must themselves be *taught explicitly and modeled regularly* with the use of the same elements of teaching discussed in this chapter. Teachers should monitor and provide guidance in these all year, every year. Of importance is that these processing moments are also opportunities to check for understanding.

Checking for understanding and engagement: "dramatic increases." These frequent "strategic stopping points" allow teachers to formatively monitor and assess learning (and on-task behavior) by calling on random students/pairs of students and walking around the room to listen and to review students' notes. During lecture, we must be "continually checking for student understanding" (Marzano, 2009, p. 87). If students are confused or don't understand the content in a particular chunk, the teacher should revisit or reteach that information before moving on to the next chunk. Again: I especially like Marzano's insistence that we must always be "scanning" to ensure, as we lecture, that all students are engaged. Ideally, teachers should strive to encourage *every student* to respond, multiple times, to questions throughout the lecture.

As noted earlier, such interactive teaching—laced with checks for understanding—can allow teachers to cover as much as four times the amount of material and will add an additional six to nine months of learning growth per student, per year (Wiliam, 2007, p. 186). Moreover, it *"dramatically increases* students' understanding of new information across content areas and at every grade level" (Marzano, 2009, p. 87).

In sum, interactive lecture can be a "marvel of efficiency" (Silver et al., 2007, p. 26). Variations on it could constitute a sizeable proportion of the curriculum—with enormous leverage for improvement. Mastering and refining these simple elements should be among the team's and school's highest priorities.

The next template is equally powerful and versatile: a simple template for literacy-based lessons that can be used in any subject area or grade level. It meshes with the approach called "Task, Text, and Talk," which we'll explore in later chapters.

Literacy-Based Lessons

Think of literacy as a spine; it holds everything together. The branches of learning connect to it, meaning that all core content teachers have a responsibility to teach literacy.

—Vicki Phillips and Carina Wong (2010)

The simple, age-old template I'll describe here typically consists of the following three activities:

- Close reading/underlining and annotation of text
- Discussion of the text
- Writing about the text informed by close reading, discussion, and annotation

For centuries, these three activities have been at the heart of both *what* we learn and *how* we learn, the keys to an education that transforms lives and can overcome the effects of poverty.

Ironically, more than 30 years of school innovation have had the bizarre consequence of driving this kind of literacy underground, almost to extinction (Schmoker, 2006, Chapter 7). Kelly Gallagher's (2009) term "readicide" (the murder of reading) aptly captures this phenomenon. So does the following trenchant observation by Jacqueline Ancess (2008), on yet another lavishly funded, overhyped school reform. Thousands of schools invested time and energy in this high-profile program failure, even as tens of thousands of students were never given the opportunity

to compose, *write, [or] revise extended analytical papers. They have never been required to analyze ideas from multiple perspectives and reach thoughtful conclusions supported by compelling evidence.* They could recall little opportunity to *discuss and debate ideas*... they had never built the habit of getting to *engage material to make meaning from it.* (p. 48)

In other words, students in these thousands of schools were *denied an education* as reformers tinkered with various school structures. Like most innovations, this one did not account for the fact that learning is typically acquired through old-fashioned, simple activities like reading, discussion, and writing.

In an ideal world, all aspiring school reformers would be required to read Ancess's (2008) lament and sign a binding agreement that they will not let this happen again. As I write this, one of the popular 21st century organizations is advancing a set of "standards" that would replace reading and writing activities with having students make websites, wikis, posters, movie trailers, or short movies with clay figures—each reflecting students' "individual personalities." Such seductive, multiday activities continue to encroach on the authentic literacy activities they aspire to replace.

We will never educate all students, or optimally educate any student, until we ensure that they engage (by current standards) in immense amounts of reading, discussion, and writing. These are the indispensable and primary means of acquiring content knowledge and intellectual skills even in the digital age (Phillips & Wong, 2010; Wineburg & Martin, 2004).

To that end, the following fairly traditional template is my attempt to demystify the integration of reading, discussion, and writing into the curriculum. It can be used with reading and writing assignments for portions of any science textbook or novel, critiques of music or art, poems, primary historical resources, magazine articles, and newspaper editorials. The template purposely reflects the same essential ingredients of effective teaching that we have been discussing.

Again, there's nothing original here. This general approach goes back further than Socrates and is the substance of most seminar-based college courses—and the very best high school courses. It constitutes about 90 percent of the daily lessons in the two-hour humanities block at Tempe Preparatory Academy and the "Great Hearts Academies" in Arizona and Texas.

As we briefly review the elements in this template, realize that its effectiveness hinges on the same factors that attract people to book clubs: the chance to acquire and refine our knowledge as we read for meaning and express and compare our thoughts and perceptions with others. An entire education can be built on these innately satisfying activities.

Teaching vocabulary. Before the reading of a text, be sure to teach any vocabulary that could impede understanding. Learning unfamiliar words or concepts before reading can increase the accessibility of a text by significant margins and make the text far more interesting (Marzano, Kendall, & Gaddy, 1999, p. 147).

Once done, we can move to the next step: establishing a purpose for the reading (which overlaps with Hunter's concept of "anticipatory set").

Establishing a purpose for the reading. To create interest in the content of the text, we will want to share some background information about the topic, read an interesting selection, or help students connect it to recent or previous learning.

Then comes the main event: a question or prompt, linked as often as possible to intellectual skills, such as those Conley (2005) recommends (drawing conclusions, analyzing and forming arguments, resolving/synthesizing conflicting opinions, or problem solving). We ask such questions because students at all grade levels will read with greater comprehension, engagement, and curiosity *when we give them a clear, analytic, or provocative purpose for their reading.* That's why author and practicing teacher Kelly Gallagher (2009) always gives his students a single final exam question *before* they begin reading an assigned novel.

Examples of prompts or questions that establish a compelling purpose for one or more subject-area texts are as follows:

• *Science.* Compare and contrast the functions of the digestive and respiratory systems/meiosis and mitosis. Evaluate arguments for the expansion of wind versus solar energy/arguments for and against human-made climate change.

• *English.* What can you infer about a character or his or her development—such as Jack in *Jack and the Beanstalk* or Antonio in *Bless Me, Ultima*—on the basis of their thoughts, words, and actions? Identify important similarities and differences between two characters—such as Old Dan and Little Ann in *Where the Red Fern Grows*—as you draw inferences about the author's message.

- *Social Studies*. Would you prefer life as a Maya or an Aztec? A U.S. or Canadian citizen? Cite the textbook, current publications, statistics, or a combination of these.
- *Mathematics*. Which multistep approach or solution to a problem is most efficient and accurate? Argue the merits of two or more countries' health care systems with regard to multiple data points.
- *Art/music*. Which artist/musician was most talented/historically significant? Compare and contrast two newspaper or magazine reviews of a movie, art show, or musical performance.

These items can also serve as end-of-unit learning targets or writing tasks. Such prompts and questions should be posted prominently and clarified thoroughly before students read one or more texts.

Good questions and prompts are essential for engagement and interest as students read, discuss, and write. Grade-level and department-level teams should make their development *one of their highest priorities*—creating databases of temporary and permanent collections of tried-and-true questions that are readily available to all teachers in a school or district.

Once we are sure that students grasp the question (by conducting a brief check for understanding), we would then tell them how their work will be assessed. Assessment can be done in any of the following ways:

- A review of students' notes or annotations (done in a quick walk-around)
- Actual writing (which can often be graded quickly or checked off as the teacher walks around the classroom)
- Participation in a discussion (see discussion rubric below)

Or we could use all three of these methods over the course of a multiday lesson or unit—always, by the way, with an eye to *reducing time spent taking home or grading papers*. (For more ways to increase writing and greatly reduce grading time, see "Write More, Grade Less" at my website—www.mikeschmoker.com/write-more.html.)

Purposeful reading normally requires active processing—whether we have students annotate, jot, take notes, or summarize their thoughts at certain points in the reading. *Students must be taught explicitly how to do such active reading*—routinely, at every grade level, and at least twice a week in every course (as they do so successfully at Brockton High School). It all starts with modeling, or "thinking aloud."

Modeling higher-order reading. Any teacher who got through college or has been in a good book club can learn to teach students to read critically and annotate. With a little practice, teachers can quickly learn to "model" such reading.

We'll see how to do such modeling in the subject areas in Chapters 4 through 7. But for now, let's suppose we are teaching 2nd or 3rd graders to read *Jack and the Beanstalk* (which I've done many times). After teaching the most challenging vocabulary words from the text, we would establish purpose by asking an inferential/argumentative question, such as

What is your opinion of Jack, based on his words and actions? Is he a noble, heroic character—*or not?*"

Variations on this question can be used with almost any work of fiction or to analyze a political, scientific, or historical figure. A variation on this assignment would be to have students read the story and then also read—and annotate—copies of two conflicting essays on another work of literature written by former students (with names blacked out). Have students discuss which paper makes the stronger argument—and why it is stronger.

We now need to show students how *we* would read the text, by "thinking aloud" as we explain how and why we underline or annotate. For example, in the first few lines of *Jack and the Beanstalk*, we find that Jack and his mother are very poor and in dire straits. Then Jack says, "Cheer up, Mother, I'll go and get work somewhere." After reading this, you might say to your students:

Well, good for Jack! Don't you think it's admirable for such a young boy to look for work to help his family? I'm going to underline that—and maybe write "young, but willing to work" in the margin. Annotation doesn't always require whole sentences—sometimes just a few words will do.

In the very next line of the story, we find something many 2nd graders might overlook: that Jack's mother says, "We've tried that before, and nobody would take you." At this point, you might say,

> Whoa... why wouldn't anyone "take" Jack—I guess that means they wouldn't hire him? Was it because he was too young? Or maybe he had a reputation *as someone who didn't work hard or wasn't very responsible?* I don't know yet—but that's OK. I'm hoping that as we read on, we'll find other actions of Jack's that might help answer my question. So let's see what else Jack does and says in the next few paragraphs. Further reading might give us a clearer impression of what kind of person Jack is.

You get the idea.

I can guarantee, from experience, that any conscientious attempt to model reading in this manner will reveal that 2nd or 3rd graders are *fully up to such truly college-preparatory tasks.* Be ready for it—and prepare to make such analytic reading a routine feature of instruction in every subject area.

Through frequent modeling of reading, underlining, and annotating, in every course, we can accelerate the attainment of core intellectual skills—by several years. Some students won't ever learn to read critically unless we show them how we do such reading several times a week with stories, poems, newspapers, or history and science textbooks. We'll see more examples of such texts and questions in the subject-area chapters—4 through 7.

After we model how we would read, underline, annotate, or take notes, students are ready to practice such reading alone and then in pairs—with our guidance.

Guided practice and formative assessment. The next step is to have students practice, by themselves, the same kind of reading, note taking, or annotation that you've just modeled—with the next paragraph or section of text. As they practice, check for understanding to see whether additional clarification or modeling is needed. Here are a few ways to do this:

• *Circulate.* This is my favorite approach; a quick one- to two-minute tour will tell you a lot. Are students underlining or taking notes appropriately? If not, you must clarify by additional modeling or instruction.

• *Have students pair up and share.* Students should frequently pair up and share their notes, annotations, or underlined text with each other. Again, talking is not only one of the best ways to digest information, it also provides a needed break and a low-threat opportunity to get feedback from peers on their ability to read for meaning. Of importance is that as students pair up, you should circulate to monitor their on-task behavior and listen to their conversations. (Again, this is not an ideal time to tutor individual students or groups, which may impede the flow and pace of the lesson; see Lemov, 2015, p. 52; Rosenshine, 2012, p. 19.)

• *Call on random pairs to share their thoughts.* This gives students an opportunity to express themselves in a more public mode while also helping you to gauge their readiness for independent practice (as well as how, if necessary, you might clarify or model active reading in a different way).

• *Ask students to quick-write responses while you circulate.* Before *or* after students pair up, ask them to quick-write their explanations or interpretations on the basis of their notes or underlinings. Remember that any form of writing, short or long, *generates and refines thought.* Quick-writing helps students to "rehearse"—that is, to formulate their thoughts before they share their insights with a partner or with the whole class in a larger discussion. I've seen the inestimable benefits of letting students share perceptions and insights. Again, such interaction mimics the pleasures of a good book club. *Remember to set time limits* for the readings, discussions, and writings—or for any of the stages in a lesson. If you don't already do this, try it; it acts powerfully to help students stay focused and on task. If they need more time, give it to them.

• *Circulate!* For all of the above, *at strategic times,* walk around for a few minutes and listen, ensure on-task behavior, and scan student work so that you can more precisely guide the next steps of learning and not leave students behind. That is, check to see what your students need from you:

—Should you do some additional modeling?

—Should you show them more explicitly how adults often *slow down or reread* to understand certain important or dense sections of text?

—Should you show them how to make connections to the question or prompt or how to collect supporting evidence for their arguments and interpretations?

For all of these, and for as long as we teach, the answer will very often be *"Yes, we do need to show them these things, sometimes several times."*

In due course, these multiple cycles of guided practice and checking for understanding maximize the opportunity for all students to succeed, to complete the day's assessment or assignment *independently.*

Independent practice and assessment. As a result of the previous steps, your students will now be prepared for the next step: to purposefully underline, annotate, or take notes by themselves as they finish reading the text or texts. If students practice these routines a couple of times a week in several courses, fewer iterations will be required before they are ready to finish reading on their own.

Keep in mind that *such analytic reading* can always be improved through continuous practice with a variety of readings. Teachers should model and conduct guided practice at the beginning of most reading assignments—at ever higher levels of sophistication and with ever more challenging texts, at every grade level. Independent practice time can also be a good time to work with those few remaining students who might require extra assistance.

Again, *execution of these processes need not be perfect.* The real power of this template is in its *frequent use*—at least twice a week in most courses, from 2nd grade through senior year. With practice, and through discussions with colleagues, you will master it in a short time and become accomplished at every aspect of it.

The preceding steps are indispensable by themselves. But they are also invaluable as "rehearsals" for the following two steps: whole-class discussion, followed by some form of writing. The close reading, annotating, and quick-writes will build students' confidence and ability to participate with newfound confidence, skill, and enthusiasm.

Whole-class discussion and debate. Students enjoy sharing what they have learned from close reading. Teachers might be surprised to know the findings of an ASCD survey in which students were asked how they like to learn: eighty-three percent of them indicated that "discussion and debate" was a method that would most "excite them" (Azzam, 2008). How often are the rudiments of effective discussion—and its immense appeal for students—taught in preservice training or reinforced in staff development? How often do administrators and evaluators reward and recognize the successful use of classroom discussion—"grounded in text"? The school leaders we'll encounter in subsequent chapters made a point of monitoring and celebrating these core educational activities.

Once students have had the benefit of close reading, annotating, and sharing notes with partners, they are eager to discuss and debate issues they find in their textbooks, historical documents, and editorials, or in print and online publications such as *TIME for Kids.* For example, students might debate topics such as these:

• The pros and cons of video games (see www.buzzle.com/articles/are-video-games-good-for-you.html)
• Whether Jack in *Jack and the Beanstalk* is a good person
• Whether the cat in Dr. Seuss's *The Cat in the Hat* is an admirable character
• Whether there could be alien beings in the universe (see www.buzzle.com/articles/aliens-are-there-aliens.html)
• The pros and cons of health care plans/legislation
• Whether President Lincoln's second inaugural address would be conciliatory or upsetting to the average Southerner of that time

• Whether we should either sympathize with Jay Gatsby's character (as a victim of the culture of the 1920s) or condemn him for his character flaws

We'll see plenty of additional examples of topics, texts, and issues in the coming chapters. We underestimate the educational power and enjoyment students derive from such discussions or debates—if they are adequately prepared for them, which they can be, if we employ steps like those described previously.

But to get the most out of discussion, we should establish clear criteria for productive participation. Remember that a good discussion is not a free-for-all; it should accord with important elements of effective exchange that, like any good lesson objective, should be explicitly taught and reinforced.

To become good listeners and communicators, students need explicit instruction in how to meet criteria such as the following:

• Cite the text when making an argument.
• When disagreeing with another's conclusions, argument, or solutions, briefly refer to or restate what they said.
• Don't interrupt; be civil and respectful.
• Be clear, concise, and on point.
• Avoid distracting verbal tics (such as overuse of "like" or "you know").

If we want students to become good listeners and articulate speakers, then listening and speaking must be demonstrated, modeled, and reinforced by the teacher throughout the interchange—in every discipline. (If these are consistently reinforced throughout the school, the benefits will be compounded.)

I observed a Socratic discussion at Tempe Preparatory Academy (in a *chemistry* class, of all places). I was impressed by how the habit of such regular discussions in most of the school's classes had made the students into such poised, confident, and effective speakers and *listeners*. The conversation was so engaging that students stayed after the bell rang.

On occasion, I would strongly recommend the "fishbowl" discussions recommended by assessment expert Rick Stiggins (1994), in which students in an outer ring observe, evaluate, and take notes on the quality of the discussion among the students in the inner ring, per the criteria. This strategy could deepen students' awareness of discussion skills—by allowing students to more fully and objectively analyze their dynamics.

These skills are critical in every sphere and, as *preparation for effective presentations, an increasingly important competency.*

Fortunately, effective text-based reading and discussion are, in turn, *the perfect preparation for writing*—which takes thinking to an even higher level. More than perhaps any other activity, writing enhances students' ability to think, make connections, and communicate with clarity, logic, and precision. Writing enables us to discern and then express critical distinctions between truth and half-truth, between sense and nonsense. Enormous power attaches to those who *do* write and *can* write (Graff, 2003; National Commission on Writing, 2003).

Student writing "grounded in text." This final part of the description of the template for authentic literacy is offered merely as a simple, general guide to writing across the disciplines; it is not exhaustive. Chapter 4—on English language arts—contains a more detailed version of the following, for which you could modify or rearrange some of the steps.

Writing, from short scribbles to more formal pieces, profits greatly from the previous processes of close reading, annotation, and discussion of one or more texts. Once completed, students should return to the text and:

• Review and reread their notes, underlinings, or annotations to select which quotes or textual material they will write about and which would best serve the purpose of the writing assignment.

• Arrange or organize the best of these thoughts, quotes, and data into a list or formal outline that makes the writing as clear and effective as possible.

Then, they write. That will require that we explicitly teach them fundamental writing skills such as the following:

• Properly integrate quotations/paraphrased material into sentences (sentence stems can be very useful here; see Graff & Birkenstein, 2015).

• Clearly explain how the quotations/paraphrased material supports and advances your argument or interpretation.

For longer, more formal writing assignments, we would also want to teach students the following skills:

• Employ transitional phrases within and among paragraphs to link each section to the subsequent section—to make your writing easier to follow and understand.

• Write effective introductions and conclusions.

You could add many additional writing skills here. But I would encourage any district to provide training in a similarly manageable set of essential—fundamental—writing skills to teachers in every subject area.

Short, informal text-based writing assignments should be a frequent feature of instruction in every subject, but these almost-daily assignments *don't always need to be formally graded*—they should be completed, checked off, or given credit only if a quick glance reveals a satisfactory attempt to cite the text and respond appropriately to a question or prompt.

In English language arts, teachers do have to ensure that students get more detailed writing instruction (more on this in the next chapter; in later chapters, we will revisit ways to employ fairly minimalist writing and scoring requirements for social studies, science, and math).

In all subjects, but especially in language arts, learning will be accelerated by having students analyze exemplar papers written by students or professionals. *Nothing enhances the power of a writing lesson like an actual example;* students need to see how good writers organize their arguments, write effective sentences, and choose appropriate language.

Because most categories of good persuasive/expository writing have the same basic elements, you can often use the same exemplar paper for multiple assignments as you build and share your "permanent collection" with colleagues. Every teacher team, in every subject, should have a good collection of papers for this purpose.

Finally, in any subject in which we assign a formal paper, we are smart to vet students' theses and outlines before they plunge deeply into the work (Jago, 2005, who also offers good practical tips on writing and on time-efficient grading practices). As a teacher, I found this to have tremendous benefits for me and my students. It is a critical but oft-neglected stage in instruction for helping students learn to get their arguments and supporting material organized. It saves them precious time and frustration—and reduces the time teachers must spend correcting papers. A focused, well-organized argumentative paper is always easier to assess at every stage, and will be a more positive, productive experience for students. (Again, for more on this and other ways to avoid the "paper load," see "Write More, Grade Less" at www.mikeschmoker.com/write-more.html.)

• • •

Throughout the next few chapters, I will be referring to the two templates discussed here, variations on which could be used countless times per year in any discipline while teachers ensure that students' skills in critical reading, thinking, speaking, and writing will advance apace.

Used right, both templates align with the English Language Arts Common Core "three shifts" and the essential intellectual skills described by David Conley (2005). Any teacher can immediately begin implementing and refining their use in team-based professional learning communities.

Let's now look at *what* and *how* we should teach in four subject areas—with a strong emphasis on literacy.

SECTION II

Curriculum, Instruction, and Literacy in the Content Areas

English Language Arts
Made Simple

Adolescents entering the adult world of the 21st century will read and write more than at any other time in human history. They will need advanced levels of literacy to perform their jobs, run their households, act as citizens, and conduct their personal lives.

—Richard Vacca

Literature makes significant life possible. [We] construct ourselves from novels, poems, and plays as well as from works of history and philosophy.

—Mark Edmundson

L iteracy skills, as discussed in Chapters 2 and 3, are foundational to an education. That makes it doubly unfortunate that English language arts (ELA), more than any discipline, has lost its way. Despite the primary place it holds in the transmission of literacy skills, it is in desperate need of clarity. We need to simplify and reconceive ELA, ELA standards, and ELA assessments.

There is a ripe opportunity for improvement here—larger than when the first edition of this book was published.

As discussed previously, state standards and assessments have had a uniquely corrosive effect on language arts. As currently conceived, they have corrupted language education and its essential mission: to ensure that students can read, write, and speak effectively. To restore sanity to literacy instruction, we should begin by honoring its first principle: that *every year, every student needs to spend hundreds of hours actually reading, writing, and speaking for intellectual purposes.*

In this chapter, I advocate for a simpler model for *how* we teach English, starting in the primary grades. It will build on Chapters 2 and 3 and make frequent references to the literacy template described in the latter. We'll revisit some of the schools already discussed and examine some additional ones—all of which have achieved exceptional success by ensuring that students engage in abundant amounts of reading, writing, and speaking every year.

There's no denying that each of the disciplines connects and contributes to success in other disciplines. But this may be especially true of ELA. As McConachie and colleagues (2006) aver, students "develop deep conceptual knowledge in a discipline only by using the habits of *reading, writing, talking and thinking,* which that discipline values and uses" (pp. 8–14); or as Timothy Shanahan avers, "English teachers take responsibility for general literacy and language skills... that can be applied across all disciplines" (Shanahan & Shanahan, 2017, p. 20).

ELA contributes mightily to career success and advancement. As we saw in Chapter 2, literacy is "the most important single goal of schooling"—a reliable indicator of general competence and life chances (Hirsch, 2010, p. 1). This is borne out by recent reports on the importance of literacy in the workplace. Corporate recruiters in every field now name the abilities to write, speak, and listen as the most sought-after skill set. The average employer ranked communication skills *twice as high* as managerial skills (Hurley, 2015). Literacy has a decisive effect on corporate earnings and workplace advancement: companies such as Cisco Systems have found that no set of skills would do more to enhance their profits than oral and written communication skills (Wagner, 2008). Or as Robert Pondiscio (2014b) tells us, precise, skillful communication skills constitute the "language of upward mobility in America." These skills allow their users to "nimbly navigate the world of organizations, institutions and opportunities." In all its aspects, literacy has immense civic, academic, personal, and professional benefits. And like it or not, literacy depends very much on what we provide in our reading/ELA courses.

In light of such evidence, how effectively are we currently imparting literacy and communication skills to our students?

Literacy Education: How Are We Doing?

Consider the situation at the National Center on Education and the Economy. Candidates for a position were recently interviewed at the Washington, D.C., headquarters. In the interviews, the hiring team was dumbfounded to discover that only 1 of 500 applicants could write an effective summary of a report. This was a key element of their interview process (they hired that person; Tucker, 2017).

Similarly, recruiters at Cisco lament that "the biggest skill that people *are missing* is the ability to communicate: both written and oral presentations" (Wagner, 2008; emphasis added). This is not an uncommon perception in business and industry. Education writer Caroline Bermudez (2016) has described, in distressing detail, the mangled language of typical business letters and emails—all written by employees with college and advanced degrees.

How can this be? And more to the point: do these issues stem from deficiencies in K–12 schooling?

Consider the fairly recent performance in language arts in the best-performing state, Massachusetts. By 3rd grade, and despite their number one academic ranking among states, *about half* of Massachusetts students cannot read at grade level (Wu, 2010). The architects of the ELA Common Core tell us that only about a third of our 8th graders are on track to be ready for the literacy demands of college (Coleman et al., 2012). That's about the same as the percentage of high school graduates who are academically prepared for college—which, in turn, corresponds to the proportion who graduate from college (Petrilli, 2016).

Such findings help explain the recent complaints of elite colleges with the highest admission standards: the faculty can't understand why students with excellent high school grade-point averages (GPAs) arrive unable to write, and who write less effectively now than ever (Bartlett, 2003). As ASCD's Laura Varlas (2016) reports, our high school graduates "hit an academic wall during their first year of college" in the areas of both reading and writing—the primary province of ELA (p. 1).

Is it churlish to dwell on these deficits, to point them out to hard-working educators? It would be—if these were the result of forces beyond our control. But they aren't. These shortcomings can be traced to eminently correctable institutional tendencies that prevent school personnel from implementing practices that would transform our ability to teach students to be literate and articulate by high school graduation. The question might be "How much juice is left in the lemon in English language arts instruction?" A lot, it turns out. There's a tremendous opportunity for improvement here.

"Juice in the Lemon": The Current State of Reading and Writing Instruction

I once heard a renowned corporate head remark that in most enterprises, there is often "far more juice left in the lemon"—more room for improvement—than we perceive. This is certainly the case with ELA instruction. Again, I'm reminded of Dick Fosbury's discovery that any high-jumper could achieve unprecedented heights—almost immediately—if they were willing to adopt a different practice (the "Fosbury flop," in which the jumper leaps backwards over the high bar). High jumping records were shattered when this technique became widely used (Burnton, 2012).

What could K–12 educators do—that they're not now doing—to equip record proportions of students for the literacy demands of college, careers, and responsible citizenship? We get an inkling from Stanford's Linda Darling-Hammond, who cites a revealing passage in Tom Wolfe's *The Bonfire of the Vanities*. A parent called the high school principal to ask why his son does so little writing in school. In responding, the principal "let out a whoop" and then said,

> Written work? There hasn't been any written work at Rupert High for fifteen years! Maybe twenty! They take multiple choice tests. Reading comprehension, that's the big thing. That's all the Board of Education cares about. (Darling-Hammond, 2010, p. 228)

Anyone who visits classrooms or monitors their children's school-work already knows this. Very few of my daughter's teachers had them write anything of substance, anything that prepared them for college. Even fewer provided actual instruction in writing. I know this from having been a middle school, high school, and college English teacher. For decades, we have known that students rarely read or write and even more rarely receive writing instruction in their English classes (see Hofstadter, Goodlad, Sizer, Jones, Cavanaugh, Olson, and multiple colleagues in Schmoker, 2006, pp. 92–96; Darling-Hammond, 2010).

And what of reading, with its reciprocal connection to writing? In the reform era, the amount, quality, and complexity of texts that students read have plummeted. On average, assigned readings are several levels below what they were even 20 years ago (English Language Arts Standards/Common Core State Standards, 2017, Appendix A; Stotsky, 1999). The average student in the 12th grade now reads books written at just above the 5th grade level (Paulson, 2014).

Students read less now than ever: Mark Bauerlein (2009) found that fewer than half of American high school students read or studied for more than an hour a week (p. 5). *The New York Times* writer Thomas Friedman (Friedman & Mandelbaum, 2011) cites findings that students don't spend much time reading, but they do spend about 7½ hours per day with "entertainment media."

If students aren't reading or writing in language arts, what are they doing? We get a glimpse of this from a young woman from Finland, who spent a year in the United States as an exchange student. Upon returning to her home country, she had to repeat the entire grade. Why? Because in the United States, instead of reading and writing (a mainstay of Finnish schooling) she and her fellow Americans spent their time preparing for multiple-choice tests or working on "projects" in which students were instructed to do things like "glue this to this poster for an hour." Students don't do such things in Finland (Gamerman, 2008, p. 2).

Are things really this bad even now—years into our multibillion dollar investment in various consortia and training around the Common Core (and similarly revised state ELA standards)?

The English Language Arts Common Core— How Much Effect?

As discussed in Chapters 2 and 3, the ELA Common Core is beset with problems—which even its architects acknowledge (Coleman et al., 2012). Its best aspects are found in its introductory and ancillary materials. But the Common Core's prominent, grade-by-grade standards are still a problem—one to which we'll return shortly. What has been the net effect of this high-profile innovation? After years of intensive investment, has it led to substantial improvements in student literacy?

English teacher and author Kelly Gallagher (2017) has been asking his audiences about their students' current writing abilities in the Common Core era. The overwhelming majority confirm what he himself perceives: that student writing abilities are "in decline." E. D. Hirsch's (2016) recent research findings appear to confirm this: that our high school seniors' "verbal abilities are *worse than they were before the new reforms were instituted*" (2016, p. 16).

When I visit ELA classrooms around the country, I only rarely find students actually reading, discussing, or writing about literature or nonfiction. I often ask my audiences what two things one is least apt to catch students doing if you pop in on an English class. After a pregnant pause, the response is always the same: reading and writing. I have quite recently visited classrooms in multiple school districts in which central office leaders spent years in Common Core consortia, attended multiple Common Core conferences, and provided professional development around the new standards. But when I visit their English classrooms, there is little or no evidence of change—skills-based worksheets and group work still predominate, sometimes with a Common Core veneer.

If such data seem too subjective, consider the findings of a report conducted after years of implementation and training in the new standards. The researchers were looking—explicitly—for classroom evidence of the "three shifts" of the Common Core (which were described in Chapter 2):

• Building knowledge through content-rich nonfiction

• Reading and writing grounded in evidence from text, both literary and informational

• Regular practice with complex text and its academic vocabulary

The rude findings: teachers themselves report that skills instruction—not the content of texts—continues to dominate. When students do read, they are provided with texts well below their grade level—instead of being helped to engage with more challenging texts (Shanahan & Duffet, 2013). In his visits to classrooms since the Common Core was introduced, Stanford's Sam Wineburg (2001) still sees instruction focused primarily on skills-based standards such as "assonance and alliteration." Old ways die hard.

And how much effect has the Common Core had on writing? According to Tanya Baker, of the National Writing Project, not much: "Kids are writing single paragraphs. It's so far from what we want for young people to be college or career ready" (Will, 2016). In the same article, we find that only 16 percent of assignments "required students to cite evidence from the text to support their thoughts and arguments"—thus 84 percent violate the essence of the Common Core. Joan Dabrowski (Will, 2016), the lead literacy adviser for the Education Trust, reports that writing in the Common Core era "rarely entails the kind of multi-paragraph, evidence-based writing that is promoted in college- and career-ready standards" (p. 6).

Kelly Gallagher (2017) cites a study by the Education Trust that demonstrated that even now, in the Common Core era, only 1 percent of assignments required extended thought (p. 25) and only 9 percent of middle school assignments were longer than a single paragraph (p. 26). Lee and Wu (2017) found that state assessments are undoubtedly more rigorous. But this has yet to have any significant positive effect on either classroom practices or performance outcomes (p. 1).

None of this should surprise us in light of what we saw in Chapter 3: that the Common Core is fundamentally at odds with itself, promoting authentic literacy in its introduction and appendixes and then—conversely—urging teachers to build discrete, skills-based lessons that are the primary impediment to authentic reading and writing. We can't seem to get past what David Pearson and Elfrieda Hiebert (2010) bemoaned upon reading the new standards: "elementitis," the tendency to reduce ELA instruction to "'pieces' of language" by which "skills are broken into elements and taught discretely" (p. 292).

Many of you don't need these studies to know this. You see it in the schools and classrooms you visit. And there are ominous indications that the lower pass rates on the new state tests won't induce much change. I recently visited multiple schools with the superintendent and assistant superintendent of curriculum and instruction in one district. They were aghast at what they saw. We saw virtually no legitimate literacy activities in the ELA classes. Because of this, they were deeply apprehensive of the results they would get on the new Common Core–based state assessments. But even when the much lower test scores came in, the improvement initiative ceased—overnight. Why? Because the scores in this privileged district were still the highest in the sub-region.

This might seem discouraging. It doesn't have to be; such data only underscores the fact that there is still a lot of juice left in the lemon: with regard to reading, writing, and writing instruction, there is an enormous opportunity for near-immediate improvement—like the kind we saw at Brockton High School, described in earlier chapters. If we're smart, we can emulate Dick Fosbury's fellow high jumpers—and adopt vastly superior methods to improve our performance immediately and momentously. The schools we'll look at later in this chapter made appreciable gains the moment that they scrapped typical ELA activities and replaced them with generous amounts of (remarkably ordinary) reading, discussion, and writing instruction. If all schools made such changes, how many more students would arrive at our colleges and career training institutes literate, articulate, and able to write well?

How do we up our game? Will it require some complex set of hard-to-learn skills that only the most talented teachers can be expected to master after years of training or experience? Not at all. It starts with reading—lots of reading.

The Life-Changing Power of Broad, Abundant Reading

If you're born poor, you'd better start reading.

—Joe Queenan

Wide, abundant reading is the surest route out of poverty and the limitations that impose themselves on less literate people. *Reading changes everything.* According to Jacques Barzun (1991), "No subject of study is more important than reading... all other intellectual powers depend on it" (p. 21). Or, as Aldous Huxley wrote, "Every man who knows how to read has it in his power to magnify himself, to multiply the ways in which he exists, to make his life full, significant, and interesting." If we could get average American children to read for even an hour a day during every school day (and we plainly could), we would change their lives dramatically. This may be the most important fact in all of education.

In Chapter 2, we learned about Paul Kalanithi, the author of the 2016 best seller *When Breath Becomes Air.* He described how his reading habits compensated for poor schooling and enabled him to attend Stanford, then the Yale School of Medicine and to become an accomplished neurosurgeon.

When Students "Read Lots"

Reading alters a child's academic and intellectual trajectory. In their often-cited study, Anderson, Wilson, and Fielding (1988) found a compelling relationship between time spent reading and reading scores: if students at the 30th percentile merely read for an additional *10 minutes per day*, they would be reading the same amount as those who read at the 70th percentile. If we added even 30 minutes of increasingly complex fiction and content-rich nonfiction, in every subject area, the effect could be historic. As Katie Haycock (2005) of the Education Trust found, three to four weeks of effective, full-day literacy instruction would allow an average student to achieve an entire year of academic growth—just by reading.

Experts almost unanimously agree that what currently occurs in English classes needs to be replaced with generous amounts of reading and being read to, on most days during the school year. I like Richard Allington's (2001) guideline: students should spend a *minimum* of 60 minutes per day reading (in all classes combined). And they should be writing for *at least* 40 minutes per day, mostly about what they read. As we saw earlier, students currently read (or appear to be reading) for only about 4 minutes per class period. Because of this, Carol Jago, former president of the National Council of Teachers of English, implores us to realize that for students to become literate, they must "read... a great deal more than students are reading today" (Gewertz, 2010b).

Or as Marilyn Jager Adams (2010/2011) puts it, students

must read lots. More specifically, they must read lots of "complex" texts—texts that offer them new language, new knowledge and new modes of thought.

Let's now look at the kinds of texts that students should be reading in abundance and why each is so vital to their education and empowerment. We'll begin with literature—key to a life that is, in Huxley's words, "full, significant, and interesting."

Reading Literature

Mark Edmundson (2004), a professor of English at the University of Virginia, is a prominent writer on the uses of literature. He knows how literature should be taught, how it enlarges us, and how it allows us to inhabit and evaluate the lives and worldviews of others as we reflect on our own. "Reading," he writes, "woke me up. It took me from a world of harsh limits into expanded possibility" (p. 1). Through literary studies, he found that his very "consciousness had been expanded" (p. 4). It is in literature that we find the private thoughts and musings of characters like and unlike ourselves, expressed in ways that are rarely found in daily discourse. Literature multiplies our exposure to every aspect of human nature and thought.

Edmundson wants all students to be enlarged by literature. Therefore, he offers an essential corrective: that it is not primarily about "figuring out" symbolism, figurative language, setting, mood, or structure. These have their place but are absurdly overemphasized in state standards—including the Common Core. Literature is primarily *about us,* as individuals, as a community of readers, seeking to understand ourselves and the world we share. Unfortunately, fiction is too often taught as though it is an abstract game or code.

Literary studies should be much simpler, more direct, and more personal: they offer us a unique opportunity to weigh our perceptions, values, and emotional resonance against those of the author and *the characters he or she creates*. Do we like, dislike, relate to, or learn from the characters or from the author's or poet's implicit messages? Do we see ourselves, our culture, or people in our lives more clearly as a result of our encounters with fictional characters from near or far, past or present? This is and has always been the primary pleasure and purpose of reading literature, plays, poetry, or memoirs.

Literature allows us to reflect, to recognize the subtle ideas and forces operating on our lives—and thus to shape them. Edmundson (2004) describes the epiphany experienced by one of his students, a college athlete, while reading *The Iliad:* she began to see herself in the character of Achilles. In reading about his single-minded focus on victory and dominance, she realized she had never consciously reflected on the value of such an obsession—her own—or its effects on other areas of her life. Was Achilles worth emulating? The experience was deeply personal for her.

Literature, writes Edmundson (2004), allows us to uncover and refine our "central convictions about politics, love, money, the good life" (p. 28). As Kelly Gallagher (2009) writes,

> I am a different person because I have read *1984*. I see my government differently, I consider privacy issues differently and I have a heightened sense of propaganda and language manipulation—all because I have read this novel. (p. 57)

I, too, am a different person, as are many of you, because of the characters and ideas we've encountered in prose and poetry. The same is true of the ideas and characters we encounter in nonfiction, literary nonfiction, and current news and opinion articles. These enlarge us as well and allow us to acquire the knowledge essential for reading comprehension and critical thinking.

Nonfiction and Literary Nonfiction

As mentioned earlier, Hirsch (2009, 2016), Willingham (2009a), and other authors have found that content knowledge and critical thinking work reciprocally. What is the best way to acquire such knowledge? Books play an indispensable role. As Willingham points out, reading *"[b]ooks* exposes children to more facts and to a broader vocabulary (a form of knowledge) than *any other activity"* (p. 37; emphasis added).

I wholly agree with Will Fitzhugh (2006) that K–12 curricula should increase the number of whole, nonfiction books that students are required to read, especially in history and social studies (see also Mathews, 2010). In English language arts, fiction and literature should always predominate. But English is also an ideal subject for students to read and acquire an appetite for content-rich nonfiction books, and so is social studies. Biographies and memoirs, the most prominent form of literary nonfiction, are rich sources of knowledge.

All students at Tempe Preparatory Academy and the Great Hearts Academies, both in the Phoenix area, read multiple, entire fiction and literary nonfiction books every year during their two-hour English and social studies block.

But books aren't enough. Willingham (2009b) adds that students also acquire essential knowledge and thinking skills "through years of exposure to newspapers, serious magazines... from a content-rich curriculum in school" (p. 2). Thomas Friedman and Michael Mandelbaum (2011) report that, unfortunately, in the past few years, the number of high school students who read newspapers has plummeted from 42 percent to 23 percent.

I'm convinced that an engaging, content-rich curriculum must include regular, in-class opportunities to read and discuss newspapers and serious magazines in every subject, from the earliest grades.

Newspapers and Magazines in the Classroom

Students enjoy current issues and events, especially when they are framed in controversy. I have seen the most indifferent students talk and write with enthusiasm when asked to read and exchange opinions about controversial issues and people such as presidential candidates, the politics of gerrymandering, or the pros and cons of nuclear energy.

For years, I recommended that teachers integrate current articles and opinion pieces into the curriculum (Schmoker, 2006, pp. 170–172). Author and high school teacher Kelly Gallagher (2009) is a master of this practice. He started doing his "Article of the Week" when he discovered that only a few of his high school students could name the current vice president. They also thought that "Al Qaeda" was a guy named "Al" (p. 28). (To see a full year of "Articles of the Week" used at Gallagher's school, go to www.kellygallagher.org/article-of-the-week.

If we can get students interested in the issues of our time (and we can), they will be more interested in issues, people, and literature of the past. Current events animate student interest in literature, politics, and history. The new norm should be something like what

Gallagher (2009) would do when teaching Remarque's *All Quiet on the Western Front:* he would juxtapose it with a close reading of two articles on the Iraq War with opposing viewpoints (p. 27). Assembling and organizing such reading materials—with good questions—should be among a teaching team's highest priorities.

For the early grades, *Weekly Reader, TIME for Kids,* and *Junior Scholastic* contain rich, readable news stories for students as young as seven. We should be reading and discussing such articles regularly.

In the upper elementary grades, a surprising amount of adult newspaper, magazine, and opinion pieces can be read and understood if we provide some background and vocabulary (and simple scaffolding procedures like those described in the literacy template described in Chapter 3). The same articles work even better with middle and high school students. I collect such articles, and so should professional learning community teams in every discipline. I have tested such articles on focus groups, asking them the grade levels for which they think the pieces would be appropriate. The groups invariably concur that with proper scaffolding, the articles could be read and discussed as early as the 5th grade and would be highly engaging.

One of my favorite sources of readable, content-rich articles is *The Week,* a summary of the week's news and opinion—from both sides, and from around the world. These articles are excellent for lessons in how to closely read and annotate (with the use, as always, of repeated modeling, guided practice, and checks for understanding). One of its regular features is the "Controversy of the Week." It starts with an arresting summary of a current issue, followed by about six brief summaries of opinion pieces from across the political spectrum—all in less than a page. This is perfect for teaching students to read analytically, annotate, and cite textual evidence as they discuss, and then write argumentative paragraphs and papers.

Kids enjoy controversy. Reading and talking about such articles may be the best and fastest way to accelerate their interest in the world and to initiate their entry into adult conversation. English teachers need to make serious room for such reading, followed by discussion and writing. Moreover, such articles make *great exemplars* for teachers to use when they teach writing.

As Gallagher (2009) writes, "We are what we read," and conversely, "We are what we don't read" (p. 45). If we want all students to be informed, well-rounded, productive citizens, they must develop "reading stamina." It's our job to *increase the amount and time they spend reading in class* (with sensible stopping points to pair up or to discuss or write briefly about what they are reading). For children in the earliest grades, we must plan deliberately—and sensibly—to help them transition from reading single paragraphs to whole pages, then two pages, and so on. Large portions of this reading should occur in language arts. And the same goes for writing.

• • •

Make no mistake: such increases—with all their manifold academic and life benefits—would require a reconception of language arts. To that end, let's take one more look at the skills and standards that still plague standard-issue literacy instruction. This time, we'll look specifically at how they unnecessarily prolong the acquisition of basic reading and writing proficiency. In this way, they subsequently delay—by years—the development of students' academic and intellectual capacities.

The Trouble with Skills and Standards

Read-i-cide, n.: the systematic killing of the love of reading, often exacerbated by the inane, mind-numbing practices found in schools.

—Kelly Gallagher

The mistaken idea that reading is a skill... may be the single biggest factor holding back reading achievement in the country.

—Daniel Willingham

I love Mike Rose's (1989) simple, ageless formulation: that we fundamentally read, talk, and write our way toward an education (pp. 32–34). But as we've seen, an emphasis on discrete standards and skills prevents reading, talking, and writing from occurring, starting in the early and upper elementary grades—when lifelong patterns of literacy are often determined.

Skills Kill: The Elementary Years

John Taylor Gatto is a two-time New York state teacher of the year. And he is outraged by typical early-grade reading instruction. Instead of ameliorating the achievement gap, typical reading instruction perpetuates it.

An educational historian, Gatto (2002) notes that literate societies of the past never underwent the inanities of modern, skills-based "guided reading" groups and regimens. Public education is culpable here: "One of the central assumptions which allow the institutional school to sustain itself… [is] the false assumption *that it is difficult to learn to read*" (p. xxxvii). Of course, the impulse to prolong the teaching of reading is encouraged by the basal textbook industry, which has enjoyed uncritical acceptance and profits from our use of its thick, skills-based texts, workbooks, and worksheets. It has much to answer for.

Long before the Common Core era, early-grade language arts instruction had become one of the most curious, counterproductive features of modern schooling. Its most insidious aspect is its tendency to elongate the process of learning to read—thus postponing "reading to learn." Obviously, schools have a duty to teach the essentials of decoding—which include phonics, phonemic units, syllabication, and related elements. But against all good sense, we teach these skills into the 2nd, 3rd, and even 4th grades. And we do it far too slowly, in compliance with the dictates of various reading programs and mass-produced basal readers. We seldom question the legitimacy of their contents: the mass of questionable activities and exercises, the insistence that we separately teach and test and record each child in small groups for the child's ability to "distinguish between initial, medial, or final sounds" or to "segment spoken phonemes contained in one-syllable words of two to five phoneme sounds into individual phoneme sounds" (the Common Core standards are bursting with such pedantry). No parent or teacher who successfully taught his or her own children to read *would ever subject them to such nonsense.*

The consequences of this small-group, skills-based focus during the typical "literacy block" should be obvious: it means that students spend the bulk of language arts, well into the 3rd and even 4th grades, waiting for their group to be taught. The implication is that students who are not with the teacher are engaged in productive literacy activities. Alas, they are not. While waiting their turn, students typically occupy themselves at "centers"—where they engage in a variety of coloring and cut-and-paste activities that make no contribution to reading—or writing—ability. We squander about two thirds of the so-called literacy block in these and similar activities (Ford & Opitz, 2002).

In combination, these factors directly prevent students from spending time reading, talking, and writing about literature—or about *nonfiction texts in history, science, and geography* (which are quietly pushed aside by the necessities of the extended literacy block).

There is a better way. We could greatly accelerate students' ability to both decode and read with comprehension. As I pointed out in Chapter 3, there are kindergarten and 1st grade teachers in challenging settings whose students are reading independently—and writing—by the middle or end of 1st grade. As we'll see, once students learn to decode, they learn to read better and acquire large amounts of vocabulary and content knowledge by reading—not by enduring more reading skills instruction.

In their book *Classrooms That Work: They Can All Read and Write*, Cunningham and Allington (2007) point out that in the highest-performing primary language arts classrooms, time is sacred: there are no coloring or cut-and-paste activities. In these classrooms, students are immersed in intensive daily instruction in the most ordinary elements of reading: the alphabet and its sounds, common blends of letters, the 37 most common spelling patterns, the 50 most transferable word chunks, and lists of high-frequency words. Students clap and chant words and syllables—as a class. They read lots of books along with their teacher, with their finger on syllables and words, as they quickly gain mastery of decoding skills.

If all students were taught in this manner, they would learn to read much earlier. Allington (2011) cites numerous studies demonstrating that *"virtually every student could be reading on grade level by the end of 1st grade"* (p. 40; emphasis added). From 2nd grade on, they could begin to read increasing quantities of text on their own as they acquire the knowledge, thinking skills, and "reading stamina" that accelerates the acquisition of knowledge and reading ability in each subsequent grade level (Shanahan, 2014, p. 187). But this can't happen if we continue to unnecessarily elongate a skills-based reading curriculum.

Virtually any student can learn the mechanics of decoding in about 100 days. That means that virtually any student could be reading simple texts by second semester of the 1st grade (Engelmann, Haddox, & Bruner, 1983).

Once students can effectively decode, we must organize time in language arts to ensure that students spend large amounts of time reading, both purposefully and for pleasure. Anything less hurts all students, but it disproportionately affects poor and minority students. When I visit classrooms and schools, I see up close how these seemingly innocent practices and products just described do long-lasting, perhaps irreparable, harm. They plainly prevent the rapid acquisition of knowledge, vocabulary, and comprehension by the bottom-performing half of the student population. They suppress student's life chances and career opportunities and deprive them of the pleasures of learning.

And it doesn't happen at only the primary level. We continue to commit "readicide" in upper elementary and secondary school as well.

"Readicide": The "Terrible Price" We Pay for Current Practices

Students aren't mature readers until they can read and recognize about 50,000 words—and the sooner, the better. But this many words *can't be learned quickly if students must sound out, syllabicate, or learn each word and its definition one by one.* The only way they can be learned is for us to ensure that they read large amounts of reading material (Smith, 2006, p. 41). As things stand, students read only a fraction of what would both narrow the achievement gap and ensure optimal intellectual growth.

From 3rd grade on, students could be reading eight to ten chapter books per year, some self-selected. If more—much more—class time were spent reading fiction and nonfiction, the students would acquire record amounts of knowledge and thousands of vocabulary words—as they build up their reading stamina.

Not all reading should be "close reading," but there should be plenty of opportunity for students to learn to read analytically and to underline and annotate, starting in the early grades with stories such as *Jack and the Beanstalk*. Students should be routinely discussing what they read and then writing paragraphs and short essays in which they advance arguments and interpretations about fictional and real-life characters. In this way, they could be *preparing for college—in the 2nd grade*. The effect of these simple changes on the bottom-performing half of the student population would be especially significant.

Despite their importance, none of them is common practice—not in the early grades, and not in the later years, when they will encounter an equally irrelevant set of language arts standards. Cumulatively, our wrongheaded emphasis on skills and standards represents what Kelly Gallagher (2009) calls "readicide."

In the upper grades and through high school, students are too often occupied with short, bloodless text excerpts and worksheets built around the most trivial standards and irrelevant literary terms, year after year (e.g., "rising action," "protagonist," "internal or external conflict"). The same goes for nonfiction: as Doug Lemov (2017) writes, "We [adults] would never read a non-fiction article because we felt it was an outstanding example of, say, 'presenting events in chronological order'" (p. 13). Why do we expect students to?

There is a cost to our somnambulant acceptance of these perverse priorities—and programs. Year after year, they directly prevent students from reading eight or more classic books per year, such as *Stone Fox; Little Women; Roll of Thunder, Hear My Cry;* or *Tom Sawyer* (see Appendix B of ELA CCSS). They will never get around to arresting nonfiction works such as Elie Wiesel's *Night* or Susan Campbell Bartoletti's *Hitler Youth: Growing Up in Hitler's Shadow*.

And they will never participate in frequent, stimulating *discussions* of these works, followed by *writing,* all in response to simple, compelling questions that can be used or varied for almost any work of literature—questions about character, culture, and theme (I'll discuss such questions shortly).

As Gallagher (2009) writes, "a terrible price is paid" when the exigencies of skills and "standards-based" instruction supersede authentic literacy activities (p. 26). Indeed, "struggling readers who do not *read voraciously* will never catch up" (p. 43). To produce a generation of "voracious readers," we must apportion class time differently.

It's worth reiterating that many teachers still cling to the belief that skills-based instruction is the key to higher test scores. They can have a limited effect—but then scores quickly plateau, especially on authentic measures. That's why state test scores have gone up on most state assessments, even as scores on the National Assessment of Educational Progress (NAEP)—a much more reliable assessment— have only inched up, stagnating in high school, where they matter most (Hirsch, 2016, p. 16).

Gay Ivey and Douglas Fisher (2006) found that "no evidence proves that an approach focused on the *technical aspects of literacy* helps students become more sophisticated in their reading" (p. 17). Others have found that this emphasis impedes students' ability to interact with text or make meaningful connections among its ideas

(McKeown, Beck, & Blake, 2009). As Harold Wenglinsky points out, high scores on the NAEP are the result of something we rarely do: ask questions and think critically about *"real texts—books and stories rather than short passages."* Our focus on language arts standards has backfired; they only succeed in "squeezing out critical thinking skills," and in this way they put "the cognitive development of our students at risk" (Wenglinsky, 2004, p. 34).

What is the way out of this morass? We must radically reconceive ELA curriculum in light of the problems just discussed. So how do we build such curriculum? As simply as possible.

How to Build a Simple, Powerful English Language Arts Curriculum

How should we organize an English language arts curriculum to ensure preparation for college and careers, as well as success on state and college-entrance examinations?

The curriculum that I recommend is similar in some ways to the middle and high school English/social studies courses at Tempe Preparatory Academy and the Great Hearts Academies referred to earlier. The Great Hearts elementary curriculum is very similar. Their curriculum ensures—"guarantees"—that every student will read the same core texts; they will have daily, analytic discussions about those texts; and all students will write the same number of major writing assignments—eight or nine, one per month—about those same texts. Moreover, every student is *taught to write,* frequently and explicitly, every year, through the use of common guides and scoring criteria. Unsurprisingly, test scores at these schools are often the highest or among the highest in the state—even though (as mentioned earlier) these schools completely ignore the state standards for ELA. Tempe Prep was recently selected as the best high school in the state. As Carol Jago points out, when you write regularly and are taught to write, test scores take care of themselves (Will, 2016).

All of this is right in line with what David Conley (2005) recommends to English and other departments—that they establish clear agreements for the minimum *number of core texts and written assignments* to assure common, quality curriculum—in the service of a simple but "intellectually coherent program" (pp. 79–82). The following applies to 2nd through 12th grade ELA—and some of it to 1st grade (in which much of the curriculum is rightly devoted to decoding).

We'll start with reading. As Jacques Barzun (1991) writes, "No subject of study is more important than reading… all other intellectual powers depend on it" (p. 21).

Reading

Teams or departments should agree on a specific—and generous—number of quality "core texts" for every course and grade level. As Conley (2005) points out, these become the basis for students to master the core skills of "annotation and close reading" (p. 79).

By building such curriculum, Brockton High School made the largest gains in the state during the very first year of their improvement effort. They went on to rise from the lowest-achieving to the top 10 percent in the state—rapidly. Their mantra was "reading, writing, speaking, and reasoning" in every course. The effort began with the discovery that students read very few books and that there were no common, required readings in English classes. As former principal Susan Szachowicz informed me,

> English teachers could essentially teach whatever they wanted… with great disparity in the rigor of the works selected. And students didn't read enough books. We used to joke that in some classes, our students studied the same book longer than it took the author to write it.

In response, and for the first time, the English department designated which challenging, complex fiction and nonfiction books were to be read at each grade level and course. It is fine to let students self-select some of their reading, perhaps with guidance from their teacher. But as Conley (2005) points out, effective English curriculum must include a sensible number of common, "foundational texts," chosen for their content, appeal, and complexity; the work of multiple scholars attests to the power of teaching students to navigate rich *common* texts (Berliner & Biddle, 1995; Rose, 1989). And others exhort us not to succumb to the pressure to "differentiate" texts for each child, with the inevitable dumbing down this leads to (Shanahan, 2014; DeWitt 2016b).

Conley (2005) recommends that most of this reading should be in the service of argument—to mine texts for supporting evidence to "construct their own arguments; agree, disagree, summarize, critique; and formulate a personal response" (p. 80). He would also have English teachers agree on the general purposes or kinds of analysis to be done for some of these common "foundational texts" (p. 82). This could be accomplished through a certain number of common questions or prompts developed by teams of teachers (which we'll expand on shortly).

In general, for every English course, we might adopt or adapt guidelines like the following as we build a simple, powerful curriculum (the actual number depending on length and lexical density of the texts):

- About 8 to 10 core books, including plays
- Numerous poems and short stories (perhaps 10 to 20 of each)
- About 10 to 20 newspaper/magazine/nonfiction articles—or speeches

These could be divided between the following:

- Fiction (imaginative literature and poetry): about 70 percent of the ELA curriculum
- Nonfiction/literary nonfiction (articles, biographies, memoirs, true stories): about 30 percent, some of which might be self-selected

These readings would be organized by grading period.

In addition, in the building of the ELA curriculum, the ratio of fiction to nonfiction derives from the assumption that **large amounts of nonfiction reading will occur in science, social studies, arts, and electives**. This will allow English to maintain its traditional (but not exclusive) focus on imaginative literature, poetry, and literary nonfiction. In our increasingly technocratic, ethically challenging culture, I believe we need the lessons, insights, and pleasures of literature more than ever.

Building Reading Stamina

Of course, such amounts of reading would be unprecedented, but we can facilitate such reading by using simple methods to increase students' reading stamina.

We can start by reading some of the initial portion of the text aloud, with students reading along with us. We would then occasionally call on random students to read a sentence or two aloud (to ensure that they are reading with us). Then we would have them read short and then increasingly longer sections of text by themselves as we alternate between reading aloud and independent reading. This is not to be confused with less-effective "round robin reading," in which students take turns doing most of the reading aloud, often in a halting or plodding manner—with the risk of interrupting the flow of the reading.

To monitor their independent reading, we would circulate to observe their underlinings, annotations, or notes—which help prepare them for the ensuing discussion and writing assignments. Of course, some reading assignments require more underlining and annotation (e.g., articles) than do others (novels or whole books; occasional notes can often be sufficient).

It is almost always helpful to allow students to pair-share their notes and perceptions at strategic points during the reading. Students who finish earlier can read self-selected books or articles online or from the school or classroom library. With a little practice, any teacher can employ this routine to good effect.

Reasonable amounts of reading can be given as homework, but we have to get this balance right: we can't count on the majority of students to complete large daily reading assignments at home, especially in communities in which parental support is often lacking. We must also remember that the opportunity for large increases in time spent reading (and writing and discussion) during the school day will emerge once we reduce or eliminate most of the movies, worksheets, poster making, and test preparation activities that often clutter the curriculum.

Columbus Elementary's "Leap of Faith"

Since writing the first edition, I have corresponded with Lynn Abeln, a 5th grade teacher at Columbus Elementary School in McMinnville, Oregon. By employing such methods, she and several members of her faculty were able to greatly increase the number of substantive, common texts that all students read in English. This "leap of faith," as she put it, meant ignoring state standards and abandoning their previously differentiated curriculum: there would be "no more 'six books [per school year] at six different levels' with most students not on task because I can only be with one group at a time." Their new curriculum would ensure that all students read, discussed, and wrote about more books and texts than ever, with some parts read aloud by the teacher. Students frequently took Cornell notes as they read—almost every day—usually around just one guiding question for each chapter or nonfiction article. For instance, for the novel *The Watsons Go to Birmingham—1963*, students would respond to chapter questions such as: "What do we learn about Kenny in this chapter?" or "How is Kenny different from his brother?" Students routinely wrote short papers and one longer, formal paper—some as long as five pages—each grading period. All of them received the same careful, explicit writing instruction—based on a clear, concise rubric used throughout the school.

Once again: during the *first year* that Columbus made this "leap of faith," the passing percentage rose from 81 percent to 88 percent schoolwide—their best scores ever; 100 percent of Abeln's students passed the test (also a first for her). Moreover, the status of the school—in which 62 percent of students qualified for free and reduced-cost lunches—rose from "Acceptable" to "Outstanding" for the first time.

This is why Richard Allington and others recommend at least 60 minutes of reading per day—across the curriculum. If we made this a priority, students could be doing—in all courses combined—at least 150 hours of reading *every year*—enough to make a life-changing difference (no matter where a student might begin).

Such extensive, purposeful reading is the basis for inquiry-driven discussion, which in turn is the best possible preparation for effective writing—as George Hillocks demonstrated as long ago as 1987.

Discussion

Talk—about books and subjects—is as important educationally as are the books and subjects themselves.

—Gerald Graff (2003, p. 9)

We greatly underestimate the value of discussion. Mary Ehrenworth (2017), of Columbia Teachers College, writes that "There has never been a more important time to teach young people to suspend judgment, weigh evidence, consider multiple perspectives and speak up with wisdom and grace on behalf of themselves." And not just any discussion, but argumentative discussion: "Argumentation," she writes, "is not just a skill for language arts classrooms—it is also a pathway to success in virtually every academic discipline" (p. 35).

Discussion is also a critical companion to reading. The English curriculum must provide plenty of opportunities for students to share, as Conley (2005) writes, their "personal experiences and values," as well as their opinions and interpretations in classroom discussion and debates, as they learn to "support their arguments and provide evidence for their assertions" (p. 81). At Tempe Prep and the Great Hearts schools, students engage in extended "Socratic discussions" almost every day during the school year. At Columbus Elementary, just mentioned, teachers now routinely conduct what they also refer to as "Socratic seminars." For instance, students read an article in *TIME for Kids* about the "tiger mom" and had a discussion about effective parenting, citing evidence to support their opinions. The principal was so impressed with these discussions that he had Columbus students do a demonstration seminar at a school board meeting.

I would recommend that students participate in at least three seminars or discussions per week *about their readings*. This work would follow the general format described in the literacy template from Chapter 3. To promote the success of these discussions, teaching teams should routinely work together to develop, test, and refine effective questions and prompts.

Students will gain immeasurably from these discussions if we use or adapt a simple rubric like the one described in Chapter 3 (or your own):

- Always cite the text when making an argument.
- Speak audibly and clearly, in complete sentences.
- When commenting on or disagreeing with another's arguments, briefly refer to or restate what they said.
- Don't interrupt; be civil and respectful.
- Be concise and stay on point.
- Avoid distracting verbal tics (such as "like" and "you know").

Using such criteria, we need to explicitly teach, model, and require effective participation in discussions. And keep in mind: once students have had the chance to read, annotate, and pair-share about a text, we can feel comfortable making liberal use of cold-calling. We can't let seminars continue to be dominated by the same minority of students who always raise their hands.

I am surprised that such discussion, and instruction in such discussion, is still so rare. When, as a guest, I conduct student seminars, it becomes obvious that it is a fairly new experience for them: they aren't used to being required to participate, asked to speak audibly—loud enough that others can hear them, or express themselves in fairly clear, complete sentences. It often seems as if I'm the first person to ever teach them these hugely important life skills. Once I do—and *if they've been given adequate opportunity to analyze the text and rehearse their thoughts with each other in pairs*—they greatly enjoy these discussions. As research tells us, it is among their very favorite activities (Azzam, 2008).

In most schools, we need to take discussion much more seriously—as they do at New Dorp High School in Staten Island.

A New Dawn at New Dorp High School

As *The Atlantic's* Peg Tyre (2012) tells us, New Dorp High School was among the lowest-performing schools in the country and was being considered for closure by New York City Public Schools. Of its freshmen, 82 percent read below grade level. We'll look at the role that writing instruction played in this school's remarkable turn-around. But, explicit instruction in the art of discussion also played a major initial role in their improvement. "Classroom discussion," writes Tyre,

> became an opportunity to push [students] to listen to each other, think more carefully, and speak more precisely, in ways that could then echo in persuasive writing [as we'll see below]. (p. 14)

Once again: their transformation didn't rely on additional funding, innovation, technology, or adherence to "standards." It began with teaching students specifically how to interact with their classmates, using simple prompts prominently displayed at the front of every classroom, such as:

- "I agree/disagree with (_____) because..."
- "I have something to add."
- "I've come to a different conclusion..."

In her article, Tyre (2012) transcribes a discussion in which students faithfully employ the stems just listed as they respond to a question about Arthur Miller's *Death of a Salesman:* "What is Willie Loman's state of mind, and what factors in his life might account for it?" (pp. 14–15). Their discussion is truly "grounded in text" (the second of the "three shifts") and exemplifies what is all too rare in our ELA classes: students carefully—and politely—listening, sharing, and commenting on each other's arguments and interpretations of literature and nonfiction. Any willing teacher can conduct such discussions with practice and through dialogue with their subject-area colleagues.

Such discussion should be a mainstay of English instruction, and of schooling itself. New Dorp faculty also discovered that these discussions, important in their own right, helped students "in ways that could then echo in persuasive writing" (Tyre, 2012, p. 14). Argumentative writing, nourished by close reading and discussion, made a decisive difference at the school.

Writing

When New Dorp was being considered for closure, the principal decided (as was done at Brockton High School) to go "all in" on literacy. In addition to analytic reading and frequent discussions around text, teachers were taught to provide explicit writing instruction in every course, on a near-daily basis.

Every student in America deserves such instruction. But too many schools tacitly subscribe to the notion, as Arizona State University's Steven Graham points out in Tyre's (2012) article, that writing must be "*caught, not taught*" (p. 10). Writing ability is indeed both "caught"—as we immerse ourselves in reading and discussion—as well as "taught"—learned from teachers who show us how to organize our inchoate thoughts into clear, logical prose.

Before their turnaround, most New Dorp faculty thought that poor students were "simply not smart enough" to write well. That changed in 2008. Without any significant staff turnover, students began to receive direct, almost daily writing instruction in how to read analytically, cite text, and support arguments—both orally and in writing. And there was never a focus on an atomized list of new or improved ELA "standards." On the contrary, Tyre (2012) points out that the school's new emphasis on explicit instruction in reading, discussion, and writing "would not be unfamiliar to nuns who taught in Catholic schools circa 1950" (p. 6). Indeed, in a "profoundly hopeful irony," Tyre reports that

> New Dorp's reemergence as a viable institution has hinged not on a radical new innovation but on an old idea done better. The school's success suggests that perhaps certain instructional

fundamentals—*fundamentals that have been devalued or forgotten*—may turn out to be the most powerful lever we have for improving school performance after all. (p. 16)

What were the results—after only two years of such explicit, traditional literacy instruction? Their English Regents passing rates rose from 67 percent to 89 percent, and the number of students who needed to be enrolled in remedial "cram courses" plummeted from 175 to about 40—in two years (p. 4). New Dorp is now regarded as a model of effective reform and is being visited by high schools from around the country.

The school's preference for proven "instructional fundamentals" is a recurring theme in these pages. Those fundamentals are strikingly similar, once again, to those of Brockton High School.

Brockton High School: Back to the Future

Sue Szachowicz was fond of telling me that their improvement effort cost nothing and involved no "innovation" or technology whatsoever; it was simply a matter of ensuring that every teacher provided good teaching and a coherent curriculum. The school's commitment to "reading, writing, speaking, and reasoning" was built explicitly into a coherent curriculum. Initially, there were designated days, every week, when observers could expect to see lessons built around writing, with explicit writing instruction. Brockton faculty members believe this was perhaps the primary reason their school made the largest gains in the state on the Massachusetts Comprehensive Assessment System (MCAS) in the first year of implementation.

In English, every grade-level team was charged with routinely assigning specific expository, interpretive, and argumentative writing assignments, all designed by teachers themselves. But once assignments were completed, Brockton faculty didn't assume that implementation was a given: Szachowicz and several faculty members "monitored like crazy" and provided frank feedback when necessary.

Of supreme importance was that the English department at Brockton regularly collected and reviewed samples of student writing. I was the beneficiary of such monitoring at a middle school where I taught in Tucson. The expectation was crystal clear: students were to complete two substantial writing assignments per grading period. Each quarter, the English department head and principal would ask us for a couple of random samples of graded student work. This gave them a good sense of how well students were writing—and how effectively we were teaching. These simple expectations and routines had a determinative effect on the quality and quantity of writing instruction at our school.

At View Park Preparatory High School in South Los Angeles, described in Chapter 2, the "guaranteed" language arts curriculum was also a function of a simple routine: every month, students wrote two argumentative papers of a defined length, using the Toulmin model of argument. Again, argumentative writing was preceded by close reading based on an essential question that drove the subsequent Socratic discussion. This was so successful in English and history that argumentative writing was incorporated into all disciplines. Teachers at View Park speak of how students gain considerably from (once again) even *one year* of argumentative writing; by the end of 9th grade, they have become confident writers who are "prepared to write in college and to think through and logically argue their points in multiple disciplines" (Hernandez et al., 2006).

View Park's student body is 97 percent African American. As described, once this routine was instituted, it was responsible for View Park's becoming the highest-achieving majority-minority school in the state of California (Hernandez et al., 2006). Ninety percent of the 2008 graduates were accepted into four-year colleges (Landsberg, 2008b).

These secondary examples are quite similar to what accounted for the success of teacher Rafe Esquith's 5th graders, who wrote an essay on most Fridays during English Language Arts. That's about 30 essays a year, on argumentative questions or prompts such as "Weigh in on George's decision to kill Lennie in Steinbeck's *Of Mice and Men*" (Esquith, 2007, pp. 51–52).

Clear Curricular Expectations: Writing

The success of these schools points to the power of a curriculum document that clarifies the core texts as well as the number and length of major writing assignments for each course. Such "guaranteed and viable" curriculum (Marzano, 2003) would ensure, at long last, that students read and write in adequate amounts in their ELA courses. Quantity counts: teacher and author Dave Stuart (2017) is especially insightful on the primary importance of "quantity"—of ensuring generous amounts of reading, writing, and discussion.

But quality counts as well. English departments should employ a common scoring guide that can be adapted for specific writing assignments (with a bias toward argumentative writing). In addition, every teacher team should collect and then integrate exemplar papers into their writing instruction. These are indispensable as both teaching and learning tools; they demystify the elements of effective writing for both students and teachers like nothing else can.

To begin the transition, I would recommend that English departments immediately establish an expectation that students write at least one—just one—substantial, polished paper each grading period (four per school year). I would also recommend that at least three of these four papers be "grounded in text"—that is, based on an analysis, interpretation, or argument in response to one or more books, plays, short stories, speeches, or poems. Instruction would be built explicitly around simple, agreed-upon scoring guides—and exemplar papers; teams should devote time to refining their use of these instructional tools. At the end of each grading period, teachers would tally up the total number of students who met or exceeded quality standards. Then they would identify common patterns of deficiency; these deficiencies would be the primary focus of the team's improvement discussions and efforts during the next grading period.

By themselves, these simple steps—more short and mid-length writing assignments, and more effective writing instruction—would ensure more analytic close reading. They would greatly enhance what Conley (2005) and Graff (2003) found to have more positive impact on college and postsecondary studies than perhaps any other factor: the ability to write coherent, argumentative prose.

In addition, although written work doesn't enable teachers to assess everything in ELA, it provides the best all-in-one assessment of language ability: it reveals how well students can read, analyze, explain, and organize their thoughts in clear, compelling language. For this reason, papers should constitute a much larger proportion of students' grades in English.

In the last section of this chapter, I will outline some suggestions for taking this a step further—by establishing a schedule of K–12 benchmark assessments that would drive essential improvements in schooling and tell us far more about students' true intellectual abilities than any standardized test. First, I will outline a provisional description of the basic features of effective writing; it is an expanded version of what I described in Chapter 3. I have found that a surprising number of English teachers find such guidance a helpful starting point as they attempt to provide explicit writing instruction.

The Major Moves of Writing

Even since the inception of the Common Core, numerous experts affirm that very few teachers learn to teach writing—in preservice education or through professional development. And many believe that it will take years of experience or in-depth training to correct this (Will, 2016).

I can't agree with that. Any individual or team could begin to teach writing effectively, tomorrow morning, simply by developing lessons for elements such as those that follow (or variations on these). This is not a manual but an attempt to describe some fairly conventional features of writing in a way that can clarify instruction. If you find what follows too formulaic, ignore it. But many of us learned to write, at least initially, from such formulas—which gave us a basis on which to improvise and thus expand our writing skills.

Introduction

There is wide agreement that the introduction, or "introductory paragraph," of a piece should contain (1) a thesis statement or argument, (2) a "hook"—to grab the reader's attention and entice them to keep reading, and sometimes (3) a "preview" that provides a brief description of the major points or arguments of the article or paper. All three can be found in the following (slightly doctored) paragraph. It was written by my niece, then in 9th grade, who was taught explicitly (for the first time) how to write an introductory paragraph:

> Do Odysseus's actions prove him to be a righteous leader? I don't think so. At times in the story, Odysseus might seem like a great leader. But he's not. He is not a good leader because he does not have his crew's best interest in mind and because he is not even a good leader of his family. His arrogant, inconsiderate, and selfish behavior repeatedly lets down his family and crew. These shortcomings reveal Odysseus' failure as a leader.

The three parts just described are readily discernible in this paragraph (some, arguably, in more than one place, which is not a problem). Could virtually any teacher or team, working from such an example, develop an effective lesson for teaching introductory paragraphs? *Of course they could.* The same goes for all of the following. All we have to do is identify, and work backward from, exemplars of good writing.

Working Outline

Building the (always tentative, "working") outline will reduce anxiety and give beginning writers an enormous practical and psychological boost. Even if we modify the outline at some point (as we often do), it helps writers to organize their thoughts so that they can move forward with confidence and coherence. An outline can consist of something as simple as a thesis statement, followed by "major points" (each clearly supporting the thesis) and maybe some supporting text, such as direct quotations or paraphrasing (each clearly supporting the major points of the paper). By teaching and vetting thesis statements and outlines, teachers save both themselves and students invaluable time and frustration—and time spent correcting disorganized prose. To repeat: there's no deep magic in this; any teacher or team could develop—and refine—lessons for explicitly teaching students to create good outlines.

Body Paragraphs

These often include elements such as the following, all taught explicitly:

• *Topic sentences*, which clarify the major point or subargument and unambiguously support the larger thesis/argument.

• *Appropriate integration of quotations*, with the use of examples and sentence stems (available from a variety of online and other sources; also see Graff & Birkenstein, 2015).

• *Exposition*, which is explanatory material that tells the reader how the supportive quotations and paraphrased material support the major point and the larger thesis/argument. This almost always requires more than one sentence.

• *Transitions*, which are phrases or whole sentences that help clarify links and relationships among ideas both within and among the major points and paragraphs; they make the writing easier to follow (you might give students an article, have them underline such transitions, and then pair up—to discuss how these expressions make it easier to follow the writer's argument).

• *Conclusion*, in which the writer seeks to summarize the writing, leave a final impression upon the reader, or both.

Terms and elements might differ, but I hope you can see that with practice, any teacher or team could successfully build and execute lessons for these basic components (or variations on them) within a semester—certainly within a school year. Such instruction would be especially effective if we "backward map" from examples of good student or professional writing. Samples of bad writing would be effective, too, because if given the chance to revise someone else's poorly written paragraph or paper, students will more readily identify and correct errors—and thereby learn valuable writing lessons.

There is no reason to delay implementing such lessons. Start tomorrow. If all teachers began to regularly teach writing using anything like this model, the impact would be swift and stunning.

At some point, the elements just described would need to be converted into learning objectives—critical components of a good lesson (Marzano, 2011a; Wiggins, 2013). In a later section, I'll describe how to do that for ELA. But first, let's address an issue that often derails efforts to promote more writing or writing instruction: the notorious "paper load." As many will ask, "Who has the time to grade all these papers?"

Fear not.

Handling the "Paper Load"

As alluded to in Chapter 3, there are highly effective ways to dramatically increase the amount of writing—and the writing instruction we provide—while *reducing* the paper-grading load. We save enormous amounts of time, for instance, when we "check for understanding"— and address student writing difficulties—before we collect any written work; when we use exemplars to inform every phase of our instruction; and when we teach students to self-assess and peer-assess by using rubrics or checklists before they hand in their work. We should also remember that both students and teachers are smart to focus our lessons on *just one* crystal-clear area or criterion, or a very limited number of them (Stiggins, 1994). That makes evaluation and scoring much faster and easier for the teacher.

Remember as well that we don't have to collect and formally grade most of the writing that students do. A lot of "grading"— assessing both individual work and our own efforts to teach writing—can be done by walking around the room and checking off work that meets the focus of the day's lesson. Deeper, more detailed assessment can often wait until a later stage of the writing.

Alas, *students don't learn about the craft of writing primarily from our comments on their papers;* the great majority of what they learn comes from carefully crafted lessons built around exemplars and scoring guides. For more information and practical tips on reducing the paper load, see "Write More, Grade Less" at www.mikeschmoker. com/write-more.html.

• • •

At this point, we might consider what activates the most engaging language and literacy instruction described in this chapter. I'm convinced that our success depends on our ability to develop compelling questions and prompts. These too must be simplified.

Guiding Questions for Imaginative Literature

The best discussions and writing about literature don't center on literary trivia; they emerge from questions and prompts that focus on character, theme, and culture, such as the following:

• What do we think of—or learn about—the people in this work, on the basis of their words, behavior, and interactions?

• What do you perceive to be the author's message or the moral of the piece? Do you agree with it and its implications for you or for people in general?

• What does the work teach us about human nature—or our own time, place, and culture—or about other times, places, and cultures?

The second and third questions work well with both fiction and poetry; all three apply to any work of fiction.

When teaching fiction, I find that students enjoy offering their opinions of literary characters and that this leads easily to helping them to discern the important themes in a work. These analyses, in turn, can help students develop arguments and interpretations that take historical and cultural factors into account.

Such questions are both open-ended and robust: they invite a variety of responses "grounded" in the entire text; students can't answer them by simply finding one place, on a certain page, with the "correct" answer. I often see teachers working from a long list of "inferential" questions that don't promote an exploration of the complete work. Questions like the ones listed earlier are richer and more complex, and students are quite capable of answering them in discussion and writing—if taught to do so.

Almost every discussion I had as a student in my favorite English classes centered on character analysis, theme, or human nature/culture. Discussions of symbolism, structure, or figurative language were infrequent—and always subordinate to these three. As a teacher, I discovered that students care more about the people in a story, about what their behavior reveals to be the essence of the work, and about their own response to it. To get them to write about these topics of interest, an open-ended guiding question is the key to unlocking a work of literature. Related follow-up questions derive naturally from such questions.

There are plenty of variations on these. For example:

- "Do you like [a certain character]? Do you approve of his/her behavior?"

- "How would you describe the relationship between [one character] and [another]?"

- "Compare and contrast the mental and moral qualities of [one character] and [another]."

- "Who would be a more reliable/interesting/admirable friend?"

- "Do you think the author likes or dislikes this character?"

- "What do you think the author wants us to learn from a certain character's experience or development?"

- "How does this historical period, or the characters' family or upbringing, influence them? Does it excuse or explain some of their behaviors?"

- "Does their experience teach us anything about our own time or place—or about human nature in general?"

Such questions form the basis of literacy studies and the employment of the (very unoriginal) procedures I refer to as a "literacy template" in Chapter 3, which applies to fiction, nonfiction, and poetry.

The Literacy Template

As described in Chapter 3, I've had great luck having 2nd or 3rd graders read, discuss, and then write short informal essays about *Jack and the Beanstalk*. In teaching the story, I employ the same "template for authentic literacy" I described in Chapter 3:

- *Teach new or difficult vocabulary* from the text.
- *Establish a purpose (i.e., a question or prompt) for the reading.* For example,

"What is your opinion of Jack?"

or

"Should the United States move toward a single-payer health care system?" (after reading an article about the pros and cons of nationalized health care).

- *Teach and model for students* how to underline/annotate/take notes in response to the prompt or question.
- *Have students discuss the work*, first in pairs, then as a class (using a short discussion rubric like the one described in Chapter 3).
- *Have students write in response to the prompt, supporting it with references to the text.* Once again, here, and for all of the above, explicit instruction must be provided on how to underline, take notes, and annotate; how to then review notes and annotations to prepare for discussion; how to participate appropriately in a discussion; how to write in response to the question with references to the text; and how to integrate supporting quotations and paraphrased material into the argumentative/interpretive paragraphs.

When I taught in this manner, almost all students made real progress on all of these activities and were able to produce a surprisingly good initial draft of their opinion of Jack. This approach will work with whole novels or separate chapters, as well as with poems, speeches, and nonfiction.

For nonfiction—articles, speeches, or essays—a simple "Do you agree or disagree with...?" or "Should we or shouldn't we...?"

question can be applied to limitless texts and controversies; they will elicit fascinating discussions of issues such as nuclear power, school uniforms, minimum wage, and alternative energy.

And there are endless opportunities to make both fiction and nonfiction studies more interesting with compare-and-contrast prompts—as the students evaluate different characters, literary works, and solutions to current problems.

Students enjoy sharing their opinions. Good questions about literature and nonfiction provide students with the opportunity to do so. I believe that such simple, inquiry-driven studies are the heart of ELA. For that reason, developing such questions for the texts we teach should be among the highest priorities for English departments and course-alike teams.

We've been examining templates and tools we can employ to simplify and increase the quality of literacy instruction. By using these, we can enhance the important role of learning objectives, which help to ensure that lessons contribute directly to the most authentic literacy skills and competencies.

Learning Objectives in English Language Arts

As we've seen, and as successful schools demonstrate, teaching students to read, discuss, and write about text must be structured—at least initially—in the form of simple, focused lessons. And again, these legitimate literacy "skills" are not to be confused with their less productive counterparts—the reading skills and standards that mimic standardized tests.

As noted in Chapter 3, learning objectives lend essential clarity and purpose to daily lessons. Most lessons—some educators would say all—benefit from such objectives. But *much more than in other subject areas,* ELA learning objectives tend to get co-opted by our inane ELA standards—many of which simply aren't essential to becoming literate and articulate. Most don't deserve to be taught at all (Schmoker & Jago, 2013; Shanahan, 2014; Willingham, 2009b).

To address this, I am providing a representative, if provisional, list of objectives that can help us to address the special challenge of writing learning targets for English language arts. You could improve on or add to this list. But notice that all are centered on authentic literacy—and are consistent with the "three shifts" of the ELA Common Core.

One last caveat: much of ELA instruction is recurrent, both within and among the grade levels. For instance, we learn and practice the art of reading analytically, discussing text, and writing effectively all year, every year—at increasing levels of skill and sophistication. If, for instance, students have been explicitly taught how to effectively participate in discussions, we may cease, at least for a time, to post a learning objective; the operative objective is to respond to the question or prompt while practicing and refining the several discussion skills that have been taught and mastered. The same principle might apply, at times, to critical reading or to writing. That said, some authors would argue that every lesson should focus on some specific aspect or refinement of a reading, discussion, or writing skill even after competence is achieved. Either view works for me.

Let's now look at a representative sample of learning objectives for ELA; many of them could be applied to any discipline. Most are written for 2nd grade and up—for students who have mastered decoding. I think learning objectives like these could occupy the bulk of ELA instruction, at almost any grade level.

Versatile English Language Arts Learning Objective Stems

In view of the nature of ELA, there is some redundancy here; some of the following samples could be included as either reading, discussion, or writing objectives.

Reading

When reading, I can...
Underline/annotate/make a list/take notes from a text in order to
- Support an argument/interpretation,
- Analyze a character's development/interaction with other characters,

- Identify/trace the development of a theme in the work,
- Develop an interpretation or thesis about the meaning of the work,
- Determine how the time, place, or culture of the work influences the characters, or
- Compare/contrast _____ (characters, ideas, solutions, etc.).

Discussion

In a discussion, I can...

Support my claims and arguments with support from the text or texts.

- Respond appropriately to the prompt/question
- Speak clearly and audibly, so that others can hear me
- Be civil and respectful
- Briefly restate classmates' remarks when commenting on them or disagreeing with them
- Be concise and stay on point
- Use (mostly) complete sentences
- Avoid verbal tics (e.g., "like," "you know")

Preparation for Writing

When preparing to write, I can...

Select or designate the most effective supporting material/quotations for my writing assignment.

- Write a working outline from my notes, underlinings, annotations, or a combination of these
- Develop an interesting thesis/argument for my writing assignment
- Determine whether/when it is best to use paraphrase—or to use direct quotes
- Conduct research and evaluate material for bias/reliability of online and other sources
- Write an interesting title for my essay/writing assignment

Writing

When writing, I can…

Describe one or more characters in writing.

- Write an effective introductory paragraph with an effective
  —Thesis
  —"Hook"
  —Preview

- Write supportive or developmental paragraphs, with effective topic sentences that support the main argument/interpretation of my essay
- Effectively integrate quotations and other supporting material into clear, coherent sentences and paragraphs
- Provide clear explanation/exposition that explains how my quoted and paraphrased material supports my arguments
- Employ effective transitional words and sentences within and among the paragraphs and sections of my writing
- Effectively address objections to my argument/interpretation
- Write an effective conclusion
- Revise an essay to improve
  —Word choice
  —Sentence quality
  —Clarity

and so forth

We would write similar objectives for writing mechanics (to be taught primarily on an as-needed basis, as teachers see patterns in student writing). For example:

When writing, I can…

- Write clear, complete sentences and eliminate fragments and run-ons
- Use proper punctuation (e.g., capitals, periods, commas, colons, semicolons)

Analogous objectives could be developed for presentations and, when necessary, for the most essential grammar, sentence structure, and mechanics.

Let's finish with a discussion of the need to make significant changes to ELA assessment, starting at the local level. Simple changes, introduced gradually, could leverage excellent ELA instruction and ensure that it maintains its primary focus on helping students to become effective readers, writers, and speakers.

Assessment in English Language Arts— Aligned with College, Careers, and Citizenship

It is hard to deny the maxim that "what gets measured is what gets done." Even now, what "gets done" in ELA is substandard because of "what gets measured" on annual state assessments: a student's ability to complete multiple-choice and short-answer test items. The quality of some of these tests has improved in some ways (that's why passing rates have plummeted). But these changes are not enough: new ELA standards and assessments have not led to the kinds of instructional changes we had hoped for (Lee & Wu, 2017; Shanahan & Duffet, 2013; Will, 2016).

That's because none of these tests adequately assess students' ability to complete extended writing and research tasks like those that students will encounter in college or careers. Our current state assessments do not measure, nor do they require, such writing. This has calamitous consequences for many students (Stiggins, 2017; Wagner & Dintersmith, 2015).

How much better could assessment be in ELA? Let's look to the past and to some high-achieving school systems to find out.

1901: A Banner Year for English Language Arts Assessment

In an eye-opening commentary, Diane Ravitch (2010) describes the stunningly simple standards for the old College Entrance Examination for English, developed in 1901. Back then, students were given the titles of 10 substantial books at the beginning of the school year (the list was revised every three years). Students knew they would be asked to write complete, coherent essays about 3 of these 10 books, scored with a common rubric. There were no multiple-choice items.

That's it.

As Ravitch (2010) points out, these "standards" had a direct effect on *what* and *how* English was taught. In 1901, no teacher would have prepared students for these extended, textually grounded essays by teaching them to "identify the 'main idea' or the 'rising action,' or to "analyze different points of view of the characters and the audience or reader (e.g., created through the use of dramatic irony)"—whatever that means (from 8th grade Common Core standards).

Instead, as Ravitch (2010) avers, such an examination all but guaranteed that students read at least 10 substantive books or novels during the school year; it guaranteed that they would receive in-depth instruction in how to analyze their reading, develop a coherent argument, and produce extended essays in clear, organized prose. For these reasons, this simple 1901 College Entrance Examination in English is obviously *superior to any state or national test produced in the standards era—not one of which requires students to read a single book or write even one extended essay.*

We could change this—right now—without abandoning state tests. The change could start locally, it wouldn't be complicated, and it wouldn't require additional time from our teachers or our school system.

We could start by reserving about two weeks at the end of selected grade levels for students to produce—and for teachers to assess, perhaps in stages—a complete essay, or research paper, or both, for which they use common scoring guides. Remember that such an assessment would not supplant or take time away from instruction: it is a pure example of what the late Grant Wiggins (1998) called "educative assessment," the completion of which is educational in its own right. Initially, these assessments could be regarded as a low- to medium-stakes supplement to state testing.

This is precisely the kind of assessment conducted in countries with the highest scores on the Programme for International Student Assessment examination, or PISA (Ripley, 2013, p. 16). Students are given several days, sometimes more, to read materials they will be tested on; then they are given several days to organize and write extended essays about the readings. And—logically enough—students take similar tests during the school year. The U.S. school system is unique in its failure to provide such rich assessments that now have a profound effect on instructional quality in the best school systems in the world (Darling-Hammond, 2010; Ripley, 2013). Such assessments would exert an immediate and positive effect on ELA instruction in the United States, and they would provide, for the first time, an accurate picture of students' true language abilities.

Moreover: within a short time, it would become apparent that (1) preparation and instruction for the new assessments would raise scores on conventional assessments far better than previous forms of "test-prep," and (2) conventional state examinations need a serious overhaul—because they now conceal more than they reveal about a student's true intellectual and expressive abilities. We owe it to students to make this seismic shift, at least gradually, away from multiple-choice and short-answer testing to our own updated version of the 1901 examination.

This proposal isn't so far-fetched. In Chapter 2, we saw how the New York Performance Standards Consortium has done something like this for years, operating on a state waiver they received in 1997. And if we're concerned about the quality or consistency of scoring, we might have state entities periodically evaluate random assessments to ensure consistency and relative reliability (as they do in the Consortium). But I believe the change would have to begin locally, prove itself, and then move up to the state and regional levels.

Initially, we might formally require that students write a multipage literary analysis or research paper, or both, at the end of the 3rd, 5th, 8th, and 11th grades. At each grade level, the length and quality of papers would be expected to meet the quality and criteria of publicly available exemplar papers. Both the passing rates and the areas of strength and weakness would be formally and prominently distributed. These data would create the basis for district, school, and grade-level improvement efforts.

In between the benchmark grades, schools could have similar, if less formal, ELA assessments. These assessments could be administered and graded by teams or academic departments, whose passing rates and data would allow them to assess their contribution to success on the more formal benchmark assessments.

Finally, during the junior or senior year, all students could complete a longer, perhaps 10- to 15-page, capstone or research paper. This might be completed in cooperation with other academic departments. This would be, furthermore, ideal preparation for students to deliver a polished, confident presentation—even a short one—that could also be part of ELA assessment.

And as I recommended earlier, one smart, simple action would ensure immediate success on these benchmark assessments: establishing a requirement that students at every grade level *are explicitly taught and are required to complete* at least one formal, substantive paper each grading period.

This is simple backward design, writ large. It would transform literacy instruction and directly address what Conley (2005) found to be the most damning weakness in our school system: our failure to teach students to write.

I'm reminded of the excellent piece by ASCD's Laura Varlas (2016) about the huge gap between K–12 instruction and the demands of college literacy. Varlas describes an English department chair, Elizabeth Gonzales, who realized that the best way to prepare students for college was to "plan backward" from the tasks and prompts found in actual college syllabi. This resulted in immediate, productive changes in the amount and length of reading and writing assignments taught at Abington High School in Massachusetts.

Simple, Life-Changing Literacy: Within Our Grasp

The evidence is clear that substantial but reasonable increases in the amount of reading, discussion, and writing would have a swift and transformative effect on student learning in ELA—as well as all other subects. To that end, imagine the effect if our curriculum spelled out and ensured that all students, in all schools,

- Read, discussed, and wrote about 6 to 10 quality fiction and nonfiction books (some self-selected)
- Read, analyzed, discussed, and wrote about dozens of interesting poems and newspaper, magazine, or online articles
- Wrote frequent, short, informal pieces and were explicitly taught to write at least one longer, formal, argumentative or interpretive paper each grading period

If these goals were matched with even reasonably good ELA instruction and aligned with authentic assessments, an unprecedented proportion of students would become truly literate and educated. It would change their lives.

This is especially certain if we can achieve a similar shift toward literacy in the teaching of ELA's traditional partner in the humanities: social studies instruction, the subject of Chapter 5.

Social Studies with Reading
and Writing at the Core

*Literacy is the key word here, because the teaching of history should
have reading and writing at its core.*

—Sam Wineburg and Daisy Martin (2004)

*Helping students learn how to distinguish truth from falsehood, how
to judge the credibility of sources, how to reason rigorously, how to
make ethical choices, and how to deal with ambiguities that character-
ize human affairs is vital to our success as a nation. Not surprisingly,
these very abilities are needed—and much valued—by employers.*

—Jim Haas

In this chapter, I'll discuss simple ways to build and deliver the
content of our social studies curriculum, with an emphasis on
the literacy and lecture templates described in Chapter 3. I will
then present an expanded section on the rich array of supplementary
sources available to us—from primary source documents to newspapers, magazines, and online resources. In the last section, I'll describe
simple ways in which we can improve social studies assessment.

• • •

Properly taught, social studies—history, civics, economics, and geography—should be among students' favorite subjects. And it may be the most important: social studies can substantially affect how we vote, and how we behave as citizens and as a society. With English, it forms the heart of humanistic studies. It is the study of *us*—of people and their interactions. In social studies, students can make the central intellectual discovery that past and present events interact inseparably. The study of history, culture, and government profoundly affect our understanding of the world and our place in it. It also contributes mightily to reading comprehension—and to higher test scores: an analysis showed that strong general knowledge is the best predictor of success on both the Partnership for Assessment of Readiness for College and Careers (PARCC) and Smarter Balanced assessments (Wattenberg, 2016).

Even so, time spent on social studies has shrunk considerably since the 1990s (Kalaidis, 2013), part of the "disappearing curriculum" that fell victim to the exigencies of testing and accountability (Walker, 2014). More disturbing still is the erosion of interest in teaching history and social studies: A University of North Carolina study demonstrated that 88 percent of elementary school teachers regarded the teaching of history "a low priority" (Markowicz, 2017).

This is most unfortunate—and unnecessary. It's time we recognize the value of history and social studies—and teach it in ways that students are sure to appreciate.

The Uses of History

In his autobiography, Norman Podhoretz (1967) wrote of the epiphany he had in his first year at Columbia. He realized that history wasn't about "other people"; it was about *him*—his country, his world, his time. "When I entered Columbia," he wrote,

> I thought history was a series of past events.... I did not know I was a product of a tradition, that past ages had been inhabited by men like myself, and the things they had done *bore a direct relation to me* and to the world in which I lived.... It set my brain on fire. (p. 33; emphasis added)

James Loewen (1995) wrote similarly of this "direct relation" between historical studies and our immediate lives. History, he noted,

> is about us. Whether one deems our present society wondrous or awful or both, history reveals how we got to this point. *Understanding our past is central to our ability to understand ourselves and the world around us.* (pp. 12–13; emphasis added)

That understanding is especially critical at a time when students are keen on being politically involved.

Informed Citizenship in an Age of Activism

Political involvement among young people has exposed an awkward fact: that many students lack an understanding of issues they feel strongly about, such as the unforeseen consequences of issuing "executive orders"; why the electoral college, not the popular vote, determines who becomes president; and the pros and cons of policies that affect free speech, free trade, law enforcement, immigration, and health care. On all such issues, knowledge about history, laws, and policies is the essential prerequisite to rational, productive debate. Without it, many citizens and students are publicly protesting solely on the basis of information furnished by partisan entities. Students are encouraged, even given class credit, to block traffic, shout down guest speakers, and throw slogans at each other in the street—often before they have adequately studied either side of an issue. Better social studies education could temper our views, induce us to seek creative compromise on urgent issues, and thus improve the workings of democracy. But as Mark Bauerlein (2009) says, many students are not only alarmingly unaware of history, government, and opposing views on current issues; they are indifferent to such knowledge.

We can correct this. We can, for instance, let students explore the history and differences among basic forms of government—and how those play out, right now, in people's lives. Students should learn about socialism, communism, and capitalism from studying at least a few nations that represent different versions of these three. They should have a chance, in an unbiased environment, to weigh the pros and cons of government policies and their effects on the economy and general welfare of countries such as Denmark, Singapore, Norway, China, Venezuela, and Japan. Without this, our instruction is irrelevant—or it devolves into propaganda.

We can ensure that they examine issues like health care, homelessness, and national defense—against the backdrop of taxation and government spending. What could be more beneficial to a democracy than to have students study all sides of such issues and discuss them in class? For social critic Christopher Lasch (1995), this is the very essence of democracy. Online sources such as ProCon.org can be enormously helpful.

Character Education

And what of developing healthy human values—or accumulating wisdom? Must we be reluctant to study the lives of historical figures whose integrity, altruism, statesmanship, or work ethic are worth emulating (as found in such books as John F. Kennedy's 1955 book *Profiles in Courage*)? According to Professor Abby Reisman (2017), an expert on social studies education, students take naturally to one of the best ways to acquire wisdom and an ethical sense: being asked to judge and learn from historical characters. Real people and events afford them the opportunity to weigh the consequences of human thought and action.

Writing for *The Atlantic*, teacher Paul Barnwell (2016) shares his discovery that many of today's students appear to possess "broken moral compasses"—a result of schooling that would have "horrified" the founding fathers. He cites studies that reveal high percentages of students who approve of violence and dishonesty. Yet on issues of character and morality, schools are largely on the sidelines. And so, "By omission," asks Barnwell, "are U.S. schools teaching their students that character, morality, and ethics aren't important in becoming productive, successful citizens?" He cites polling data indicating strong public support for such teaching and has found that his students "crave more meaningful discussions and instruction relating to character, morality and ethics" (Barnwell, 2016).

If taught properly, social studies, along with English and literary studies, would surely promote a wiser, more informed citizenry.

Once again: both English and social studies help us understand ourselves; they reveal the hidden or unquestioned cultural and political influences that act on us, often without our conscious consent. Social studies, which includes *current* issues and events, allows students to understand those influences. And like literature, it broadens their vision and sensibilities beyond the limits of direct experience. In this way, it allows everyone to have a greater hand in the history we all help to make—in our own world, nation, town, or temple.

How can ordinary teachers fulfill the promise of social studies with students who might seem indifferent to it? There is a way.

For social studies to "set the brain on fire," it must have authentic literacy—and controversy—"at its core" (Wineburg & Martin 2004, p. 44). Wisdom, enthusiasm for learning, and preparation for college, careers, and citizenship can come only from intensive, frequent reading; talking (*lots* of talking); writing; and arguing about the people, issues, and events of the past and present. Facts are essential here. Kevin St. Jarre (2008) speaks for many of us when he writes that students must know the pertinent facts that precede and inform the issues of our time. But he also begs us to recognize that intellectual engagement, not rote learning, is the key to a much-needed reset in social studies: "What [students] need are more Socratic discussion and reading, more analysis, more writing and *more reasons why they should care*" (p. 650; emphasis added).

If we want students to care about social studies, we must put literacy at the core (Wineburg & Martin, 2004).

Social Studies with Language and Literacy at the Core

Next to language arts, social studies is perhaps the most literacy-intensive of the disciplines. Both help us understand people and cultures. Both require us to read closely and carefully—so that we may become wise consumers of language that is so often used for commercial, political, or self-aggrandizing purposes.

It's all about language. As Stanford's Sam Wineburg (2001) writes,

Language is a medium for swaying minds and changing opinions, for rousing passions, or allaying them. This is a crucial understanding for reading the newspaper, for listening to the radio, for evaluating campaign promises, or for making a decision to drink a NutraSweet product based on research conducted by the Searle Company [which manufactures NutraSweet]. (p. 83)

Wineburg believes students must be taught to "argue with the text"—with textbooks *and* with current or historical documents. This makes all students and adults "historians... called on to see human motives in the texts we read; called on to mine truth from the quicksand of innuendo, half-truth, and falsehood that seeks to engulf us each day." Social studies is the place to learn this, to "think and reason in sophisticated ways" (Wineburg, 2001, p. 83).

We learn to "mine truth" from a curriculum rich in opportunities to argue and dismantle written and spoken arguments. Wineburg and his colleague Daisy Martin (2004) call for an "investigative curriculum" that consists of a "two-part equation... the teaching of history should have *reading and writing at its core*" (p. 44; emphasis added).

That "equation" has yet to prevail in our social studies instruction. I recently worked with members of a central office team who were convinced that students in their highly rated schools were doing lots of reading and writing in social studies. To test this, they fanned out and observed social studies instruction in over 40 classrooms around the district, chosen at random. They found students reading or writing in only two of those classrooms.

James Banner is the cofounder of the National History Center in Washington, D.C. After studying history teaching in representative states, he and several national experts found that it was deficient in precisely the skills that are "fundamental to historical knowledge and thought: writing well, constructing arguments, reading critically, assessing evidence" (Banner, 2009, p. 24).

Students won't acquire historical knowledge (or care about it) without abundant opportunities to read, write, and talk. As McConachie and colleagues (2006) write, "Students can only develop deep conceptual knowledge in a discipline by using the habits of reading, writing, talking, and thinking which that discipline values and uses" (p. 8; emphasis added).

The stakes are high. As Wineburg and Martin (2004) write, "Our democracy's vitality depends on... teaching students to be informed readers, writers and thinkers about the past as well as the present" (p. 45). We don't adequately appreciate this fact. If we did, we would do more to preserve its soul: literacy, analysis, and argument. As with language arts, we must rescue social studies from "readicide" and an activities-based curriculum that leaves students "engaged but illiterate" (Wineburg & Martin, 2004, p. 45).

Skits, Posters, and Social Studies Illiteracy

In observing social studies classrooms, Wineburg and Martin (2004) found that analytic, argumentative reading and writing have been replaced by activities that focus on "multiple intelligences and learning styles." They found (as I have) students performing skits, making posters, and doing an excessive number of PowerPoint presentations (p. 45). I wish more teachers knew that Howard Gardner himself is dismayed by such nonsense in the name of his research on "multiple intelligences" (Traub, 1998). Such practices supplant our efforts to equip students for careers and college, ensuring that they will never learn to read and write about social and historical issues—such as "defending an argument on why the U.S.S.R. [Soviet Union] disintegrated" (Wineburg & Martin, 2004, p. 45). We would rather entertain students than teach them.

Wineburg and Martin would instead take us back to the future— to the *old* stuff that ought to inform the *new* core of 21st century social studies.

An "Old-Fashioned" Message

"We are aware," write Wineburg and Martin (2004), "that we have crafted a decidedly old-fashioned message for a technologically savvy world" (p. 44). They advocate for a social studies curriculum that equips students to participate in "the literate activities that our society demands. This means teaching students to be *informed readers, writers, and thinkers* about the past as well as the present" (p. 45; emphasis added). For them, "The place to teach students to ask questions about truth and evidence *in our digital age* is the history and social studies classroom, and we should not delay" (p. 42; emphasis added).

This emphasis on "truth and evidence" must be rooted in common curricular content—in an organized schedule of essential topics and standards. Good social studies curriculum might approximate the following:

• Essential topics and standards, divided by unit and grading period (to ensure roughly common pacing and depth)

• *Selected* textbook pages (*not* the entire book—or all of every chapter) that are aligned with units and topics

• About 30 or more supplementary or primary source documents, including current magazine and news articles, to be read closely and discussed about once a week (a variety of available resources for this are described at the end of this chapter)

• Some prepared interactive lectures for each unit to reinforce or supplement the textbook (see the interactive lecture template)

• Guiding questions that inform both interactive lecture and the study of various texts

• An agreed-upon minimum number of end-of-unit or semester papers, essay assessments, and research papers (with specifications for their approximate length)

• Routine use, for all of these assignments, of something like the literacy template in Chapter 3

That's basically it. Any team of social studies teachers could outline the units, topics, texts—and some preliminary text-based questions or prompts—in a single session. They could then implement the new curriculum without delay. Once the curriculum is outlined, teams can continue to refine it, especially during the initial year of implementation. From then on, its effective delivery must become our active priority: the focus of professional development, faculty, and team meetings.

How do we build such a curriculum?

Building Social Studies Curriculum

Offered a list of standards, we should scrutinize each one but also ask who came up with them and for what purpose. Is there room for discussion and disagreement?

—Alfie Kohn

In Chapters 2–4, we examined the shortcomings of standards—especially literacy standards. But, again, standards in all other subjects and content areas have more merit than those in ELA: despite their imperfections, they provide a useful starting point for building a coherent, "viable" curriculum. We are wise to consult them—but not to commit to them in their entirety. As you build social studies curricula, I encourage you to revisit the more detailed process described in Chapter 2.

To briefly recap that process:

• Determine the approximate number of days you have to teach the curriculum (your "instructional budget").

• Review standards documents for each course—and approximate, in pencil, how many days it would take to teach each one.

• Add up the number of days. If it exceeds the number you have to teach (and it often will), you must subtract topics and standards until you achieve "viability"—an approximate match between the standards and the number of days you have to teach them.

• Apportion the topics that you will use by week or grading period, with due consideration for holidays and other interruptions on the school calendar. Write these topics in a column on your curriculum document.

- Begin selecting and matching interesting texts to units and topics; place these in a column adjacent to that of the topics.
- Add guiding questions or prompts that provide purpose for the reading, lecture, discussion, and writing tasks.
- Write numerical expectations for major writing assignments, such as the number and length of major written assignments for each grading period or semester.

When these steps are complete, the curriculum document is ready for use (but always subject to adjustment). Again, it is probably a good idea to leave two or three weeks "free" each semester for individual teachers to pursue their favorite topics or interests (DuFour et al., 2006, p. 65).

The steps just described should furnish the course-alike team with a working curriculum with which to begin creating daily lessons. Blank templates for building such curriculum are available in Schmoker (2016) and online at www.ascd.org/ASCD/pdf/books/SchmokerAppendixB.pdf.

Let's now look at how we would work from this initial curriculum map to develop lessons and units.

Organizing Around "Task, Text, and Talk"

Once we have assembled our curriculum, then what? For social studies, I find Stephanie McConachie and colleagues' (2006) formula for content area literacy very helpful—their notion of "task, text, and talk" (although not always in that order). Their scheme aligns seamlessly with the literacy template in Chapter 3 and facilitates the successful execution of a literacy-rich curriculum.

First, we establish which topics or sets of topics can best be taught with the use of a selected text or texts (a textbook selection, an article, a primary resource). Then we establish the task: what McConachie and colleagues (2006) call the "questions/prompts," which guide the actual text-based work that students will complete—the analytic reading, the pair-share and whole-class discussions, and text-based writing (which often doubles as an assessment).

We can build much, if not most, social studies curricula around these core activities. The best schools always have (Cookson, 2009).

Of course, these critical literacy skills and social studies tasks must be taught explicitly to students. We must *"apprentice them* into each discipline's way of thinking" (McConachie et al., 2006, p. 2; emphasis added). The term "apprentice" nicely reinforces the elements of good teaching. For example:

• The teacher demonstrates—"models"—in small, manageable chunks, how to address the task (e.g., how to underline or annotate the text) and then provides the student-apprentices with an opportunity to try it themselves (guided practice).

• The teacher circulates to *observe and evaluate* students' efforts to underline or annotate (to check for understanding). If students aren't succeeding on that chunk (as is often the case), then...

• The teacher adjusts or reteaches that step or chunk of the lesson—and then has students make yet another attempt to effectively underline/annotate (guided practice) and checks for understanding and reteaches again if necessary.

The cycle repeats as the teacher continues to check for understanding and reteach until students are ready for "independent practice"—which can also serve as an assessment (and can often be graded or evaluated quickly as the teacher circulates during the lesson).

These teaching and learning processes are applied to critical reading, note taking, discussion, and writing—that is, to all of the elements in the "literacy template" described in Chapter 3.

Suppose, for instance, that our topic for elementary or middle school students will be the three branches of government. We're always smart to begin with some background on the topic both to pique interest and help make the text(s) accessible.

According to the "task, text, and talk scheme," the texts that correspond to this topic might be (1) certain carefully selected pages (*not* an entire chapter) from the textbook (describing the branches of government), or (2) a primary source document about the separation of powers, or (3) both.

The student's "task" would be to underline or take notes from the text or texts and then provide arguments in response to this question:

"Should we give more—or *less*—power to any of the three branches of government?"

Before students read the texts independently, the teacher would review any potentially difficult vocabulary terms. Then he or she would implement multiple cycles of the bulleted steps described earlier: read a portion of the text aloud while "teaching/modeling" his or her own thoughts as a critical reader—showing them how he or she would underline, annotate, or take notes—in small, manageable steps. For each step, the teacher would provide an opportunity for "guided practice"—for students to attempt their own underlining and annotating (both independently and in pairs). During and after this step, the teacher would circulate to "check for understanding"—and reteach that step if additional instruction or modeling are needed. When students are ready, the teacher would let them finish underlining and annotating the text independently. This is a good time to work with students who might still be struggling to underline or annotate appropriately.

The talk in the "task, text, and talk scheme" occurs (1) during the modeling and guided practice, as students pair up to discuss and compare their notes and impressions or when the teacher calls on random students as part of her effort to check for understanding, and (2) when a formal or Socratic discussion follows the completion of the reading assignment. (See the section "Whole-class discussion and debate" in Chapter 3.)

This discussion, in turn, would be followed by either a short or a more formal writing assignment—all taught with the same effective elements of good teaching.

The same basic approach would work with chapters and selections from a quality textbook. I happen to be very impressed with Joy Hakim's (2007) *Freedom: A History of US*. It is an informative and highly engaging read for students in upper elementary school, middle school—and possibly high school (if you can find a better text, use it).

Let's look at one more example of task, text, and talk—for middle or high school.

Task, Text, and Talk in Middle and High School "World History"

Let's suppose that the curriculum topics for a course have been allotted on the calendar and that during one grading period, the following units will be taught (as they are in a district I once worked with):

- Renaissance
- Reformation
- Age of Revolution

Each unit is two to three weeks long. Let's also suppose it is the beginning of the grading period and we are preparing to teach about the Renaissance. The major topics to be covered are prominent Renaissance writers and artists and the evolving relationship among church, society, and science. The work would be similar to that in the lower grades, described previously.

First, the team would develop a **task**—in this case, a somewhat more elaborate one, such as the following:

> Write a three- to four-page paper in which you evaluate or rank-order the merits of the Renaissance. Be sure to cite some of the art, writings, and major historical figures of the period. Make some connections and comparisons to other historical periods— or to our own.

The **texts** could include a 12-page excerpt on the Renaissance from a world history textbook, some samples of art (by da Vinci, Raphael, and so forth), and some primary resources that could include selections from Machiavelli's *The Prince;* Castiglione's *The Book of the Courtier* (a Renaissance-era guidebook for gentlemanly behavior); George Washington's "Rules of Civility and Decent Behaviour in

Company and Conversation" (available online at http://gwpapers.
virginia.edu/documents/the-rules-of-civility/); and Froma Harrop's
2010 opinion piece "Slobs and American Civilization," which is
about modern manners and the decline of culture and civility. Students would underline, annotate, and take notes on these texts.

The **talk** in this case would begin between pairs of students as
they learn from each other and their teacher how to annotate and
take notes on the art and readings (and, as we'll be seeing, from
"interactive" lectures). These conversations would prepare students
for whole-class discussions focused on questions about the established church versus the scientific community of the time; medie-
val versus Greco-Roman values and culture; and Machiavelli and his
provocative writings. There is plenty to discuss around these topics
and documents. Student participation in these discussions could be
evaluated with a simple rubric like the one in Chapter 3.

These text-based discussions are the ideal preparation for the
papers students will write, which could also have a research component whereby students supplement the common readings with a
specified number of sources they would find on their own (like those
we'll see in the last part of this chapter).

All of the activities just described would be broken down into
simple "learning objectives" that address whatever students need to
successfully complete the reading, discussion, and writing assignments and lessons; for example, "I can…" statements for learning
to underline and annotate; selecting supporting quotations; supporting remarks in a discussion with reference to the text; paraphrasing;
integrating supporting text into their writing; and explaining how
quotations and paraphrased material support their arguments. I have
provided samples of such literacy objectives in Chapter 4. And for
social studies in particular, some representative samples and stems
for learning objectives are provided at the end of this chapter.

• • •

Any teacher or team could master the basic framework of task,
text, and talk. In my experience, students find such activities vastly

more engaging than typical social studies, which seldom challenges their intellect or includes opportunities for them to discuss and share their thoughts and opinions as they read and learn. As mentioned earlier, discussion is among students' favorite ways to learn (Azzam, 2008).

Much in this scheme hinges on the quality of the tasks. Let's now examine some representative "tasks" from U.S. and world history, geography, economics, and civics. Then we'll look more closely at how these can be addressed through interactive lecture and close reading.

Simple, Replicable Social Studies Tasks

As Abby Reisman (2017) avers—and my teaching experience confirms—the best tasks often consist of just one robust question or prompt for one or more given texts. Good questions are almost always argumentative: they require us to provide evidence and details to support our claims and interpretations. Argument can take various forms, requiring us to evaluate, propose, compare, and contrast, or rank-order the relative importance of different factors, people, or events—from the past or present. Before students even begin to read—or listen to a lecture—such "argumentative" tasks create curiosity and lend purpose to every page of a written assignment.

The meteoric rise of Brockton High School's performance, referred to earlier, began in the social studies department. Many excellent argumentative tasks are built into their social studies curricula. Here are a few of them, several of which demonstrate the power and versatility of compare-and-contrast tasks—an easy, highly effective way to infuse content with intellectual engagement (and that ranks very high on Marzano and colleagues' [2001] list of effective teaching methods):

• Compare and contrast the three branches of government at the state and national levels.

• Read excerpts of Chinua Achebe's *Things Fall Apart* to assess the impact of European expansion on village life.

- Evaluate two contrasting news articles describing the 1886 Haymarket riots in Chicago.
- Compare and contrast the Homestead riot to the recent events in Charlottesville and elsewhere.
- Compare and contrast the Italian and German national unification movements.
- Compare and contrast the Articles of Confederation and the U.S. Constitution (or parts of each).
- Write a news article or editorial about attending the World Anti-Slavery Convention of 1840.

Such tasks are far more engaging than merely learning *about* the topics themselves. Students always enjoy sharing their thoughts and having them taken seriously, which happens when they read and talk and write in response to questions and prompts like the following:

- *Evaluate* U.S. behavior during the westward movement, including the Mexican-American War, the Louisiana Purchase, and the acquisition of Oregon.
- *Evaluate* Roosevelt's handling of the Depression and the major New Deal programs and compare with Harding's handling of the depression of the early 1920s (a *very* interesting comparison).
- *Evaluate* the ethics of walking away from an "upside-down" mortgage. (Lots of pro-con articles on this topic are available online.)
- *Evaluate* life among the ancient Maya, Aztec, or Incas.
- Which African, Asian, or European country do you deem to have the highest quality of life, according to readings and demographic statistics?
- Describe a realistic post–Civil War Reconstruction program that is based on your own ideas and a synthesis of the plans you learned about in your textbook and other readings.
- As a public official, defend a system of government—or a synthesis of systems—with reference to each of the following: socialism, communism, and democratic capitalism. *In defending your preferred system, conduct and cite research on at least one country that represents it (e.g., Denmark, China, Singapore, the United States).*

• As an expert on a historical period (the Reformation, World War I), write an abbreviated history of that period; feel free to offer *your interpretations and opinions* of events and people along the way. (This one could be used and repeated liberally, for any unit or historical period at *any* grade level.)

• After reading journals, diaries, and newspaper accounts of three early explorers of Northern Canada, discuss whether these explorers were heroes or not (from Wagner & Dintersmith, 2015, pp. 203–204).

• Rank-order the factors that contributed to any major event or turning point in history: the American War of Independence; the Industrial Revolution in Britain; the abolition of slavery (this versatile task can be applied to any historical period, event, or epoch). Justify your rankings in writing.

The last task could easily be applied to any and all wars; we might also ask our students to study and then respond to the simple question "Was this war justified?" or "Could we have avoided this war—and how?"

Before we look at sentence stems that can help us to build tasks for any text or topic, I will highlight tasks in one more category: geography. Historically, we haven't done justice to this fascinating aspect of social studies.

Geography Tasks

Most students leave school (as I did) with an inadequate knowledge of geography and its profound effect on the social, cultural, and economic development of nations and continents. In "geography," I include the following:

• Physical features: mountains, rivers, weather, oil and mineral resources, the absence or presence of natural harbors, access to coastlines—all of which affect trade and transportation

• Ethnic, racial, tribal, political, religious, and cultural makeup; relations among various groups; relations with neighboring countries

Geography matters—in myriad ways in the life of nations. But our students often betray a surprising ignorance of its influence. An excellent recent resource is Tim Marshall's (2015) *Prisoners of Geography*. It lays out the most compelling, consequential geographical facts affecting 10 countries and every continent. Africa, for instance, has many scenic rivers, but they are frequently punctuated by waterfalls that often prevent them from being useful for shipping or transportation; this has had a significant effect on African trade and development. There is an arresting section on how the geography of Western Russia makes the country exceptionally vulnerable to attack—and how that helps explain Russian history and politics (Marshall, 2015). Any one of its chapters will alter the way students look at the countries and regions they study (Marshall, 2015).

Geography-related "tasks"—which could guide reading, discussion and writing—might entail the use of prompts or questions like the following, all rooted in argument:

• For any country or continent we study, what are the most significant factors that have affected this country's/continent's development?

• What do you think are the most significant effects of this country's/continent's relations with its neighbors?

• Rank-order and explain three characteristics of a nation's or region's physical geography that have had the greatest effect on its history or culture.

• Compare/contrast two states or countries with regard to geographic advantages and disadvantages.

This sure beats asking students to memorize the names of capital cities, rivers, or natural resources—*without weighing their enormous and interesting significance*. We can do better.

In addition, tasks like these address Conley's (2007) intellectual standards and rely on readily available resources—textbooks and supplemental readings that are easy to access online. All of them address core content, stimulate thought, and give students considerable freedom in how to respond to them.

Let's now take a closer look at the kind of close reading that such tasks require.

Close Reading in Social Studies

For McConachie and colleagues (2006), the capacity for "genuine historical inquiry" can be imparted only "by *modeling and making explicit* the ways [teachers] want students to argumentatively and analytically read, interpret, and talk about the documentary evidence before them" (p. 12; emphasis added). As we've seen, the key to such slow, careful engagement with text is the employment of an argumentative, interpretive prompt or question.

Close Reading Stems

In addition to the other prompts and questions in this chapter, any teacher or team can develop their own "close reading" questions from variations on the following suggested stems:

- Do you agree/disagree with _____ [writer/author]?
- Draw parallels between _____ and _____ [past and *current* issues, people, or events].
- What present-day, real-world lessons can we learn from _____ [text or texts]?
- What *stands out*—what important inferences, interpretations, or connections can you make from your close reading of _____?
- Do you approve or disapprove of _____ [policy, person, or movement]? What lessons can we learn from it/them?
- What real-world problem or problems does the study of _____ [person or policy] help us solve?
- What important inferences can we make from this text about a particular time, place, or culture?
- Compare and contrast _____ and _____ [historical figures, events, or epochs].
- What are the most/least attractive or largest contributors to _____ [wars, movements, political/cultural developments, and so forth]?

- How does geography affect _____ [culture, economic development] in a country or region?
- Determine how _____ [any historical event or development] caused or contributed to subsequent events.

Questions and prompts derived from such stems will invariably promote stimulating engagement with text. All of them encourage the kind of close, purposeful reading that prepares students for college, careers, and citizenship (Conley, 2005; Graff, 2003). And they are right in line with the new (if still imperfect) breed of state English language arts assessments.

I have seen how such purposeful, close reading can stir students' curiosity, reflection, or moral sense. We have to stop indulging in the misconception that K–12 students don't care about ethics, human rights, war, climate change, global trade, and the best and worst of popular culture. Almost all of them care—greatly—about past and present issues if they are given the opportunity to do a "close reading" of a good text and if they know they will have a chance to discuss it with others. Here are two examples of how such reading might be taught.

Two "Close Readings"

Suppose, in the first case, that you gave 5th or 6th graders the following argumentative task as they read assigned textbook material:

> "As you read about the Maya and Aztecs, write an argument for why you would prefer to have been a member of one tribe/group or the other."

The learning objective might be "I can take notes from a text to support my argument."

The actual text is about five pages (once you exclude illustrations) from an upper-elementary history textbook I'm looking at. It could be read in three or four segments, with breaks to review notes, pair-share, or briefly discuss.

Modeling Close Reading

You would start by reading the first paragraph or section—out loud—as students read along; you might occasionally call on random students to read a sentence—to ensure *that they are reading along with you.*

As you read, students hear that 1800 years ago, in the Mayan city of Tikal (present-day Guatemala), the buildings were so stunning they looked like a "snow-capped mountain range." You tell students to look at the picture in the textbook of the ruins of an imposing Mayan temple. Then you read that the city "had a population of 50,000." At that point you would "model" your thinking—and note taking—on a document camera or overhead projector, like so:

> Hmm. Impressive. That was about 200 CE—almost 2,000 years ago. Such a huge city, with gorgeous, sophisticated architecture! This tells me the Maya had a strong appreciation for beauty and order and were an advanced civilization for their time. I will jot this down—*very briefly*.... Remember, students, that notes are rarely written in complete sentences. I'm only going to write "beauty/order!—advanced civilization for the time" on the text. These facts directly address our question [as you point to the question on the board] and might cause me to want to be a member of this tribe. But I will continue to look for the answer to our guiding question as I read the next section.

A few sentences later, after reading some material that is less germane to your task, you would share your impression that it doesn't adequately address it—so you won't take any notes for that portion. But then, as you read that Mayan temples were built "to ask their gods for success in battle," you might stop and say something like the following:

> This tells me that the Maya were religious and that they may also have been warlike. I'm going to briefly jot these facts down because they directly address our question [as you literally point to the question] about which tribe we would prefer to live among.

I will also write, *"How* warlike? More or less than Aztecs or Incas?"* I'm writing this down—see?—because it would affect my decision as well. In other words, I'm not sure I would want to be a member of a group that devoted most of its time and resources to wars of conquest.

The routine use of such modeling would have inestimable intellectual and academic benefits. It is as important for elementary school students as it is for secondary students. I find that many high school students underestimate the legitimacy of their own thoughts and are thus hesitant to formulate them. Listening to teachers think as they read and take notes demystifies these critical abilities.

Middle or high school students could be given a task like the following:

> "Evaluate the Progressive Era (1890–1920). Do you agree with, disagree with, or have a mixed opinion of the Progressives' agenda?"

This period is loaded with interesting controversy. Before the reading, you would provide a hook or anticipatory set—perhaps by providing some background information or by comparing this era with our own (with regard to the current income gap, unemployment rate, political movements). You would tell students they will be reading one textbook selection and one article about the Progressive Era. Then you might read from the first paragraph of a textbook selection.

You would do the same kind of modeling as described previously. After reading a paragraph or two about the "muckrakers"—the Progressive Era journalists—you would stop to tell students something like this:

> I like the fact that the muckrakers were looking out for the poor and those without a voice in the early 20th century. I admire that. But it also says here that there were "fierce circulation wars" and competition between newspapers during this time. Editors paid a lot of money to writers who could dig deep for "the dirt that the public loved to hate." I'm going to jot that quote down in my notes [which you then do, modeling and explaining how

you usually only jot down brief phrases, not whole sentences]. I'm wondering—aren't you?—whether the desire for money and the editor's demands would cause some of the "muckrakers" to exaggerate some of their stories —to sell papers...? So: I'm going to keep reading, but first I'll jot down "muckrakers distorted truth to sell papers? Could hurt people's reputations"—because that fact may be part of my evaluation of the Progressive Era.

You get the idea. You could conduct the same processes for virtually any reading task and text that involves note taking—or, if it's a text that students can write on, underlining and annotation—and copies of current articles, opinion pieces, primary historical documents, and demographic tables on various countries, states, or cities. We'll discuss such texts in a moment.

When we routinely model and make explicit how we adults read, think, and make connections, students will learn to do it, too. And they will begin to see that such close, insightful reading *is well within their reach*—but only if we follow such modeling with the other elements of effective instruction.

Guided Practice and Checking for Understanding

Modeling is essential, but so are the other routine components of good lessons—guided practice and checks for understanding.

For example, after you model your thinking for the Maya/Aztec assignment, you would let students read the next paragraph or two while you circulate and observe their note-taking efforts—their guided practice. You would look for patterns of strength or weakness: are students recording important information (like the fact that one of the tribes had mastered very sophisticated farming methods)? Do they know how to abbreviate their notes and annotations to save time— but in a way that they can make sense of later? Do they need you to do more modeling? They often do—sometimes more than once.

Or perhaps they are close enough to mastery that you can now have them pair up and compare notes—and learn from each other. At this point, you can call on pairs of students randomly to see how well they can explain the connection between their notes and the demands of the task. Their responses will provide you with invaluable information on how much more instruction they may need.

When you believe they are ready, you would let students finish taking notes on the remainder of the document independently. They could pair up one last time to compare their notes and then have a whole-class discussion. These discussions could culminate—perhaps on the following day—in a brief paragraph or a short paper that addresses the question or prompt.

As with note taking, both discussion and writing would be taught explicitly, in accordance with learning objectives (if students haven't learned these skills yet) for how to paraphrase, integrate quotations, write an explanation for how their citations support their argument, and so forth. By just walking around with a grade book or clipboard, the teacher could grade these short writing assignments for logic and content.

Thus is a worthy education acquired—by employing something like the simple, unoriginal literacy template described in Chapter 3. *By design,* this template shares some of the same elements as those of interactive lecture. Both templates incorporate underlining or note taking, discussion, and writing into learning. Both provide a stimulating opportunity for students to address meaningful intellectual tasks—the enemy of boredom. I will now briefly review the high-engagement elements of "interactive lecture" as they apply to social studies. It applies to all grades; I've had success using it with 1st graders.

Interactive Lecture in Social Studies

As noted in Chapter 3, interactive lecture is "a marvel of efficiency" (Silver et al., 2007). It allows us to impart essential content knowledge that may not get adequate treatment in the textbook or other assigned readings. It can be a highly engaging way for teachers to share what they deem most important—without treating students as passive recipients.

Interactive lecture incorporates the same "routine components" (Marzano, 2007, p. 180) of good lessons referred to in these pages. In social studies, it requires something like the following (described in more detail in Chapter 3):

- Begin the lecture by providing essential or interesting background knowledge and an open-ended question or prompt (similar to the "close reading" questions we've been looking at).
- As students listen and take notes, circulate and observe to ensure that they are on task and taking effective notes for each brief chunk of the lecture.
- Talk or lecture for no more than five to seven minutes at a time, then give students an opportunity to review/revise their notes against the question or task—and to compare their connections and perceptions in pairs (for perhaps one or three minutes at a time).
- Reteach or clarify whenever checks for understanding indicate that students need guidance in how to take appropriate notes; move on when they are ready for the next portion of the lecture.

This template, like the literacy template, could be followed by a whole-class discussion. In these discussions, it is always important that we do an adequate amount of cold-calling in order to ensure that all students are engaged and participative—and are practicing and refining critical communication skills.

Whether based on readings, lecture, or both, the discussion would typically be followed by some form of writing—short or long. This writing can also serve as an assessment.

Writing and Assessment in Social Studies: A Realistic Approach

I would love to see writing occupy an increasingly larger portion of both instruction and assessment in social studies. At Brockton High School, students routinely completed short written assignments and assessments—a designated number of times each week, in every course.

Brockton students wrote longer papers as well. As former principal and social studies chair Susan Szachowicz told me, they wrote a designated number of college-style papers in every social studies course. Their curriculum explicitly directs teachers to provide instruction in how to do the following (which could easily be converted into literacy-based "learning objectives"/"I can" statements like those in Chapter 4:

- Write thesis statements.
- Take notes.
- Paraphrase.
- Properly integrate quotations and citations.
- Organize and outline material.
- Employ basic research skills.

Szachowicz attributes Brockton's historic gains to the school's explicit focus on writing more than to any other factor.

Importantly: we can incorporate writing into social studies without requiring teachers to devote inordinate time to grading papers. As we've seen, students' underlinings, annotations, or notes can double as assessments of what they are learning and (just as important) how effectively we are teaching. Similarly, we can have students regularly convert their annotations and notes into short, focused written assignments that meet that day's learning objective. I contend that such writing constitutes the best form of assessment in social studies. But it is worthwhile for us to consider paper grading in social studies for a moment.

Grading Papers in Social Studies

First of all: short, everyday writings don't always need to be handed in. Teachers can assess student work as they circulate, conducting checks for understanding and (by extension) giving credit for adequate completion of the day's writing task. We should also remember that such frequent, if imperfect, assessment is always better than highly accurate but *infrequent* writing and assessment (Lemov, 2015, p. 35; Stuart, 2017).

The same goes for longer papers. Again, most of such writing should be done in class, with supervision, and with the benefit of multiple checks for understanding and reteaching—before any written work is actually turned in for corrections. If longer papers are completed in this way, in manageable steps and phases, much of the work can be assessed as the teacher circulates, recording scores or credit for completion of many of the stages. All of this maximizes efficiency and quality, inasmuch as students receive far more timely and therefore productive whole-class feedback, even as teachers spend less time grading and correcting papers.

In addition, these efforts ensure that the quality of the writing, when turned in, reflects this cumulative feedback, making it much easier to score. Our goal is to avoid having students turn in written work until the class has achieved success on each phase of the writing and only after each student and a peer have evaluated their writing against an exemplar and a checklist of *very clear* criteria (each of which has been taught explicitly).

I still believe that English teachers have the primary responsibility for teaching students the finer elements of a writing rubric. The primary focus of social studies is for students to learn and grapple intellectually with content and to discuss and write clearly and effectively about what they learn. In teaching and assessing the fundamental elements of writing, you may want to consult portions of the "Major Moves of Writing" section in Chapter 4. For more suggestions on how to increase the amount and quality of writing even as we significantly reduce time grading papers, see the article titled "Write More, Grade Less" on my website at www.mikeschmoker.com/write-more.html.

Writing should be a routine feature of social studies instruction—and its assessment. It is high time that essay assessment becomes a more prominent feature of history, geography, and civics courses.

Essay Assessment: You Get What You Assess

If we want to move beyond an emphasis on isolated facts and promote true intellectual engagement in social studies, then we have no choice but to convert more—and eventually most—of our social studies assessment into a set of content-based but open-ended essay questions.

The transition would not be that difficult. Ideally, students would be given the assessment questions at the beginning of a unit or grading period, knowing that not every question will be on the test but that they should be prepared to answer any of them. In this way, every lecture, text assignment, and lesson constitutes the best kind of "test prep." For some of these assessments, or certain portions, we might allow them to draw from their texts, notes, and research—in an "open-book" environment; we could even teach them to organize their materials for the day (or days) of the test. Even *as they take the test,* they would be reading, writing, analyzing, and reviewing the content they learned that unit, grading period, or semester. And they'd be learning like crazy. If that is really our goal, such assessments would promote vastly more learning than asking students to memorize isolated facts for a multiple-choice test.

Some of these assessments might be conducted over multiple days—or an entire week. Once again, this would not be an interruption of learning; it would constitute the kind of "educative assessment" that Grant Wiggins (1998) advocated for years ago. I would point out that educators from numerous countries outside the United States have informed me that essay assessments—not multiple-choice tests—are the exclusive form of social studies assessment in the countries with the highest scores on the Programme for International Student Assessment (PISA) test (Ripley, 2013). Students in those countries spend several class periods in productive preparation for these intellectually robust exams.

We could extend the benefits of such assessments. A few times per year, we might let students expand on one of their responses to an assessment question—with the requirement that they supplement it with some independent research.

And in our Internet-driven age, we had better teach students, as Sam Wineburg and Sarah McGrew (2016) urge us, to be discerning users of online sources. As they demonstrate, our students are surprisingly unreflective about what they come across on the World Wide Web. On the one hand, most can identify the grosser forms of "fake news." But they must be *taught* to distinguish between objective and biased sources and to pay attention to who is writing what on behalf of which entities and for what purposes.

Finally, I reiterate the recommendation I made in Chapter 4: that students should complete a lengthier, formal writing assessment for social studies at certain grade levels—possibly at grades 5, 8, and 12; the intervening grade levels would contribute to the success of these major benchmark assessments by the building of similar but less formal assessments into their curricula. These might be completed in cooperation with the English department.

If instituted, such an assessment regimen would transform social studies and have a game-changing effect on students' reading, thinking, and writing abilities—with equally powerful effects on student preparedness for college or careers.

It all begins with an acknowledgement of the central role of *texts*. Textbooks—used selectively—should be part of the mix. But we must also seek out and integrate a much richer variety of supplementary sources that could enrich and enliven social studies instruction.

Supplementary Texts—and Tasks: Making Social Studies Relevant

I'm convinced that social studies could be on the cusp of its greatest moment—a subject that students love and look forward to. To that end, we must supplement textbooks and lectures with other interesting texts, both current and historical. Such documents should include primary source documents, alternative histories, and newspaper and magazine articles, which illuminate the past and help students better understand and connect to the present. We should introduce such texts no later than the upper elementary grades.

There's a real opportunity here. To make these good things happen, teams of teachers must become avid, systematic collectors of compelling documents (and then match them with equally compelling tasks and questions). Many such documents should be tied to instructional units, but we should also make room in the curriculum for timely documents that will provoke curiosity and interest in the world.

I have divided the following documents into my own somewhat arbitrary categories—and only as suggestions. The categories overlap. For each, I briefly explain how it would contribute to greater richness in social studies and history courses.

Historical and Primary Source Documents

At most grade levels, students should have regular opportunities to read from eyewitness or contemporary accounts or from official or notable documents from the historical periods they are studying. These materials will give them an up-close, unfiltered sense of people's thoughts and actions at the time the pieces were written. Their understanding of people and their cultural milieu will be deepened in a way that no textbook, by itself, can achieve.

For instance, every student should have the chance to read General William Tecumseh Sherman's 1864 letter to the mayor and council of Atlanta—sometimes titled **"War Is Hell."** In it, Sherman forcefully justifies his scorched-earth tactics during the Civil War. It is a revealing glimpse into the mind of a 19th-century warrior. Sherman's logic is brutal but compelling—and it invites comparison to recent and current wars.

When studying the early explorers, students can read selections from **Christopher Columbus's personal diary** (1492), which is written in clear, concrete language (4th or 5th graders could read it). These provocative entries tell us a lot about the mind of Columbus himself, as well as about late 15th-century European culture.

Students could defend or debate those values against our own or against the backdrop of his era. Or we might have them analyze the sometimes-damning contents of the diary against Dimitri Vassilaros's (2008) article **"Columbus Was a Hero."**

When studying the rise of industrial America, they could read an excerpt of Harriet Hanson Robinson's (1898) *Loom and Spindle*, her account of life as a mill worker in Lowell, Massachusetts, where even 10-year-old girls worked *14-hour days*. (A two-page excerpt of Robinson's text can be found, along with many other fascinating historical documents, at Fordham University's "Internet Modern History Sourcebook," available online at https://sourcebooks.fordham.edu/mod/robinson-lowell.asp). A good question for this and similar texts: "What differences and similarities do you see, between then and now, in our attitudes toward women and girls—or working conditions?"

Abraham Lincoln's **second inaugural address** (1865) abounds in implications about "just war" and the case for the Northern cause. Students could write an analysis of the speech from the perspective of a Confederate official.

The Analects of Confucius (circa 500 BCE) make very interesting reading: Confucius's simple aphorisms have had a profound, enduring effect on China's history, culture, and development. *Many of these could be read by most 3rd or 4th graders*—even though many contain thoughts of remarkable depth and subtlety. Students could argue about their merits and compare Confucius's perspective to current notions of wisdom (available online at www.indiana.edu/~p374/Analects_of_Confucius_(Eno-2015).pdf).

Andrew Jackson's message to Congress **"On Indian Removal"** (1830), which led to the Trail of Tears, captures the mind-set of Jackson's era. No textbook summary can convey that mind-set like a one- or two-page selection from this address to Congress.

Selections from President Ronald Reagan's **"Tear Down This Wall" speech** (1987) have a fascinating (and somewhat controversial) backstory—and are an excellent supplement to the study of the Cold War.

Martin Luther King Jr.'s (1963) **"Letter from a Birmingham Jail."** The logic, context, and arguments of this pivotal, highly readable letter address the core issues of the Civil Rights movement.

Supreme Court decisions. These primary source documents are rich in history and *can be made quite accessible to students*—if we provide background, vocabulary, and scaffolding before and during the reading. I have had great luck teaching portions of *Plessy v. Ferguson* (1896) to 7th graders.

The Internet has made it easier than ever to find and then match compelling primary source documents to periods we are studying, which would enlarge students' understanding of human nature and provide a more global perspective on the past and present. They are an obvious, critical supplement to textbook reading, but there are other secondary source documents that would also greatly enhance social studies: short biographies and excerpts from alternative histories, current events articles, and other accessible sources.

Short Online Biographies

Even short, one- or two-page biographies can provide a deeper look at historical figures than do most textbooks (though some, like Joy Hakim's *A History of US,* contain excellent short biographies). For each, students could carefully read and annotate as they answer questions such as "What do we learn from this person's life about [his or her] time and place—and our own lives, time, or current issues?"

At Brockton High School, World History students learn and write about utopian theorist Robert Owen, 18th-century demographer Thomas Malthus, philosopher Karl Marx, and other writers. Their life stories abound with opportunities for debate, discussion, and writing. But keep in mind that though Clara Barton, John Brown, Frederick Douglass, Genghis Khan, Akbar the Great, Malcolm X, Helen Keller, Cesar Chavez, and Aristotle are fascinating people, we must, as always, teach, model, and "apprentice" our students in how to read such biographies—how to mine their rich implications for their time and ours.

Alternative Histories

There are many excellent alternative histories, in short or long forms:

Howard Zinn's (2003) left-leaning *A People's History of the United States* takes a critical stance toward American origins and history. It has now been published in a form appropriate for elementary and middle school (Zinn, 2007/2009).

Thomas E. Woods Jr. writes about the Great Depression and the New Deal from a conservative perspective. He makes the case against government intervention in the economy as he compares the depressions of the 1920s with those of the 1930s and between these and our more recent "Great Recession" of 2008 (see online at https://mises.org/library/forgotten-depression-1920.

James W. Loewen's (1995) book *Lies My Teacher Told Me*, is packed with provocative interpretations of U.S. history. It includes a fascinating study of Helen Keller, whose ardent embrace of communism is seldom found in traditional history books (see www.thirdworldtraveler.com/History/Hero-making_LMTTM.html). Many education experts rightly note that conventional textbooks tend to avoid controversial information and perspectives. Not these sources. Why not supplement our textbooks with excerpts from books like Loewen's (1995) or Zinn's (2003), or Larry Schweikart and Michael Patrick Allen's (2014) *A Patriot's History of the United States*. These would guarantee lively discussions—and writing assignments that students would care about.

So would articles about current events.

Current Issues, Events, and Late-Breaking News

Students should have opportunities to read and discuss articles on both sides of issues such as trade agreements, health care policy, animal testing, the use of military and domestic drones, alternative energy, the pros and cons of globalization, the increasing cost of college—and school uniforms. (If you don't think this is a compelling issue, examine the pros and cons of it at the always helpful ProCon. org (http://school-uniforms.procon.org).

ProCon.org is a cornucopia of highly readable, attractively organized information on both sides of numerous current and enduring topics. It provides background on the issues and brief "Top 10" lists of reasons for and against, followed by clear, concise paragraphs with quotes and access to articles and bibliographic information— all to promote objective, impartial examination of important issues, which they update regularly. The 2017 additions to the site include the pros and cons of building a border wall, of a vegetarian diet—and the impact of increasing the minimum wage on young people's summer employment opportunities (see http://minimum-wage.procon. org/). Many such issues affect students where they live.

FactCheck.org is an excellent source for resolving conflicting views in the media on current and ongoing issues. It exposes the ways various entities distort facts for commercial and political reasons.

IndexMundi.com has a variety of demographic and life quality statistics for nations, states, and cities.

The Wall Street Journal and *The New York Times* editorial pages furnish students with an opportunity to compare conservative versus liberal treatments of the same issue. *The New York Times* "Room for debate" features opposing op-ed pieces on timely topics.

The Week, mentioned earlier, has numerous readable summaries of a range of national—and international—opinion on the week's prominent controversies.

At the elementary level: **TIME for Kids** and similar publications feature current events written at 2nd- and 3rd-grade reading levels. In an article about President Trump's address to a joint session of Congress (on February 28, 2017), his proposals are described in plain, engaging language, and then the Democratic response is presented— with areas in which Democrats disagree with Trump and Republicans. *TIME for Kids* has an equally accessible companion article on the Republican effort to repeal and replace the Affordable Care Act. Great stuff.

Again, an important caution: *please ignore—or carefully vet—the ever-present questions, activities, and worksheets that accompany such sources and materials—they are seldom worth your time. Instead, simply provide students with a good guiding question that will inform their close reading, discussion, and writing.*

Lastly, students' own historical writings can be an interesting resource for students. At every grade level, we should collect good examples of student papers that are worthy of analysis and discussion. Since 1987, Will Fitzhugh's quarterly **The Concord Review** (www.tcr.org) has published the best examples of high school historical writing you'll find anywhere.

History, as we know, is always repeating itself—*with differences.* Students need to develop a sense of these historical patterns and differences; they will soon be our voting citizenry. Whether they are informed or ignorant of domestic and international issues will matter greatly.

The addition of such texts would revolutionize social studies. Their inclusion in the curriculum would enliven students' interest in current events and create opportunities for us to help them to see vital connections between past and present.

A Whole New World

Social studies is the study of the world.

—Teacher Eugene Simonet in *Pay It Forward*

Let's take stock. If students read, wrote, and talked for anywhere near the amounts suggested in this chapter—and if they closely read, argued, and wrote about the issues they encountered in textbooks, primary source documents, newspapers, magazines, and online articles every year—the cumulative benefits would be unparalleled. Average students in the United States would be more intellectually informed, articulate, and ready to make their way in the world than ever. We can make this happen.

Let me end by sharing two brief stories that convince me of this. Not long ago, I was doing a demonstration lesson in a middle school history class. I had students read the majority opinion in *Plessy v. Ferguson* (1896), in which Justice Henry Billings Brown wrote his reasons for believing that people of color should not be allowed to sit on the same trains as white people. Here we have a bright, educated man explaining, on behalf of several other bright, educated men, why we should (of all things) separate the races on trains and in public places.

After reviewing some vocabulary, sharing some background, and modeling my own reading and underlining of the first couple of paragraphs, I had the students closely read the next couple of paragraphs. As they read and underlined, I circulated to make sure they were on task and to see how well they were doing. After a few such iterations of modeling, guided practice, and checks for understanding, they were ready to read and underline the rest of the document on their own (while building up all-important reading stamina). When they finished, we had a lively discussion in which every student participated. I then had them write their best arguments in a couple of paragraphs, which they did eagerly. Almost all of their written work met the demands of the writing task. Their experience mimicked my experience when teaching *Jack and the Beanstalk* to 2nd graders.

I did nothing exceptional—I'm always a little rusty and off-balance when I come in cold to teach a class to students I've just met. With a little bit of practice, any teacher could have done what I did. But when the class was over, *the students clapped.* Not (believe me) because of anything I did, but because they plainly enjoyed such activities far more than most of what they typically do in social studies.

A while later I was in a high school leading a similar discussion about a controversial document with 11th graders in a U.S. history class in a relatively high-scoring school. Again, every student seemed to enjoy the opportunity to read, underline, annotate, share thoughts in pairs, and then discuss the issues as a class. Everyone participated—eagerly. I later found out that most of them, up through the 11th grade, *had never done anything like this before.* Can you imagine the effect on students' lives, careers, and college readiness if we addressed this?

There's an enormous opportunity here.

• • •

Representative Social Studies Learning Objectives

(See also literacy-based learning objectives in Chapter 4.)

I can...

• Write one/several paragraphs explaining/arguing/interpreting _____.

• Participate in/contribute to a discussion about _____.

• Explain/describe _____ in writing/discussion.

• Respond to a higher-order prompt/question in writing/orally [e.g., about a historical figure, or one or more historical events].

• List (best/most/least important) reasons/factors for _____ [an historical or current event/development].

• Write a [paragraph/short paper*] explaining most important (causes/effects) of _____.

• Create a written plan/solution for _____ [controversial issue or problem from past or present].

• Take notes on _____ [most important people/events] from a text or lecture—to be used for _____ [written assignment/ presentation].

• Write an argumentative paper* describing a solution to _____.

• Compare and contrast _____ and _____ in writing/ in _____ [number] paragraphs.

• Present a __-minute persuasive PowerPoint report* on _____.

• Create a timeline depicting/comparing _____'s rise and fall with _____'s rise and fall.

• Write a ____-page paper* that compares and contrasts _____ [character/historical figure/event] with _____ [character/ historical figure/event].

*Could constitute a short "unit" of instruction *or* presumes considerable previous/preparatory learning of antecedent skills.

Redefining Inquiry in Science

Inquiry science occurs when students use reading, writing, and oral language to address questions about science content.

—Susanna Hapgood and Annemarie Sullivan Palincsar

Hands-on… activities may have overshadowed the importance of developing science content ideas.

—Kathleen Roth and Helen Garnier

"How the World Works"

There's nothing complicated about what science education should impart. I like Wagner and Dintersmith's (2015) fresh expression: that science education should enable students to "understand how the world works" (p. 129). That understanding will prepare students to be informed citizens and consumers and to pursue advanced science studies—or science, technology, engineering, and math (STEM)–related careers if they choose. It should inspire curiosity, a desire to know how to apply scientific knowledge in work and daily life. These goals are within our reach—but only if we build our efforts around a "viable" number of essential science standards.

Too Many Science Standards

In countries with the highest achievement in science, the number of core concepts taught in their standards document is less than half that of the United States. Education policymakers know that in-depth learning in science is impossible if we impose a set of standards that goes beyond the most essential concepts at each grade level (Roth & Garnier, 2006–2007).

There's been a positive development on this front: the publication of the New Generation Science Standards (NGSS), which have been adopted by 18 states as of this writing (Loewus, 2017). The NGSS calls for "a limited number of core ideas in science and engineering… a reduction in the sheer sum of details to be mastered." This is to discourage "shallow coverage" and to ensure greater depth of understanding (Next Generation Science Standards, 2018, Appendix E: Progressions, p. 1).

The NGSS K–12 "Progressions" (in Appendix E) appear to live up to that claim. The document also emphasizes the application of science in engineering, agriculture, and technology. And there is a strong emphasis—once again—on argument, writing, and communication. There is time for all of this because the "Progressions" focus on a much-reduced body of essential knowledge.

Where the document goes wrong is its "complicated format" (Loewus, 2017). It insists that teachers work from three additional documents, each with multiple items explained in several pages of bulleted paragraphs, columns, and boxes: in addition to the Progressions, there are seven "Crosscutting Concepts," eight "Science and Engineering Practices" and seven "Conceptual Shifts"—a total of 22 long, repetitive lists and paragraphs. It is outlandish to believe that average practitioners can be expected to work from such a clumsy assemblage of documents, written in the usual "standards-ese."

I would recommend that science educators focus their efforts on the admirably concise core content in the NGSS K–12 "Progressions" (Appendix E) or on any other concise set of science standards—such as those published by the *Core Knowledge Foundation* (www.core-knowledge.org/); in Marzano and colleagues' (1999) *Essential Knowledge;* or from their own reduced version of their state standards. This essential reduction will allow for deeper treatment of each topic.

Once we select the grade-by-grade standards we will teach, we would simply integrate something like the following into core content instruction (which represents my own reduced, provisional synthesis of the 22 NGSS practices, concepts, and shifts):

- **Applications:** real-world problem solving, solutions, interconnections (among engineering, design, construction, and so forth)
- **Modeling:** graphic, physical, or computer-based
- **Hands-on activities:** experiments, investigations, fieldwork, laboratory sessions, and so forth
- **Analysis and interpretation:** of data and evidence of natural or human phenomena (e.g., human actions, policies)
- **Argument:** oral and written communication of all of these activities

If schools actually taught only the most essential K–12 "Progressions" informed by something like the items just listed, students would receive an excellent science education. And as we'll see, it could be taught through very ordinary methods: through active reading, writing, interactive lecture, and (in appropriate measure) science investigations and activities.

Literacy is crucial for success in science. For that reason, we should be alarmed that by the time students are in high school, their *literacy skills are weakest—by far—*in science (ACT, 2010). To remedy this, students need to learn core, essential science content through reading, discussing, and writing. These are finally being acknowledged as essential to authentic, *inquiry-based* science.

Content-Based "Task, Text, and Talk"—in Science

Learning in every discipline requires large amounts of "task, text, and talk" (McConachie et al., 2006). Science activities are essential, but prominent science educators are urging a healthier balance between science activities and content-based literacy.

Kathleen Roth and Helen Garnier are senior research scientists at the LessonLab Research Institute at UCLA. They found that the highest-achieving countries had a crucial element in common:

their "science lessons focused on content," on "engaging students with core science ideas." Not so in the United States, where content is often pushed aside in favor of "a *variety of activities*"—with little connection to essential science content (Roth & Garnier, 2006–2007, p. 16).

Throughout these pages, we've heard from cognitive scientists that content knowledge is essential to critical thinking in the sciences (Hirsch, 2008, 2016; Willingham, 2009a). Science educators concur. In "Characterizing Curriculum Coherence," Roseman, Linn, and Koppal (2008) stress that for students to make connections between the life and physical sciences, they must acquire a coherent "central core" of science knowledge (p. 17). Similarly, science professor James Trefil (2008) has little patience for those who underestimate the importance of essential science content to scientific thinking. "In the end," he writes,

> you cannot think critically about nothing—the concepts you manipulate have to be in your mental arsenal.... There is no point teaching students to think critically about global warming if they don't know the basics of planetary energy balance. (pp. 176–177)

This doesn't mean we can't teach content and critical thinking simultaneously; indeed, the optimal way to learn subject matter is to analyze and evaluate it *as we learn* (Silva, 2008; Willingham, 2009a). If we don't know the essential concepts that inform a scientific issue, we are at the mercy, in any argument, of those who do.

But once again: less is more; we must keep our focus on only the most essential science concepts, which creates time for us to integrate literacy into the curriculum. This is central to both mastering science and learning to think critically about it.

Literacy, Laboratories, and Science Content— in Proper Proportion

Laboratories and investigations are vital to science education. But some science educators underestimate the equal importance of reading and writing about science content. That's the conclusion of a two-year study by Timothy and Cynthia Shanahan (2008). Many scientists told the Shanahans that much of the "essence" of science was learned from close analytic reading of *science textbooks* (p. 54)— which I'll describe in a later section.

We can restore this balance. The effort begins with building a coherent, literacy-rich curriculum for each course and grade level— the NGSS "progressions" are a helpful source for this. Or we can derive essential content from our own state standards documents, using procedures such as those described in Chapter 2:

- Reduce the number of concepts and skills to a manageable amount.
- Organize them into grading periods.
- Determine where in the curriculum it is most appropriate to conduct science labs, investigations, and projects.
- Assign science-related texts that support topics in the curriculum.
- Establish the parameters for the approximate number, length, and frequency of common writing assignments.

Once completed—even provisionally—we must resist the false imperatives of multiple-choice teaching and testing. The best way for students to learn is not by having them memorize disconnected science facts. It is by providing frequent, focused opportunities for analytic reading, talking, and writing about science concepts.

Science Inquiry—Through *Literacy*

Even I was surprised at the number of prominent science educators who are calling for a redoubled emphasis on literacy. As Louis and Kimberly Gomez (2007) argue, science education is in dire need of "an intensive reading in science infusion" (p. 225).

The National Research Council supports these findings:

Being science literate entails being able to read and understand a variety of science texts to form valid conclusions and partici-pate in meaningful conversations about science. (Zmach et al., 2006–2007, p. 62)

One of the report's key recommendations was for teachers to ensure that they "engage students in extensive reading of content area texts" (Zmach et al., 2006–2007, p. 63), which echoes Shanahan and Shanahan's (2008) finding that a meaningful (though not excessive) proportion of science knowledge can—and should—be acquired from science textbooks.

Literacy is also integral to "inquiry-based" science. In "Where Literacy and Science Intersect," Susanna Hapgood and Annemarie Sullivan Palincsar (2006–2007) make clear that true science *inquiry* occurs when students engage in "reading, writing and oral language to address questions about science content." In this way, students learn "to build their capacity to engage in scientific reasoning... to generate claims [arguments] about a phenomenon" (p. 56). Their article also affirms the importance of science textbooks—and the importance of showing students how to read and write about science content.

One of the best science lessons I ever observed was an expressly "Socratic discussion" in a high school chemistry class. The day before, students had read, from their textbooks, about the molecular basis for how water changes forms under different conditions. They were asked questions about condensation, fog, and evaporation (e.g., "What do you think happens if... ?"). The teacher would occasionally nod or interrupt briefly to indicate that they were on or off the right track. Students listened to each other intently and worked hard to articulate their thoughts as they questioned and corrected each other, always building on or responding to each other's remarks—or the teacher's cues.

For almost an hour, these students were expanding both their mastery of the concepts they learned from the textbook as well as their powers of listening, thought, and expression. They clearly enjoyed the discussion, and all of them participated (which, once again, reinforces Amy Azzam's [2008] finding that 83 percent of students find discussion their *favorite way to learn*).

Now multiply this experience by about 50 (which is about how many such discussions occur in that chemistry class *each year*); then add writing, as well as the right amount of investigations and lab activities. What do you have? An exemplary chemistry education—simply achieved.

Reading and Writing in Science

Language is the medium of thought—and its refinement. Inquiry-based reading, writing, and discussion are integral both to science education—and to science-related activities. That means we must explicitly teach students, starting in the early grades, to read science texts as we "consistently model how to read critically and question ideas presented in the text," according to Hapgood and Palincsar (2006–2007), who found that students who "used textbooks" and wrote purposefully about what they read "learned the most content" (pp. 57–58). I'm reminded of Timothy Walker, mentioned earlier, the American teacher who writes for *The Atlantic*. He discovered that a surprising amount of the common curriculum in high-achieving Finland was "textbook-driven" (Walker in Stoltzfus, 2017).

But we can't just *assign* textbook reading (or selected excerpts; we should never assign entire chapters). As Courtney Zmach and colleagues (2006–2007) found, we must explicitly *teach* students how to do close, purposeful reading in science. Such lessons must include "think-pair-share, paraphrasing[,]... modeling, guided practice and chances to apply the [reading] strategy independently"—the same "routine components" of instruction we've discussed in each chapter (p. 63). Strategic reading, talking, and writing are among the truest forms of "active learning" in science.

And *students will enjoy this*. Hapgood and Palincsar (2006–2007) found that students are "eager to talk, read, and write" about what they learn in science. They love to "compare their thinking with others' thinking, actively communicate with one another and express their ideas through words and graphics" (p. 56). Zmach and colleagues (2006–2007) similarly discovered that students were "eager and engaged" during their reading in science lessons and that the readings themselves "stimulate lively discussion."

Good things will result from such literacy-rich science instruction: "significantly higher" scores on both reading and science tests, more positive student attitudes toward science, and "more confidence in [students'] capacity to learn science" (Hapgood & Palincsar, 2006–2007, p. 59).

Maybe that's why, in the high-achieving schools of the Netherlands, science teaching is grounded in literacy.

Science and Literacy in the Netherlands

In Dutch science classrooms, as in Finland, literacy plays a central role. In the Netherlands, specific textbook readings are a routine feature of instruction. The lesson begins with a five-minute orientation to the text—precisely the kind of "anticipatory set" that should always precede instruction. This piques curiosity and ensures that far more students will comprehend and retain what they learn from the text (Marzano, Pickering et al., pp. 92–96). (The crafting and sharing of such "orientations," by the way, should be a high priority for course-alike teacher teams working in professional learning communities.)

After the brief orientation, the reading of the text is interwoven with explanations by the teacher—opportunities to discuss answers to the text-based questions. Students read for a manageable 20 minutes or so, *as they write* in response to these questions. This is followed by an opportunity for students to revisit their answers and to elaborate on their initial written responses (Roth & Garnier, 2006–2007, p. 20).

Many U.S. teachers have yet to discover the power of having students periodically review their notes and annotations, which invariably allows them to clarify, extend, and refine their thought as they "think on paper." This is the "miraculous power" that writing has to make students better thinkers in any subject (R. D. Walshe in Schmoker, 2006, p. 64). This simple routine could be used several times per week, in any science course—as it is in the Netherlands.

Strategic reading, writing, and talking have never been prominent features of U.S. science instruction. How does this affect prospects for scientific learning and careers?

Why We Fail: The Early Erosion of Literacy

The erosion of literacy is one of the most insidious developments in modern schooling. And as we saw earlier, levels of literacy are lowest in science (ACT, 2010).

Gomez and Gomez (2007) found that students' difficulties with reading textbook material were among the chief reasons for low performance in science and social studies. Having fallen out of fashion, textbook reading is "abandoned early"—as it was in my two daughters' science classes. With each passing year, students fall further behind in their ability to read challenging, content-rich text: the kind they will encounter if they attend college. No one sounds the alarm, even as teachers cease to regard the textbook as "an active, meaningful ingredient" in science instruction (Gomez & Gomez, 2007, p. 225).

In their article on science education, Hapgood and Palincsar (2006–2007) note similarly the "dearth of informational texts" and "impoverished reading diets" that students receive the moment school begins (pp. 56–57). Zmach and colleagues (2006–2007) implore science instructors to make explicit content-based literacy lessons the core of science instruction in the early grades (pp. 63–65). But few do. As a result, middle school students can't read "demanding text... [in] their textbooks and content-area materials in science" (p. 62). Rather than redress this aggressively, both middle and high schools collectively abdicate this responsibility, as "students engage in *little reading of content texts in secondary classrooms"* (p. 63).

Thus does the American aversion to text quietly diminish aptitude and interest in science and STEM careers. You can't learn a discipline without being a habitual, close reader in that discipline (Alberts, 2006–2007; McConachie et al., 2006). Such reading—and note taking—is essential for understanding the essence of science (Shanahan & Shanahan, 2008).

Real scientists know this. Let's listen to two of them—acquaintances of mine—as they share their perspective on the vital (if unfashionable) importance of science textbooks.

Real-Life Scientists—and Textbooks

An Astronomer's Point of View

Jeff Hall is the director of Lowell Observatory in Flagstaff, Arizona. He speaks almost reverentially of the role of textbooks in his life as a student and successful scientist:

> Where I'm sitting, I can see the spines of some of my favorite textbooks. These books improved my grades greatly by helping me to understand material better. Some of these are real gems, immortal texts I can still learn from... they gave me a deep understanding of quantum mechanics, general relativity, thermodynamics, the interaction of light and matter. These are topics that underpin the modern field, and to understand them you have to do *a lot of reading* (emphasis added).... Scientists don't just "do" science; you can't do scientific work without being a regular reader of scientific articles. Reading textbooks prepares you to read scientific articles. In research, you need to have read enough textbook material to read scientific material with skill, to stay abreast of and maintain currency in the field.

For Jeff, reading science textbooks literally "sets the stage for future success in scientific pursuits." This is precisely what it did for another renowned scientist and acquaintance.

An Evolutionary Biologist's Experience

Paul Keim is a world-renowned biologist and professor at Northern Arizona University in Flagstaff, Arizona. He was the lead researcher who helped pinpoint the origin of the Washington, D.C., anthrax outbreak of 2001.

Keim speaks of the complementary powers of reading and lectures and of the value that science textbooks had for him as a student:

I shape my lectures around the content in the textbooks, so that they reinforce and complement each other, so that the text supports and clarifies my lectures. For students, this approach is invaluable.

Keim doesn't have his students read all of the textbook (I strongly concur). He *does* want them to read deeply and slowly, the way he did as a student:

There is too much material in most textbooks. I have them read about 25 percent of the text. The body of facts and concepts they will learn from lectures simply don't stand by themselves.... How can we talk about the nucleus of a cell without understanding cytoplasm? *The textbook is one of the few places you can go to learn more depth about these concepts; it gives you the total story.* The big downside for those who don't read the textbook is that they don't get the critical supportive details. No matter how effective your lectures are, there is so much good auxiliary material students will miss if they don't read the text.

That vital "auxiliary material," read slowly, gave Keim himself a crucial advantage. As he explained, "The textbook can be an equalizer for slower students.... In college *I would often read only one page in my biochem book at a time.* I had to read and reread the most difficult material. That gave me an advantage, being able to reread parts of the text until I understood it" (emphasis added).

Clearly, we should consider making carefully selected portions (not whole chapters) of textbooks a larger element of science teaching—starting in the early grades. And it is worth remembering that most of this reading should occur *in class,* with instruction and oversight adequate to the reading task. In this way, more students will complete assignments successfully. We'll now look more closely at how to teach textbook reading effectively.

Close Reading of the Textbook: Sound Waves

According to Shanahan and Shanahan (2008), we need to explicitly instruct students in how to navigate science texts. Even more than in most subjects, there is a close interdependence between words and their accompanying graphics. To understand the concepts, readers must do what some students find unnatural: they must often reread and alternate between the written text and any illustrations or statistical tables. In this way, as one scientist points out, students "learn the essence of science" (p. 54):

> For instance: *I am looking at two pages in a textbook on the impact of temperature on the movement of sound waves. On a first reading, I don't understand the concepts. So I slowly reread one paragraph that seems particularly important. It tells me that as the upper part of the sound wave travels upward, it enters cooler air, and that this colder air causes the upper portion of the sound wave to slow down. This in turn allows the lower portion to gain on—to get ahead of—the slower upper portion—and to reach its destination sooner. I am starting to get it, but not as fully as I'd like. So I look at the illustration. Now I can actually see what the sound waves look like at the upper and lower end as they travel from warmer to cooler air. The illustration illuminates the concept but I return to the text again because I want to better understand what is called the "silent zone" at the bottom of the arc of sound that I see in the illustration. So I reread that portion—sentence by sentence— as I revisit the illustration. I'm starting to see that the combination of sound waves and temperature explains why someone closer to a source of sound may not hear it— even though someone further away can. I just learned something quite interesting about how sound travels— from a textbook.*

These are the simple but essential operations that mature adult readers perform automatically to master complex material. But they are not automatic for students. If we want all of them to learn science, we need to employ the same basic moves and methods described previously—with (as always) several iterations of modeling, guided practice, and checks for understanding. Such close reading needs to be explicitly taught, at increasing levels of sophistication, every year in *all* science classes.

Such text-based instruction would prepare students for the next important step: to share their now much clearer, more refined thoughts in whole-class discussions—whether they are about molecular theory or the pros and cons of wind energy. Later in the chapter, we'll see how to align textbook readings with the curriculum.

But we should also build a variety of other texts into the curriculum: supplementary and current science readings. The use of such texts will enliven science learning for all students.

Choosing Supplementary Texts

Science textbooks can tell us a lot about "how the world works." But a variety of texts can bring science even closer to students' lives and potential aspirations: articles about late-breaking STEM-related discoveries and prominent scientists—from the Pasteurs to Steve Wozniak (Steve Jobs's partner and "tech wizard") and late-breaking STEM-related developments. Every week or two, we could have students read and discuss such biographies and articles.

It's never been so easy. Interesting, readable texts for every level can be easily found in an array of science journals, news magazines, and online sources. Ideally, these should connect to the science content that students are studying. Perhaps 10 to 20 percent of the curriculum should be focused on such readings, accompanied by discussion and writing—about their real-world implications and applications. I can't imagine a better way to imbue scientific studies with relevance.

There is time for this. If, in the spirit of the NGSS, we focus only the highest-priority science standards and scrap the least-essential laboratory sessions, activities, movies, and worksheets, there will be far more opportunity for students to read, talk, and write about the content in such texts. And as we've seen, students are "eager to talk, read, and write" about science topics—if we set the stage for it (Hapgood & Palincsar, 2006–2007, p. 56).

The following are examples of supplementary texts and sources that could be integrated into the science curriculum. There is some unavoidable overlap among the categories. And again: these must be more than mere "reading assignments"; they will promote science inquiry only if they are accompanied by guiding questions, discussion, argument—and some form of writing, in which students distill their evolving insights and conclusions into prose (most of which—remember—does not need to be formally graded).

Early Elementary Texts

There are several good sources appropriate for the elementary grades—such as **TIME for Kids, Junior Scholastic**, and **Science Spin**. They contain articles about recent dinosaur discoveries, what working scientists do, the science of caffeine, and how three-dimensional printing can be used to create body parts. These publications are written for students as young as 1st grade, in clear, readable language. They are often accompanied by statistics, tables, and graphs.

Again, a caution: *please ignore most of the ever-present questions, activities, and worksheets that always accompany such materials; they are the enemy of true inquiry.* Instead, simply have students read them purposefully—in response to good analytic or guiding questions as they learn to read, underline, take notes, or annotate.

Biographies. Plenty of excellent short biographies of scientists are available online. And researchers have discovered some surprising academic benefits of reading about the lives of scientists: such reading *significantly increases* overall achievement in science. The effects are particularly strong if students read biographies that *describe the personal or professional struggles* that scientists encountered and overcame in their life and work. Gains were especially pronounced for low achievers (Lin-Siegler, Ahn, Chen, Fang, & Luna-Lucero, 2016).

We should seek out biographies that feature, for instance, Gregor Mendel's arduous experimentation in his garden that led to our modern understanding of heredity; the Wright brothers' years of trial and error that led to their historic plane flight; or Barbara McClintock's seminal, persevering work in genetics. Because the research community was slow to recognize the accomplishments of women, McClintock received the Nobel Prize decades after her discoveries, when she was 79. Aspiring engineers—or anyone—would enjoy reading about one of the great engineering odysseys of the 20th century: John Rust's years-long struggle to invent the cotton reaper. Rust's epic perseverance is dramatically chronicled in excerpts from David Halberstam's bestseller *The Fifties* (pp. 454–457).

Biographies don't always fully capture the most dramatic episodes in science or the lives of scientists, inventors, and engineers. For that reason, we should also collect articles that contain compelling narratives of scientific discoveries themselves.

Science stories. Stories—read or heard—are a great way to learn about science. Students would enjoy reading about the romance and partnership of Pierre and Marie Curie, which led to their Nobel Prize–winning work on radioactivity. Or about the curious, often troubled relationship between Steve Wozniak and Steve Jobs as they reinvented personal computing. The details behind the troubled Apollo 13 mission are full of implications for engineering and human ingenuity. Excerpts from *The Double Helix*—about Watson and Crick's discovery of DNA—make great reading. So does the account of Thomas Edison's unsuccessful lawsuit against Granville Woods—sometimes referred to as the "Black Edison"—over patent rights for an invention they collaborated on. This story points up the often cumulative, collective nature of scientific work. Students would be intrigued to read about the significant physical effects of being in space for an extended time, as they read about biochemist and astronaut Peggy Whitson (who has spent the most time in space of any American). David McCollough's account of the obstacles overcome in the building of the Brooklyn bridge are riveting—and rooted in basic scientific and engineering principles.

Engineering/medical health breakthroughs and stories. For secondary science, the website Greatest Engineering Achievements of the 20th Century (www.greatachievements.org) contains a multitude of concise, well-written articles describing the origins of the greatest engineering feats and accomplishments of the modern era—with a helpful timeline of each invention's development, the obstacles overcome, and major contributors to the discovery and application of such things as transistors, air conditioning, nuclear technology, spacecraft, the Internet, household appliances, agricultural mechanization (e.g., the cotton gin and McCormick reaper), and airplanes.

Students are bound to enjoy reading about the science and engineering behind Hoover Dam, the electrical grid, x-ray technology—and the development of simple but important inventions such as the zipper, luggage with wheels, toasters, dishwashers, and microwave ovens. David Halberstam's account (1993) of McDonald's restaurants—the actual "engineering" behind its "Speedee Service System"—is a page-turner, full of implications for manufacturing design, plant layout, efficiency, and continuous experimental refinement of time- and money-saving processes (as emphasized in the NGSS). The story of W. Edwards Deming's work in revitalizing industry in Japan after World War II is inspiring; it transformed engineering, manufacturing, and industrial processes throughout the world.

All of these stories illuminate "how the world works" in captivating detail.

Current and Controversial Science Articles

Current articles about late-breaking discoveries have the power of "now"; they focus on timely, urgent issues. There are plenty of good online sources. These don't always have to be tied to the current unit; they have value in themselves for inspiring curiosity about science and the work of scientists.

Science News for Students (www.Sciencenewsforstudents. org) stays very current on science news, such as the increasing popularity —and dangers—of "vaping."

As mentioned in Chapter 5: **ProCon.org** is an excellent, free source for any teacher and certainly for any science teacher. In its science and technology section, you will find abundant materials arguing both sides of issues such as the following:

- Alternative energy versus fossil fuels
- Are cell phones safe?

- Is nuclear power practical?

And it's added an important new feature: a rating that helps students make judgments about the authority or bias of their sources. The website also provides an explanation for its rating system, which students and teachers can read and critique, in which they candidly admit the difficulty of assigning a hard value to any particular source.

For many of the topics, you can click to go to related pages. For example, the alternative energy page contains links to short, readable bullet points for and against the use of biofuels and of nuclear, solar, and hydrogen power. Each topic also has a "one-minute overview" that provides background for the issue in clear, easy-to-read language. With a click, you can consult the "expanded background" for each topic. Either of these would be perfect to construct anticipatory sets and pique student curiosity.

Below this overview are 10 short, argumentative paragraphs in each of two columns—"pro" and "con." Each summarizes the important facts or conclusions from one article; citations for each article are provided (if students want to look them up online).

The format itself is compelling: students can review the arguments in close juxtaposition, which makes comparison, evaluation, and synthesis of the arguments easier. By themselves, these concise, well-written paragraphs provide students with abundant opportunities to learn essential content, to read closely to analyze competing claims, and to argue and communicate—all recommended in the NGSS standards and practices.

Another source of good articles for middle and high school science courses is *The Week*, which I discussed in Chapter 5. *The Week's* "Health and Science" page typically contains about five short, readable pieces on recent breakthroughs. I've found short articles on the following topics:

- The myth of the multitasker
- The academic benefits of chewing gum
- How Facebook use may adversely affect students' grades

The January 20, 2017, issue includes a piece on the discovery of a "new human organ" (the "mesentery," which brings the total number of organs to 79); another brief piece describes the prospect of building igloos on Mars—whose insides could be kept at a comfortable 72 degrees. Another notes a spike in reported cases of mumps—and lists several theories for why this is happening. This single page is consistently arresting, and the brief articles connect meaningfully to life, earth, space, and medical science at every grade level.

In such articles, we encounter the same patterns and opportunities for close analytic—and argumentative—reading, discussion, and writing:

• Most of the pieces reflect the interesting and recurring issue of *cause versus correlation,* which students enjoy debating. (Is gum chewing the cause of higher grades, or do smart kids like to chew gum? Does Facebook cause lower grades, or do underachieving students just spend more time on Facebook?)

• In many of the articles, the authors admit that the featured discoveries are inconclusive about root causes. (For example, in the gum-chewing piece, some scientists speculate that chewing gum stimulates mental activity because it promotes blood flow in the region of the brain... *but they have no proof.*)

• Pieces often invite analysis and debate about *the way the studies were designed.* For example, multitaskers in one study were identified as those who merely happen to use the greatest variety of media and technology; nothing is said about using them simultaneously. If taught to read carefully, many students will ask whether this is really the best way to identify "multitaskers."

• All the articles invite us to think and discuss connections among science disciplines. (The gum-chewing article has implications for both chemistry and biology, and the Facebook article connects both behavioral and biological/neurological science.)

The range and appeal of these short articles are bound to promote students' interest in science courses and in scientific and technical careers.

The Week also contains readable, full-page articles on major scientific issues. I am looking at one on nuclear energy. I will now use it to describe how to model and teach effective reading of such articles—as I did previously with textbook reading. Once again, teachers would show students how to reread some portions, annotate and refer to graphics in the text (if there are any) to achieve understanding, form arguments, and make connections as they navigate the "lexical density" that typifies science textbooks (Shanahan & Shanahan, 2008, p. 53). Any teacher can learn to teach these effectively. Such instruction would demystify such intellectual work and allow students to master the art of reading nonfiction closely and critically.

Close Reading: A Science Article

First, regardless of what we're reading, we're always wise to teach the vocabulary that is critical to understanding the text before we ask students to read it (per the literacy template in Chapter 3, on which this section is based). Doing so is key to addressing the range of reading abilities in a classroom and to ensuring that all students can engage and comprehend a challenging text. Don't skip this essential step: the net result is the equivalent of an increase in comprehension of *33 percentile points*. Words taught (even cursorily) before reading will be learned much faster, even as they aid comprehension. This is a critical part of "scaffolding" any text-based lesson (Marzano et al., 1999, p. 147).

I'm looking at an article from *The Week* that lays out the pros and cons of nuclear power plants. After briefly teaching—and providing definitions for—about a dozen vocabulary words from the text, I always provide a brief (three- to five-minute) anticipatory set to stir interest or establish the relevance of the topic.

Next, I establish the specific purpose for the reading—by providing a guiding prompt or question that helps readers to focus their attention as they read. It sometimes doubles as the learning objective. A versatile, dependable form of such a question is one that simply asks the student to take a side or to agree or disagree; for example:

"Should we or should we not build more nuclear power plants?"

Then, I would model—"think aloud"—as I read a short portion of the text. For instance, in the first paragraph of this article, I would note—aloud—that the United States has gone "30 years without building a new nuclear plant" but is now "preparing to build as many as 29 in the next several years." I would say to my class:

> This gets my attention. Does it get yours? Why did the United States wait so long to build more plants—and then decide to build so many *so fast?* I have mixed feelings about nuclear power. And the fact that we didn't build a plant for 30 years makes me nervous. Is it because these plants *are dangerous?* That's a reason for me to be *against* building any new ones [as I point to the guiding question on the board]. On the other hand, the fact that 29 plants are now being built might indicate that these plants are safer now—maybe the technology is better? If so, maybe we *should* consider building more plants. I haven't yet reached a conclusion about whether I'm for or against building more plants, but I'll underline these phrases [or possibly model how to annotate them] and read on as I come to my own conclusion based on the text evidence.

After modeling, I would then ask students to engage in "guided practice"—by having them read the remainder of the paragraph on their own and underlining any evidence that argues for or against the building of such plants. While they are reading, I would circulate to "check for understanding"—to see whether they are underlining appropriate evidence. If, on this first attempt, they are overlooking the best evidence in the paragraph (as many do) I might have them pair up and look for evidence together. Or I would model once again, being even more explicit in explaining what I would underline and why.

After such "reteaching," I would circulate again to check for understanding. I would continue in this cycle until I see evidence that they can underline an adequate number of examples from the text on their own ("independent practice"), which I now allow them to do for the remainder of the text. And I continue to circulate during independent practice—or to work with the students who still need assistance.

Once they have finished underlining the text, I would have students share and explain their underlinings with each other in pairs—as rehearsal for a whole-class discussion.

If we consistently implement such simple processes, from the earliest grades, science students will learn to read, think, and articulate with increasing skill and sophistication. But they must also write, for writing takes students to even higher levels of clarity and precision in their powers of thought. There is no better preparation for effective writing than the close purposeful reading and discussion just described (Hillocks, 1987).

Writing in Science

As often as possible, lessons like the one just described should culminate in an opportunity—however brief—for students to respond to a question in writing. It is in writing that students convert what they have learned from reading and talking into more coherent, logical, precise language. In writing, new thoughts are often born, which build on the insights gleaned from reading and talking. As we've seen, writing has a "miraculous power" to take our thinking to the next level (Walshe in Schmoker, 2006, p. 64). Hapgood and Palincsar (2006–2007) found that the students who learned and retained the most content in science were those who wrote about what they read (pp. 57–58).

For Bruce Alberts, former president of the National Academy of Sciences, writing has a transformative effect on learning. According to Regina Nuzzo (2005),

> Alberts and his colleagues noticed that their students were studying only to pass the multiple-choice examinations, [so] they changed the test to include short-essay answers. It was amazing, Alberts says, to see how this small change *caused students to think so much more deeply about the material.* (p. 1; emphasis added)

Doug Reeves's (2008) organization conducted a study that demonstrated that regular writing and note taking contribute significantly to mastery of science content. In schools in which writing and note taking were rarely implemented in science classes, approximately 25 percent of students scored proficient or higher on state assessments. But in schools where writing and note taking were consistently implemented by science teachers, 79 percent scored at the proficient level (Reeves, 2008).

Writing matters. With this much at stake, students should regularly convert notes or annotations into cogent arguments and explanations, if even in one or two paragraphs. It is also critical for science students to write both short and more formal research papers, from single-source to multiple-source assignments each year—with their length increasing at each grade level. Even one substantial research paper per year would prepare students for the kind of writing they will do in any number of STEM-related fields.

Students could write short or long papers about topics such as the following:

- Careers in science
- Competing theories on scientific topics
- The history and development behind the engineering of the electrical grid, dams, the space shuttle, internal combustion engine, assembly lines
- Papers on potential solutions to engineering, scientific, or environmental problems—obstacles to the use or cost-effectiveness of alternative energy; the encroachment of invasive fish species in Lake Michigan
- Compare-and-contrast papers (e.g., two or more animal anatomies, competing theories for natural phenomena, rocks and minerals)
- Biographies of scientists, past or present
- Position papers on scientific issues such as

—Cloning

—Fracking

—The recent argument that "Zealandia" should be considered a continent

   —Most promising forms of alternative energy

   —Animal testing

   —Climate change

   —Vaccines for kids

—Cell phones' connection to cancer

See ProCon.org (www.procon.org) for resources on these subjects.

In high school courses, at least one of these papers should be three to five typewritten pages—mostly completed in class, so that teachers can monitor and guide student efforts to ensure success. As David Conley (2005) found, students need to write far more three- to five-page papers in K–12 to be prepared for college.

But science teachers shouldn't be expected to teach writing in precisely the same manner as English teachers. In science, perhaps the emphasis should merely be on producing sound, readable papers that will be evaluated primarily for clarity and content—for the student's ability to cite written sources to support a scientific argument or conclusion with evidence. The finer points of writing can be left to the language arts teacher.

We've been looking at literacy and the elements of instruction that empower the teaching of literacy. Let's now look at how those elements apply to "interactive lecture" and related practices. Executed effectively, interactive lecture complements textbook reading, as it does for Professor Keim. As Bybee and Van Scotter (2006–2007) point out, "reading, lecture, and discussion" are among the essential elements for promoting scientific reasoning and literacy (pp. 44–45). For James Trefil (2008), lecture is one of the most powerful, efficient ways to impart essential scientific knowledge.

Interactive Lecture

An adolescent doesn't learn by listening. To really learn, a student needs to be constantly thinking, articulating points of view, and responding to and asking great questions.

—Kevin Mattingly, dean of faculty at Lawrenceville School

(in Wagner & Dintersmith, 2015)

Students thrive in settings where their opinion matters and they engage in meaningful debate.

—Wagner and Dintersmith (2015)

Tremendous academic benefits accrue to the right amount of "interactive lecture" in every content area (Marzano, 2009). Done right, lecture is a "marvel of efficiency"—an engaging means of ensuring that students retain *and engage with* the knowledge and skills that the teacher decides to prioritize (Silver et al., 2007, p. 26). But done wrong (as it often is), lecture is among the most boring and ineffective modes of instruction.

To be effective, *interactive* lecture has to contain the same "routine components" described at length in Chapter 3: modeling, guided practice, and continuous, same-day formative assessment. I encourage you to revisit the more detailed treatment of interactive lecture in Chapter 3, but here are its essential steps:

• Begin the lecture by providing essential or provocative background knowledge and an open-ended question or prompt.

• Ensure that the lecture provides sufficient information for students to respond to the question.

• As you lecture, circulate and observe to ensure that students are on task and taking effective notes for each brief chunk of the lecture.

• Avoid lecturing for more than five to seven minutes at a time, then give students an opportunity to review/revise their notes against the question or task—and to compare their connections and perceptions in pairs (for even one to two minutes at a time).

• Reteach or clarify whenever checks for understanding indicate that students need guidance in how to take appropriate notes; move on when they are ready for the next portion of the lecture.

Because it is active, efficient, and engaging, this form of lecture can be a regular staple of instruction—and could therefore have an outsized positive effect on learning. Because it contains frequent pair-share opportunities, it ensures the inclusion of discussion and writing in students' learning.

Eric Mazur, the Harvard physics professor mentioned in Chapter 3, had tremendous success with interactive lecture, which he adopted when he realized that even his highest-scoring students didn't understand the underlying concepts of physics—those which even "plumbers and electricians know like the back of their hands" (Wagner & Dintersmith, 2015, p. 200). So he crafted his own versions of interactive lectures, with an emphasis on what he calls "Concep-Tests": after lecturing on a concept, he would project one or more multiple-choice items on a screen. Then he would have students select, discuss, and then defend their answers with their peers—while he circulated, listening for their understanding or misconceptions (think "check for understanding"). Then he would reteach or clarify as needed. As a result of this approach, Mazur's students achieved "dramatic gains" on his tests of conceptual understanding as well as on "conventional tests of narrow and procedural problem solving" (Wagner & Dintersmith, 2015). Success rates soared, especially for the previously lowest-scoring subgroups (Mazur, 1997).

At its best, interactive lecture addresses a provocative question or prompt—in response to which students take notes, discuss, and write (or write and then discuss; either way is effective). All the following questions and prompts address the NGSS emphases on acquiring core content, identifying patterns, making arguments, and modeling and communicating understanding. And all of the following could be easily converted into clear, effective learning objectives (e.g., "I can compare and contrast _____", "I can argue/justify/explain _____.").

A representative set of sample science objectives and stems is presented at the end of this chapter.

Compare and contrast. Instead of simply lecturing students on various science topics, ask them, as you lecture, to take notes and pair-share their perceptions of the similarities or differences among the types, features, or functions of the following:

- Different kinds of clouds
- Reptiles and amphibians
- Objects that float or sink
- Plants and animals
- Unicellular and multicellular organelles
- Floor spreading and plate tectonics
- RNA and DNA
- Systems (respiratory, cardiovascular, etc.)
- Various sources of alternative energy
- Eukaryotic and prokaryotic cells
- Two different manufacturing processes
- Designs for testing the effectiveness of a product

While students are taking notes, reviewing their notes, and pair-sharing, circulate to assess, for instance, if they are noting simple patterns—such as the fact that both wind and solar energy work better in some geographic areas than in others; that natural fluctuations in wind and sunlight can be a problem; that both wind and solar energy are free, abundant, and clean. They might also note that nuclear power is also clean but that it generates dangerous waste that is hard to dispose of; that it is more prone to fatal mishaps than wind or solar; and so forth. We might allow a moment to evaluate and give reasons for which form of energy we think would be most practical or cost-effective.

After lecturing on prokaryotic and eukaryotic cells, we could have students identify three things that are different and three that are similar, on the basis of the lecture (which could include visual or videographic aids).

ConcepTests—with written explanations. As we lecture on a particular topic or concept, and as students take notes, we might stop at certain points to ask them a short-answer, multiple-choice, or true–false question that requires an understanding of that concept, such as

• Gases, liquids, and solids all have which of the following properties? (multiple-choice)

• What will happen to _____ [water; ice; oil] if we _____ [expose it to freezing temperatures/heat; mix it with other substances]? (short-answer)

• If you mix _____ with _____, it will [evaporate; explode; change color]. (true–false)

• Which of the following factors would do the least/most to help/harm _____ [a certain animal; lake; ecosystem]? (multiple-choice)

• Which of the following weighs more…? (multiple-choice)

• _____ is better suited to its environment than _____. (true–false)

• Plant and animal cells are different in which important way(s)? (short-answer)

• Which of the following characteristics pertain to eukaryotic cells? To prokaryotic cells? To both? (multiple-choice)

• How might the extinction of _____ [predators, such as piranhas, lions, wolves] affect the food chain or ecosystem we are studying? (short-answer)

• Which of the following best explains why _____ [baking powder and vinegar; hydrogen and oxygen; hydrogen peroxide and sodium iodide] react chemically? (multiple-choice)

For the true–false or multiple-choice items, students would be asked to explain their answer in writing—so that the teacher can circulate and review the responses to check for understanding. If there is confusion, the teacher could address it or have students pair up to compare their written responses and work toward clarity. The teacher could then cold-call on individuals or pairs to gauge understanding—and reteach if confusion persists.

Evaluate and justify. These open-ended prompts would allow students to write informed judgments that are based on the content of the lecture, for which they have taken notes:

- Topic: the conditions most favorable to organic life
  —Ask them to justify which planet other than Earth is most likely to contain life.
- Topic: sources of energy
  —Ask them to justify which one would be most practical for our region/a particular region/all regions.
- Topic: certain animals/plants
  —Ask them to justify which one is best suited to its environment.
- Topic: various elements in an ecosystem
  —Ask them to justify which one they think is least or most important to the health and continuance of that ecosystem.
- Topic: the criteria for planet status
  —Ask them to justify why Pluto is/is not a planet.
- Topic: the engineering that culminated in the following achievements (e.g., nuclear power plants, hydroelectric plant, electrical grid, internal combustion engine, hybrid engine, wind turbine)
  —Ask them to justify their rank-ordering of these engineering achievements, from most to least impressive.

Simulations. As the teacher lectures and/or shows a video simulation, periodically ask inferential or if/then questions and alternate between having students write or pair-share their thoughts about

- States of matter
- Radioactivity
- The solar system
- Solar system/orbits/seasons
- Characteristics of light
- Earth's major layers

Good simulations can be found on such sites as https://phet.colorado.edu or Vimeo.

These are all variations on "interactive lecture." Note how the lectures are designed to ensure that students are not just listening and taking notes: they are thinking, sorting, ranking, comparing, evaluating, deciding, and justifying (all forms of argument) as they listen, talk, and write. This too is active, inquiry-based learning. Hands-on science activities and investigations, however, are also critical. They should constitute a generous portion of the science curriculum.

But first, a caveat.

Hands-On Science: A Caution

Good science activities, connected to science content, are essential. But as we've seen, less time tends to be devoted to hands-on science in countries with the highest science achievement than in the United States, where science instruction often consists of an excessive "variety of activities." And many of the science activities conducted in U.S. schools either did not support essential content or "contained no explicit science content at all" (Roth & Garnier, 2006–2007, p. 20).

Roth and Garnier are not alone in this view. The National Research Council found that most high school science laboratory sessions were "poorly integrated into the rest of the curriculum" (Bybee & Van Scotter, 2006–2007, p. 44). Prominent science educators are calling us to reevaluate the profusion of disconnected "cookbook laboratory exercises" that are still too common in schools (Wenglinsky & Silverstein, 2006–2007, p. 25). These are of limited value to science learning because they focus primarily on "procedures rather than learning goals" (Perkins-Gough, 2006–2007, p. 93).

One of my daughters took an advanced high school science course from a teacher who proudly proclaimed that no textbook would be used in the course—it would consist entirely of hands-on activities. My daughter saw little value in most of those activities but was deeply grateful for a different science teacher who combined carefully selected hands-on activities with liberal amounts of science articles and textbook readings. This deliberate combination of reading, writing, and hands-on activities equipped her for the laboratory work, field studies, and research she did in college and now does as a working environmental researcher.

But this is not the norm. In his interviews with students and teachers, James Trefil (2008) found that most "labs" are carried out pro forma. Students told him that they typically "game" the activity by merely working backward from the correct results, without learning much in the process (pp. 188–189).

Bruce Alberts, the former president of the National Academy of Sciences, had similar experiences in high school and then at Harvard. He found science content fascinating but loathed the years he spent completing "tedious cookbook... boring laboratory exercises." Amazingly, he writes, "the same boring laboratory exercises continue at most of our universities today, nearly 50 years later!" (Alberts, 2006–2007, p. 18).

The lesson here is that *hands-on science activities are critical in good science education* but should (1) occupy a reasonable portion of the curriculum, and (2) be driven by a clear purpose that connects to the content of the discipline.

Hands-On Science Investigations and Activities

From the earliest grades, hands-on activities, investigations, fieldwork, and computer simulations can powerfully inspire interest in STEM-related careers. They can cultivate a logical, scientific mindset and convey science concepts vividly. Such activities might constitute between one-third and one-half of the overall curriculum (the other half to two-thirds split between active reading, writing, discussion, and variations on inquiry-based, interactive lecture).

Science activities should be informed by the science and engineering concepts or content that students are learning as they read, write, and discuss science and its implications for the real world. All these elements should contribute to students' increasingly sophisticated understanding of "how the world works"—and how that understanding can make our lives better.

The following activities are adapted from different science sites; they align strongly with NGSS assessment item banks I've reviewed but go beyond them (I believe) in terms of intellectual authenticity and real-world connections. They could be adapted for any level of schooling—elementary, middle, or high school.

- Test or compare various products for actual quality—or against their advertiser's claims.
- Conduct fieldwork and gather data on plant and animal life, weather, human behavior, and so forth—to make generalizations; draw inferences; identify patterns. Then represent the data graphically and describe observations and conclusions in writing.
- Collect, categorize, analyze—and then generalize or make inferences about—natural specimens, such as insects, soil, plants, rocks, and animals.
- Create models (drawings, computer simulations, apparatus) that clarify science concepts and relationships (regarding sound, weather, physics, and so forth).
- Employ CAD (computer-assisted design) software to design a product or address an engineering task within given parameters.
- Teach students about various inventions and improvements (e.g., McDonald's efficiency methods, wheels on luggage, cupholders in cars, just-in-time inventory). Then have students

  —Brainstorm in pairs or small groups to generate lists of problems, challenges, needs, or opportunities for incremental improvement of any process or product in any sphere.

  —Identify one of these and brainstorm, sketch, design, or build solutions or prototypes to address the problem or challenge.

  —Test or evaluate a solution and refine design on the basis of results.

- After learning about cell life, anatomy, biology, or another subject, hypothesize about ways that we might make progress against various diseases, disabilities, and other problems.

• Draw or create simple models or prototypes to better understand and communicate an understanding of products or concepts.

• Use microscopes to analyze air, water, rock, or soil samples to determine their content, quality, and significance with regard to their ecosystems.

• Dismantle, analyze, and describe the design and functions of the components of small appliances, machines, or electronic devices.

   —Develop and sketch tentative/potential improvements for any of these, on the basis of perceived need/opportunity.

• Brainstorm and then construct a functioning apparatus using limited resources (after watching the clip from the movie *Apollo 13,* in which astronauts repair their ship with materials available on their ship).

• Design, build, and then refine designs for weight-bearing bridges, towers, supports—or simple devices and machines.

• Participate in competition to design and build the farthest-flying paper airplane, the sturdiest popsicle/paper clip bridge, the fastest rubber-band powered car.

• Perform experiments with plants—to test the effect of different variables on growth or yield.

Ideas for similar STEM-related activities can be found at a variety of websites, which I came across in the Marshall Memo (2017). For example:

• Odyssey of the Mind: www.odysseyofthemind.com/materials/2015problems.php#p1

• National Academy of Engineering Grand Challenges: www.engineeringchallenges.org/challenges.aspx

• Museum of Science, Boston, Engineering Everywhere: www.eie.org/engineering-everywhere/curriculum-units

• Museum of Science, Boston, Engineering Is Elementary Curriculum Units: www.eie.org/eie-curriculum/curriculum-units

• eGFI Dream Up the Future: http://teachers.egfi-k12.org/ideas-for-using-egfi-cards

• PBS's Design Squad: http://pbskids.org/designsquad/

- TeachEngineering: https://www.teachengineering.org
- Rutgers Today: https://news.rutgers.edu/media-advisory/engineering-students-demonstrate-projects-solve-real-world-problems/20141201

Such activities would richly address (the essence of) the 22 concepts, shifts, and practices of the NGSS. And all of them both support and are supported by essential science content and science literacy—the reading, discussion, and writing that must be liberally integrated into every aspect of the science curriculum.

Good science curriculum contains just a few critical elements—adequate content, interactive lecture, higher-order literacy, and the right amount of hands-on laboratory activities and experiments. With these important elements in mind, let's now look at how we can bring them together to build coherent, teacher-friendly curriculum that teachers will actually use; the key is to make it so simple and clear that teachers would *want* to use it. We'll finish this chapter with a look at how science assessment can better support the curriculum and help us improve its delivery.

Achieving Coherence: Science Curriculum

First: curriculum must be "viable" (Marzano, 2003); the best science instruction is highly focused on a manageable number of only the most essential skills and topics, taught in adequate depth.

Second, the curriculum must explicate "what to teach and when": a schedule that adequately designates which science topics should be taught in each grading period, in approximately what order (Darling-Hammond, 2010, p. 295). Nothing is more important; we've seen evidence that the implementation of a coherent, literacy-rich curriculum may have more effect than any other in-school factor (DuFour & Marzano, 2011; Hirsch, 2016; Marzano, 2003).

Once again, we are assisted in this effort by the relative concision of the NGSS K–12 Progressions, which are impressively clear and concise; I count only about 30 major topics that are to be taught in all of grades 6–8.

There are other such concise sources, all of which overlap considerably with each other and with the NGSS Progressions. Marzano and colleagues' 1999 compendium of standards contains only about 30 topics for all three middle school grades (1999). The K–8 Core Knowledge Foundation's science standards are similarly concise and well written. And science educator James Trefil (2008) has produced a list of only 18 major (and fairly predictable) science concepts to be taught across K–12.

Whether you start with any of the sources listed earlier or with your own state standards, you will then need to follow a process like the following to create a coherent curriculum—a schedule of "what to teach and when" (this process is described in greater detail in Chapter 2):

• Estimate the number of days it would take to teach each topic in your standards document in adequate depth, inclusive of science activities and literacy activities (your time/day "budget").

• Add up the days; if the total exceeds the number of instructional days available to teach the content (approximately 140 to 150), reduce the number until you arrive at a "viable" set of standards.

• Organize the content and skills into grading periods (without overcrowding any of them).

• Determine and designate the most appropriate times to conduct science investigations and activities.

• Assign and record science-related texts that support the curriculum.

• Establish parameters for the approximate number and length of writing assignments—at least major writing assignments—for each grading period.

Blank templates for building such curricula are available in Schmoker (2016) and online at www.ascd.org/ASCD/pdf/books/Schmoker-AppendixB.pdf.

Both during and after this process, you may want to evaluate your curriculum against a manageable synthesis—like the one I created earlier in this chapter—of the 22 items found in the appendixes to the NGSS (the "Crosscutting Concepts," "Science and Engineering Practices," and "Conceptual Shifts").

- *Applications*. Real-world problem solving, solutions, interconnections (among engineering, design, construction, and so forth)
- *Modeling*. Graphic, physical, or computer-based
- *Hands-on activities*. Experiments, investigations, fieldwork, laboratory sessions, and so forth
- *Analysis and interpretation* of data and evidence of natural or human phenomena (e.g., human actions, policies)
- *Argument*. Oral and written communication of all of the above activities

As indicated earlier, I think a short, intuitive list like this one can be stored in working memory as we create curriculum and lessons. But I have less faith that teachers can be expected to integrate 22 detailed, highly abstract conceptual elements into their curriculum. As *Education Week*'s Liana Heitin-Loewus (2016) avers, figuring out how to incorporate these NGSS shifts, concepts, and practices into clear, cogent curriculum will be "quite hard to do"; as she points out, there is little guidance on which element should inform which topics and at what grade levels.

I would encourage schools to review these 22 items and then develop a concise, manageable synthesis like what I have attempted above.

When these steps are complete, the curriculum document is ready for use (but always subject to adjustment) as the basis for the team to create common lessons, reading assignments, questions, and writing assignments. Again, it is probably a good idea to leave two or three weeks "free" each semester for individual teachers to pursue their favorite topics or interests (DuFour et al., 2006, p. 65).

We should also leave time to conduct more extended authentic or open-book assessment at the end of units and grading periods. Let's look more closely at the role such cumulative assessments could play in both assessing learning and driving quality instruction.

Science Assessments

Today, assessment in our schools has become the bitter enemy of learning.

—Tony Wagner and Ted Dintersmith

School and district assessment in science should mirror our priorities, with due consideration given to the new breed of state assessments—students' ability to read closely; make models; analyze both text and data; develop solutions; and construct arguments—all rooted in core content. Such complex tasks can't be assessed adequately with multiple-choice items—and, indeed, there will be far fewer such items on the new NGSS and other state assessments. These new assessments will contain far more reading, writing, and analysis (Loewus, 2017).

Such assessment will require more time, but it won't be an interruption to an education; it will be an extension of it.

Educative Assessments

The best science assessments can't be conducted in a single class period and then scored electronically. Ideally, assessments should allow students time to more fully demonstrate their ability to analyze, organize, and express their knowledge in writing. At the least, we should begin to supplement objective testing with increasing amounts of short-answer and essay responses.

A simple way to achieve this is to provide students with open-ended questions at the beginning of each unit, grading period, or both. We would then inform them that what they read, write, and learn—from lectures and activities—will directly contribute to their success on short-answer and essay assessments at the end of each unit.

As we teach, we would call attention to these questions and show students how to organize their notes, readings, and other materials to facilitate success on the written exams. These short, frequent assessments would be designed to provide practice for the longer summative—and state—assessments.

Together, such assessments would lend purpose to daily instruction and would have far more academic and intellectual benefits. We could make the transition to such exams by gradually increasing the written component as we become comfortable—and faster at— scoring such assessments.

To ease the burden of scoring, such exams could be conducted in stages, even over several days, as would be done with any written assignment. And even if we graded them in a cursory, imperfect manner, the academic benefits of such tests would far surpass the meager benefits of multiple-choice testing. Both the preparation for such tests and the actual test itself are indisputably "educative"—a seamless extension of learning itself.

In conclusion, all of these benefits could be amplified if these assessments were used as the basis for more extended research/ writing assignments. Students could choose one or more of the open- ended questions from their assessments and supplement the work and writing they have already done with additional sources to pro- duce a two- to five-page paper (depending on grade level). If, from the 3rd grade up, students completed even two such papers per year, it would contribute substantially to their preparation for any kind of college or professional writing tasks in any STEM field. In this case, too, science teachers would not be expected to teach the finer points of writing: that is still the primary province of English language arts.

• • •

I hope this chapter makes clear that we could truly transform sci- ence education—by integrating the teaching of content with simple, powerful literacy, lecture, and science activities. If such a transforma- tion occurs, it will begin with a commitment to creating coherent, teacher-friendly curriculum—and to the same "routine components" of good teaching that apply to every discipline.

Representative Science Learning Objectives

See also the literacy-based learning objectives in Chapter 4.

I can...

- Explain the similarities or differences, or both, between _____ and _____ [e.g., species, phylum].
- Create/Construct _____ to represent _____.
- Design and model a more efficient procedure/process for _____.
- Develop and describe, in writing, a test for refining a product or process.
- Compare and contrast the major subsystems of the human body.
- Rank-order and justify, in writing, five forms of alternative energy.
- Explain, in writing, what I think are the most significant effects of biodiversity—or its degradation.
- Predict, in writing, how I think _____ will affect _____.
- Evaluate the relative effectiveness or potential of ___ [products, innovations, medical discoveries].
- Compare and contrast, in writing, the relative struggles and accomplishments of _____ scientists.
- Demonstrate understanding of _____ with a _____ [graph, illustration, diagram].
- Explain/describe/evaluate/compare and contrast _____ in writing.
- Compare and contrast the challenges faced by two scientists who study the same or similar phenomena.
- Accurately observe, measure, and describe _____ in writing/graphically [e.g., field notes, the effect of an experimental variable].
- Conduct _____ steps of scientific method in an experiment.

7

Making Math Meaningful

It is not yet clear whether the best option for all is the historic algebra-based mainstream.... Teachers need to focus on the interplay of numbers and words, especially on expressing quantitative relationships in meaningful sentences.

—Lynn Steen, former president, Mathematics Association of America

I can no longer imagine teaching math without making writing an integral aspect of students' learning.

—Marilyn Burns

The need for mathematics is *pervasive*. We should want all students to become confident, capable users of math: who know how to apply it to the real world they will enter as citizens, scientists, doctors, engineers, nurses, business owners, salespeople, or accountants; as they create and analyze budgets, calculate the soundness of an investment, buy homes, shop intelligently; and as they make the myriad calculations that life and work require. Students should have abundant opportunities to learn the kind of math they will need to succeed in the most common science, technology, engineering, and mathematics (STEM) careers.

Unfortunately, current math education doesn't address this issue very effectively. In this chapter, I will argue for significant, perhaps long-term, changes to math education that build on the best aspects of the Common Core math guidelines but go beyond it.

But first, I will concentrate on the present—on the most effective, immediate ways to both improve math outcomes *and* make math more enjoyable to learn. These actions will enable record numbers of students to succeed on state assessments, on college entrance exams, and in those K–12 math courses that prepare them for coursework in STEM-related college majors.

Before we examine those actions, let's look at how well—or poorly—our students perform in mathematics. It will reveal a ripe opportunity for improvement.

The Immediate Problem—and Its Solution

More students fail in math than in any other subject (Singham, 2005; Steen, 2007). Failure in math is among the primary causes of high school and college dropout rates. At our community colleges, *more than 75 percent* of students fail their required algebra course; most of those who fail also drop out of college (Hacker, 2012). Students receive *twice as many D*s and *F*s in math as they do in all other subjects (Hacker, 2012). According to Mano Singham (2005), a professor of mathematics education at Case Western Reserve University, math has "the lowest pass rates on proficiency tests for all ethnic groups" (p. 84). In Cleveland, where he lives, only 20 percent of high school students pass the state math exam the first time they take it (p. 15). With the advent of the Common Core math standards (and similarly revised) state assessments, passing rates are now lower than ever (FairTest Examiner, 2013).

What steps can we take to ensure significant, immediate gains in mathematics? Let's start with the most obvious: the implementation of effective, soundly structured lessons.

Effective Instruction: No Longer an Option

Many of you reading this can well remember, as I can, the self-recriminating feelings we had when we simply did not understand what was being taught in certain math classes. By the third or fourth step in the lesson, we realized that we didn't understand the first or second step. We knew this—but the teacher, who typically made no attempt to conduct even the most cursory "check for understanding" as he or she went through the lesson, didn't. The pace of instruction was dictated by the interactions between the teacher and the best math students—who *raised their hands,* were called on, and then praised for their correct answers. Then it was on to the next step, with the rest of us falling further behind by the minute.

I continue to observe these practices in hundreds of math lessons in dozens of states representing every socioeconomic level. This is essentially how math is taught in America. And it accounts for much of the failure we see in math classes.

To change this, we need to provide in-depth professional development in sound instruction to every math teacher: on how to write clear learning objectives (some representative learning objectives for math are provided at the end of this chapter); on how to teach in *small* instructional chunks; on how to follow each chunk with an immediate opportunity for students to practice that one small step— as the teacher circulates to check on student progress; and on how to modify instruction if needed (*as it often will be*).

Such instruction changes everything. The effect of such lessons—as we saw in Chapter 3—is among the very most powerful, proven interventions, *especially in math.* It appreciably increases both the number of students who would succeed in math and the speed at which they would learn it. These practices would vault U.S. math achievement from the about 18th to 5th place on international math assessments (Wiliam, 2007, p. 189). In view of such evidence, it is unconscionable to withhold these practices from students who would so clearly benefit from them. And it is foolish to think that the right kind of explicit instruction conflicts with the Common Core.

Explicit Instruction *and* Practical, Conceptually Based Math Instruction

We should disabuse ourselves of the recent misconception that such step-by-step instruction is at odds with the Common Core's sensible emphasis on letting students "struggle" or "persist" without undue intervention as they try to solve complex problems. Common sense dictates that such opportunities must alternate with or be preceded by explicit instruction that abets their success on messier, more complex problems. And it should be just as obvious that letting students struggle is itself a form of "guided practice," but it must be accompanied by checks for understanding—and additional guidance when necessary. That is, if students are struggling for an extended time *without producing visible evidence of progress,* we plainly need to adjust and scaffold instruction appropriately—and then let them struggle (practice) once again. There is no conflict here.

Troy Preparatory School, mentioned in Chapter 3, offers a timely case. In 2011, the statewide passing rate in math for high-poverty schools was 40 percent. But at Troy Preparatory, a member of Doug Lemov's school network, the math passing rate was 100 percent—the result of the school's emphasis on explicit teaching practices similar to those just described (Lemov, 2015, p. 24).

So what happened when the new Common Core math tests were administered? According to some Common Core advocates, Lemov's model is the outdated antithesis to the more rigorous, conceptual nature of the new standards. But that's not the case at all: the first year of Common Core testing, the New York state passing rate in math plummeted to 28 percent. But at Troy, it was 74 percent—two and a half times the success rate for high-poverty schools.

Proper amounts of explicit instruction do not conflict with—and are vital to success in—Common Core, project-based learning, or independent learning. When will we learn this?

If all teachers implemented such instruction, the effect would be profound—and often immediate—within the first year of implementation. This would be especially probable if such instruction were accompanied by frequent opportunities to read and write as we administer a coherent, agreed-upon curriculum.

The Interplay of Numbers and Words

The late Lynn Steen was among the wisest and most widely-respected mathematicians of our time. He was president of the Mathematics Association of America and chairman of the Conference Board of the Mathematical Sciences. In Part II of this chapter, I will expand on his critique of the algebra-to-calculus sequence that dominates high school and college mathematics.

For now, consider the case he made for educators to liberally incorporate language into math education. According to Steen and the legion of mathematicians he influenced, reading and writing are just as important to quantitative education as numbers and algorithms. As he put it, "to make mathematics meaningful, the three *R*s must be well blended in each student's mind" (Steen, 2007, p. 194). This not only makes math meaningful, as we'll see, it *raises test scores considerably.*

According to Steen, reading and writing—the first two *R*s—are the missing key to better math education. Deep, practical learning depends upon the reciprocal "interplay of numbers and words, especially on expressing quantitative relationships in meaningful sentences" (Steen, 2007, p. 10). To prepare citizens and workers, both language and numbers must be interpreted and applied to "serve human purposes" (p. 10). Students need frequent opportunities to express their quantitative interpretations in arguments, reports, and proposals. Such *literate/mathematical thinkers* are precisely what employers seek—those who can read, speak, and write for practical purposes "in the natural and social sciences" (Steen, 2007, p. 11).

And we need not worry about incorporating language at the expense of higher test scores. The new breed of state and Common Core math tests incorporate far more word problems, reading, and writing into test items than ever. Moreover, recent evidence points to the advantages of giving concrete word problems priority over abstract equations. Historically, word problems were introduced only after students had learned how to solve equations. In fact, word problems should be the primary means by which we introduce formulas and algorithms, wherever possible.

In a University of Wisconsin study, two groups of students were compared: for one, word problems were the primary mode of instruction; for the other, equations. In the word problem group, 91 percent of students succeeded on the assessment; in the group taught with equations, only 62 percent did. The researchers found that "word problems provide powerful, informal problem-solving strategies, and language itself provides an entry point to mathematical reasoning that is *highly superior to the algebraic equation.*" When will we learn? "Word problems," the study concludes, "should be given *at the start* of the lesson" (Sparks, 2014; emphasis added).

Language is the "clothing" of thought—including mathematical thought. This is particularly true of mathematical argumentation.

Quantitative Arguments

Math is a marvel of order and elegance. But its primary purpose, wrote Lynn Steen (2007), is to help us make and dismantle oral and written "quantitative or logical arguments." These arguments touch on every aspect of our lives: "Virtually every subject taught in school is amenable to some use of quantitative or logical arguments that tie evidence to conclusions" (p. 12).

Our ability to interpret, analyze, and calculate—in the service of argument—helps us more effectively weigh, convey, and synthesize demographic factors; vote intelligently and understand election data; effectively market goods and services; gauge two nations' comparative social or economic health; make predictions; evaluate campaign pledges; or take intelligent risks on a business, a stock—or a professional athlete. We need numbers to make and monitor intelligent budgets, determine how much economic pain we can sustain as we attempt to reduce greenhouse gases, predict future employment needs, assess actuarial factors on insurance benefits, and calculate dosages for medical treatments and pharmaceuticals.

These common, practical "word problems" and applications require certain amounts of algebra-based mathematics. But they depend just as much on our ability to skillfully read, write, articulate, interpret, and explain quantities, percentages, ratios, charts, and trends.

Whenever we can, we should teach math through such real-world, language-rich applications. Data, in a variety of forms, can provide engaging opportunities for mathematical analysis and argumentation. Students could be asked to make inferences and arguments for questions such as the following, with multiple data points provided for each:

• Using multiple data sources, which of five companies or stocks appears to be healthiest in the short or long term? Rank-order from best to worst, with clear written explanations.

• Which country appears to get the most value from its health care system? In making your argument, take cost, mortality rates, waiting periods for health services, and so forth into account. Write a report defending your conclusions.

• After reviewing tables of statistics on profits and production costs for the most popular movies, write an explanation for which movie genre (e.g., horror, drama, action) appears to be the best investment.

These instructions could be converted easily into simple, versatile "I can" statements that integrate numbers and language, such as "I can read/review/analyze _____ in order to argue/explain/model/demonstrate/interpret _____ in writing."

Authentic "word problems" like these would excite interest and engagement in mathematics. And such math "texts" lend themselves to what the Common Core calls "modeling": the creative employment of (usually several) equations and calculations to solve mathematical problems. We'll focus on modeling, and many more examples follow.

Professional learning community (PLC) teams can help each other to build up their collections of such texts and scenarios—perhaps in consultation with working professionals in the community. Such resources are a great way to get students reading, analyzing, and then developing their own quantitative arguments, graphs, and written explanations in ways that transfer readily to the modern workplace.

It all begins with reading—with teaching students how to tackle math and related texts successfully.

Close, "Slow" Reading in Math: The Textbook

In Chapters 5 and 6, we looked at Shanahan and Shanahan's (2008) two-year study on the use and value of textbooks. As mentioned, they recommend reiterative reading in all subjects. The Shanahans found that mathematical text must be read most carefully of all. Math procedures, explanations, and story problems must always be read slowly and repeatedly—and never for mere "gist or general idea." The meaning in math text often pivots on a single word; in many word problems, inattention to the distinction between "a" and "the" will result in miscalculation. They note that the ideas and operations in a math text or story problem "require a precision of meaning and each word must be understood specifically in service to that particular meaning" (p. 49). Or as Braselton and Decker (1994) write,

> Mathematics is the most difficult content area material to read because there are more concepts per word, per sentence, and per paragraph than in any other subject; the mixture of words, numerals, letters, symbols, and graphics requires the reader to shift from one type of vocabulary to another. (p. 276)

I am looking at an elementary grade word problem for which students are to interpret a Venn diagram that represents polling data. Only after I read the story problem twice, and then slowly reread certain phrases, did it become clear to me that the correct answer hinges on the use of the single word "might" (as opposed to "is"; the diagram reveals that certain individuals in the poll might [or might not] belong in both polling categories).

If I were teaching students how to read such text, they would need to hear my thought processes as I read such a problem—out loud, to see where I would choose to reread the text, where I became puzzled, and how, even as an adult, I still read such dense text very methodically to reach a solution.

The average student simply isn't sensitive to language at this level of precision. They don't readily employ such slow or repeated reading strategies to acquire meaning. To ensure that they acquire these habits, we must model such reading on a frequent basis.

Let's look at an example of such close reading—one that will both increase conceptual and real-world understanding and also raise math scores.

Teaching the First *R* in Math: Reading

Arthur Hyde is a professor of mathematics education at National Louis University. He is convinced that dramatic improvement will occur in all schools when we embrace an "essential change": we must put close, word-by-word "reading comprehension" lessons at the center of math instruction (Hyde, 2007, p. 44). Math educators must redouble their efforts to "infuse language and thought into mathematics" (p. 46).

Let's look at his simple example of how he and his K–8 teaching partners achieved dramatic success on open-ended, extended-response, and word problems.

The 2nd grade lesson begins like any good reading lesson, with the teacher providing real-world context for the problem and a review of potentially unfamiliar words that might impede understanding of the text (in this lesson, the word "freight").

In the next step, the teacher posts the word problem on the overhead projector. She then guides students through a carefully scaffolded, *sentence-by-sentence analysis* of the problem, as she models how she would analyze and then develop equations derived from her reading of the text. This would be followed by students' attempts to do the same as they engage in "guided practice." For each sentence, she has students read it and then write their thoughts and equations as she circulates, stopping the lesson when necessary to reteach or guide their reading, writing, and problem-solving efforts. This is precisely the kind of "interplay of numbers and words" that makes math meaningful (Steen, 2007, p. 10). It is not unlike the line-by-line treatment we would devote to a poem or to the Declaration of Independence.

In this way, Hyde (2007) and his K–8 teachers have been able to get 2nd grade students to succeed on complex, multistep math problems that most would deem too challenging for 2nd graders. As a result of such "adapted reading comprehension strategies," performance in math at this school "improved dramatically"—once again, in a single school year (p. 45).

Such teacher-directed, whole-class approaches have been shown to work with students at all levels in Singapore for students "who perform on, above, or below grade level" (Hoven & Garelick, 2007, p. 30).

Such instruction could and should be followed by opportunities to more independently apply these analytic skills to a different situation—to purposefully "struggle" and "persist" (as the Common Core recommends) with a different text or situation alone or with peers, *using the tools they have now acquired from the more explicit teaching and modeling* just described. These skills won't be learned by most students if we ignore the need for explicit instruction in this scheme.

The second *R*—writing—is just as critical, as we saw in Arthur Hyde's classroom. We must be mindful that writing is not only a form of communication, but is perhaps our best tool for problem solving, in math as in all areas.

The Second *R* in Math: Writing

It is unfortunate that so many teachers leave our teacher preparation programs without learning that writing is arguably the most powerful form of thinking, clarifying, and problem solving in any subject. Multiple scholars concur with Ted Sizer's observation that "writing is the litmus paper of thought" and should therefore be "the very center of schooling" (Schmoker, 2006, p. 61).

The act of writing allows us to grasp conceptual relationships, to acquire insights, and to unravel the logic of what was previously murky or confusing. When students must explain or evaluate a solution or algorithm in writing, they achieve a deeper understanding of its meaning and application.

The effects of writing on learning and problem solving can be dramatic—and immediate. In one middle school, 186 students were given multiple opportunities to explain and problem solve—in writing— as they learned math concepts (Zollman, 2009). As a result, the percentage of students who met or exceeded performance standards on the state assessment rose in three areas:

- In math knowledge, from 4 to 75 percent
- In strategic knowledge, from 19 to 68 percent
- On math explanations, from 8 to 68 percent

As the author writes, "good teaching in reading and writing is good teaching in math" (p. 11). And as Steen (2007) pointed out, employers will always "seek graduates who can interpret data... and can communicate effectively about quantitative topics." Therefore, he writes,

K–12 students need extensive practice *expressing verbally* the quantitative meanings of both problems and solutions. They need to be able to *write fluently in complete sentences and coherent paragraphs*; to explain the meaning of data, tables, graphs and formulas, and *explain their reasoning*. (p. 12; emphasis added)

Unfortunately, K–12 students rarely get such "extensive practice" in these critical skills. As a result, college students in the natural and social sciences have a hard time "expressing in precise English the meaning of data presented in tables and graphs." From the earliest grades, students need far more opportunities to write and thus develop "quantitative arguments" on topics like global warming, health care, or teen smoking (Steen, 2007, p. 12).

Writing may be the most vital missing ingredient in current math education. As math expert Marilyn Burns (2004) writes, "I can no longer imagine teaching math without making writing an integral aspect of students' learning" because it "requires students to organize, clarify, and reflect on their [mathematical] ideas" (p. 30). There are plenty of simple ways to write in math. All of them exercise students' mathematical reasoning capacities and the ability to give verbal form to numbers and equations. Tim Kanold, mentioned in Chapter 3, is a math textbook author and former superintendent of Adlai Stevenson High School. At Stevenson, students were given credit for incorrect answers on their tests if they could explain, in writing, why their answer was wrong and why the correct answer is right.

To deepen conceptual understanding, Marilyn Burns (2004) has students write explanations and descriptions for any math concept they are taught. She has 3rd graders write an explanation for concepts such as "equally likely"; 4th graders are asked to write about how multiplication and division are similar and different; 5th graders are asked to *write short essays* on the topic of "What I Know About Fractions So Far" (p. 32).

Burns (2004) provides another simple, all-purpose writing strategy: give students regular opportunities to explain why one answer or approach to a math problem is superior to another. She suggests a simple prompt with endless applications at any grade level (p. 33):

- I think that the answer is _____.
- I think that because _____.
- I figured this out by _____.

Such exercises should become routine components of math curriculum. I wish my daughters could have done such writing in their math courses. I wish they had learned fewer algorithms but more about how, in Steen's (2007) words, to "write fluently... explain their reasoning [and]... communicate effectively about quantitative topics" (p. 12).

Reading and writing—the first two *Rs*—are essential for success in math. But neither of them can be implemented in an overcrowded curriculum. This brings us to the third large factor that could have significant and immediate effects on math achievement.

Coherent Curriculum—Less Is More

As we saw in Chapter 2 (and in every chapter since), the implementation of an agreed-upon, "viable" curriculum may have more impact on achievement than any other factor. There's a ripe opportunity here—because very few schools currently implement such a curriculum (Berliner, 1984; DuFour & Marzano, 2011; Hirsch, 2016).

Stanford's James Milgram is convinced that the "unbelievable success" of the highest-achieving countries in math can be directly attributed to the severely limited number of math topics they allow in their curriculum (Milgram in De Vise, 2006). In Chapter 2, we saw schools that significantly reduced their math standards—and saw dramatic increases in achievement as a result (Hammond, 2009, p. 1; Landsberg, 2008a; Leinwand & Ginsburg, 2007).

For decades, mathematics professor William Schmidt (2008) has been at the forefront of efforts to reduce the number of U.S. educational standards and to teach them more meaningfully. Good standards, he writes, "need to focus on a small enough number of topics so that teachers can spend *months, not days,* on them" (p. 22; emphasis added). Right now, the U.S. penchant for packing each grade level with excessive, overlapping topics makes that impossible. As Schmidt once wrote, "everything is covered everywhere" (p. 23). This profusion of standards forces each teacher to make ad hoc selections from their standards documents, which eventuates in a curricular disaster, that is "great variability among courses with the same title" (p. 24).

To address this, Chapter 2 describes a simple process for selecting only the most essential standards for inclusion in the curriculum, along with evidence that any good-faith, collective attempt to do this will add quality and increase test scores—significantly, usually within a single school year. Moreover, when we reduce standards, we increase the odds of having a "guaranteed and viable curriculum"—one that allows for sufficient depth and that will *actually be taught.*

The following process is explained in more detail in Chapter 2. To recap that process for math: school or district course-alike teams could:

- Determine the approximate number of days you have to *actually teach* the math curriculum (minus days for testing, assemblies, and so forth).
- Review state or national mathematics standards documents, or both, for each specific course—and approximate, in pencil, how many days it would take to adequately teach each one.
- Add up the number of days. If the total exceeds the number you have to teach (and it often will), you will need to discuss, then thoughtfully subtract topics and standards until you achieve "viability"—at least an approximate match between the skills and topics you want to teach and the number of days you have to teach them.

When this is completed,

- Apportion the topics by week or grading period, with due consideration for holidays and other interruptions on the school calendar. Write these topics in a column on your curriculum document.
- Begin selecting and matching textbook pages/instructional materials to math topics; place these in a column adjacent to the topics.

When these steps are completed, the curriculum document is ready for use (but always subject to adjustment) as the basis for the team to create common units and lessons together.

These procedures should furnish the course-alike team with a working math curriculum with which to begin creating daily lessons. Blank templates for building such curriculum are available in Schmoker (2016) and online at www.ascd.org/ASCD/pdf/books/SchmokerAppendixB.pdf.

A few years ago, my wife's high school math department took deliberate steps to select and agree upon only the most essential math topics, determine the amount of time to devote to each, and then identify common textbook pages to optimize student success. At the end of two years, the school received an award for being among three schools in the state with the largest math gains. Such achievements attest to the "incredible success" we might have if we intelligently reduced and then focused our instruction on the most essential math standards (Milgram in De Vise, 2006).

Which brings us to the Common Core—or similarly revised state math standards (in non–Common Core states). We would expect them to reflect the need for fewer standards and greater emphasis on conceptual understanding and application. But do they?

Common Core Math: The "Good, the Bad, and the Ugly"

The Common Core got some things right. Its architects set out to create standards that were fewer, clearer, and more applicable to the real world. Indeed, there appears to be a reduction of standards at the elementary level and a new emphasis on conceptual understanding, application, and the integration of language into the math curriculum. And the eight "Math Practices" that accompany the standards do reinforce these new emphases.

But problems remain. In describing the "good, the bad, and the ugly" aspects of the Common Core math documents, Jennifer Bay-Williams (2016) of the (decidedly pro–Common Core) Fordham Institute writes that the new standards "have also had some regrettable collateral consequences" (p. 1). Though there appears to be a reduction in the number of standards at the elementary and middle school level, the eight "Math Practices" complicate both curriculum and instruction. Despite their merits, the eight practices are lengthy, ambiguous, and overlapping. Each disquisition on the eight practices is packed with (often murky) details. And the document is particularly deficient in clarifying how and when these practices should be applied—and to which grade-level standards. I was struck by this the first time I read them—and reread them. There is, writes Bay-Williams (2016),

> little guidance on which problem-solving strategies to prioritize, how many might be appropriate for a particular topic and (most importantly) *why* students benefit from knowing more than one approach. (p. 1)

In view of the prominence given this document, it is inevitable that it will override—and thus postpone—the more critical, consequential task of organizing a coherent curriculum. It is just as inevitable that many teachers will apply the practices haphazardly or inappropriately. Either way, the intent of the new standards is compromised.

· To give you a sense of this: I've observed so-called "model lessons" by earnest, "Common Core–trained" instructional coaches in districts where the eight practices were strongly emphasized. Most of these lessons were pure chaos. They abound in buzzwords and activities supposedly derived from the math standards and practices. In such lessons, a misappropriation of the "math practices" overrode the teacher's concern with any attempt to *monitor student progress during each phase of instruction.* Letting students "struggle" (which is essential, in proper proportion) often gave way to overlong, confusing instructional segments, with most students desperate for guidance they never got. At the end of the lessons, when students were asked to complete problems independently, hands flew up everywhere—no one knew how to complete the assignment. But the teachers were able to get around to only a few students before the bell rang. This is what happens when standards documents are launched prematurely—before being properly vetted for clarity—or piloted and then refined.

Don't take my word for it. I interviewed William McCallum, the lead writer for the Common Core math standards and the eight practices. He could not have been more kind or candid. He believes that the elementary standards were indeed reduced, as promised, and that they do more than previous standards to promote conceptual understanding (I see evidence of this myself).

But McCallum agreed with me that despite their merits, the eight practices are still bloated and ambiguous. I read several portions of the math practices out loud to him, as I asked a simple question: would the average practitioner understand this language? He not only shared my perception that they wouldn't, he chuckled along with me as I read to him. And he confirmed my suspicion: that the committee members fiercely resisted attempts to change the language or remove topics from the final document.

So: large problems remain with regard to the eight practices, at all levels. But what of math education at the high school level—the traditional algebra-to-calculus sequence that purportedly aims to prepare students for the academic and working world? Did the Common Core achieve their goals in high school?

They did not.

High School Standards

I got an inkling of this when my wife, a high school math teacher, told me that she and her colleagues saw no evidence of a reduction of high school standards. When I shared this with McCallum, he agreed: there was no reduction. "Algebra is algebra," he told me.

This is a profound problem. As we saw in Chapter 3, math leaders like William Schmidt campaigned for significant reductions in the number of standards taught at every level. Schmidt (2008) urged U.S. math educators to "focus on a small enough number of topics so that teachers can spend *months, not days,* on them" (p. 22; emphasis added). People like Schmidt and Stanford's James Milgram (in De Vise, 2006) called our attention to countries whose world-class math achievement was a result of teaching about half as many standards.

At the high school level, Common Core math, by its own logic and criteria, failed. It has made it more, not less, difficult to integrate conceptual understanding and application into the high school curriculum.

For all this, we still have the opportunity to significantly increase math achievement, right now, by focusing on the practices already described here. We should begin by building a coherent curriculum calendar for every math course, all of which ensures that instructors of the same course teach only the most essential standards and topics for about the same amount of time and thus prevent the "great variability among [math] courses with the same title" (Schmidt, 2008, p. 24). It would also *make time* for teachers to enrich math instruction with additional opportunities for students to engage in real-world mathematical modeling that integrates reading, writing, and quantitative arguments into problem solving.

Lastly, all math teachers must implement the essential elements of sound instruction consistently. Rightly understood, these elements apply directly to the best kind of complex, application-based mathematical modeling and problem-solving—inclusive of regular opportunities for students to "struggle" and "persevere" as they work on conceptual and real-world problems. As we've seen, the combination of effective curriculum, literacy integration, and soundly structured lessons all but guarantees significant gains on any kind of test, especially in mathematics (Wiliam, 2007).

But let's now focus on the possibilities of mathematical modeling itself, which is prominently emphasized in several of the math practices. In correct measure, it may have more impact on authentic math ability than anything else we do.

Modeling

In modeling, math meets the real world. In the "Eight Math Practices" of the Common Core, we are told that modeling allows students to "apply the mathematics they know to solve problems in everyday life, society, and the workplace." It enables students to "identify important quantities in a practical situation and map their relationships [by] using various tools."

In an article on math modeling in *Education Week,* Liana Heitin cites several experts, including William McCallum, who appear to define it simply as the application of mathematics to actual situations, using any combination of equations, calculations, measurements, or visual representations. Such "modeling" is especially helpful for those "big messy problems [which] tend to have multiple entry points and no single right answer" (Heitin, 2015). But as Heitin points out, such modeling is "unlike much of what students learn in math class."

We have to hope that will change. Let's now look at some examples of such real-world, complex situations that lend themselves to mathematical modeling and would convince students that math matters.

Not long ago, my brother and I tackled just such a complex situation: he had to make a decision about whether he should buy or rent office space for his small business. To make this decision, we had to consider the following data, some of them estimates and projections—and all surrounded with language: with conversation about the amount he currently paid in annual rent; the estimated increase in rent over a 15-year period; the down payment and other purchasing costs for the office he intended to buy; comparative square footage; the annual mortgage payments and the number of years he would be making these payments; the estimated amount he could charge others to rent space from him (and the approximate number of months per year that he could assume this rental space would be occupied); the tax advantages of buying versus renting office space; and estimated projections of current and future real estate values (which were rising). All of these data were used as we deliberated, estimated, wrote, and calculated our way toward a solution.

We were "modeling"—solving a complicated, multistep, real-world problem, with both of us thinking, talking, scribbling, and calculating—with calculators—until we felt we could make a wise decision (he did buy the office building). The point here is that such "mathematical modeling" (by this or any other name) is engaging, hugely practical—and crucial to a student's education.

Do students learn to do—or get much practice doing—such modeling in their math classes? Not even close. Both of my daughters did well in math and took advanced math courses in high school and college. One day I discovered that one of them, despite her high grades in high school math, didn't know where to begin to tackle real-world problems; she had never been asked to do so—or shown how. As Heitin (2015) points out, such modeling is "unlike much of what students learn in math class."

We can change this. Math educators can regularly integrate real-world problems and scenarios like the following into every math course, starting with simple problems in the early grades. And we might also notice that these don't require much algebra or advanced algebra. They do require imaginative combinations of arithmetic, estimation—and some algebra (especially ratios and proportions).

• The class wants to buy pizza for a class party. Determine which pizza restaurant would offer the best value by comparing cost, size of pizzas, and distance from school (Heitin, 2015).

• Create a realistic budget based on your weekly allowance or a defined annual income with regard for present and future needs and desired purchases.

• You want to buy a new bicycle. To decide which one, compare different bikes for cost and (numerical) quality ratings per your criteria. Determine which bike is the best value for the money within various budget categories ($100–$200; $300–$500).

• After deciding on approximate amounts of space you need for a home, yard, and garage, calculate and then record on graph paper how you will optimize the space available on your 0.4-acre lot.

• For various scenarios, decide—and defend, in writing—why a pie, scatterplot, or bar chart would be most effective or accurate in communicating data on _____.

• Make data-based arguments for or against minimum wage, forms of alternative energy, the North American Free Trade Agreement (NAFTA), and so forth. (See ProCon.org for data.)

• Write an argument for which cell phone plan/college/ insurance policy/car is the best value, on the basis of the data.

• Using actuarial tables and statistics on three individuals, defend, in writing, the best age for each of them to collect Social Security.

• Pick and explain, in writing, which of five players you would like to contract for your professional team, on the basis of the following data: team salary cap, player's age, history of injuries, performance statistics, and so forth.

• What would have been the best strategy for Hillary Clinton to have won the 2016 election for president? For example, which states and counties would have given her the maximum number of votes in the minimum number of campaign stops? Examine data on polling, electoral votes, demographics, and party affiliation within states/counties.

• Make an argument for which country has the highest quality of life—the United States or _____ (e.g., Canada, Finland, United Kingdom). Make your argument on the basis of taxes, average household income, health costs, hours worked per year, and so forth (adapted from Hacker, 2016, p. 201).

• Rank-order the cost-effectiveness of several charities on the basis of selected criteria (lives saved, people cured of debilitating diseases, people brought out of poverty, etc.). Explain your rankings in writing.

• Write a rough business plan that reflects analysis of data for critical factors (e.g., demand for your product/service, rent/overhead, estimated income, anticipated profit margin, labor costs).

• Decide which job you would accept among several options—on the basis of any or all of the following: initial salary, local cost of living, cost/length of commute, benefits, estimated increases in salary, or other factors.

• Write an explanation for why you should or should not remodel a house—or which rooms you would remodel—before selling it. Consider current home value, expense of remodeling, projected added value, value of other homes in the neighborhood, and so forth.

These are only suggestions. Teams of teachers could develop and refine better tasks and problems than these. They could be aligned, wherever possible, with quantitative occupations such as accounting, finance, bookkeeping, real estate, architecture, engineering, catering, construction, supply chain management, event planning, project management, banking, and purchasing/inventory control. In this way, we could help students to discover their hidden aptitudes and give them a taste of possible future occupations. If such activities were conducted even every week or two, students would acquire unprecedented amounts of real-world math proficiency.

New Hampshire has built a large component of such activities into their curriculum—and their state assessments. Students are asked to do modeling for tasks such as designing a water tower—which requires them to "draw models, do calculations, analyze results and write a proposal all in one exercise" (Cavazos, 2016). One New Hampshire teacher claims he's never seen students so focused while they're taking such tests: "When you give kids a real-world problem," he enthused, "they get incredibly motivated. If you walked into my room, during PACE [the state test], you could hear a pin drop" (Cavazos, 2016).

• • •

As we've seen, there is a strong case for judiciously reducing the number of mathematics standards, for more language-rich math instruction, and for additional modeling. Combined with effective instruction, these changes would result in more meaningful math education *and* in higher test scores—especially on the new breed of state math assessments. This may be more than enough to ponder for many math educators, for now. If you are among them, you may not need to read the rest of this chapter.

But there is also a case for even more profound—and controversial—changes to math education. They would go beyond, but build on, the best aspects of the Common Core. The last part of this chapter will explore the case for such a shift in greater depth. Some find this case unpersuasive. But others contend that it would repair a "failed math curriculum" and prepare record numbers of students for the real-world mathematical demands of the future. According to one mathematician, such changes could make the United States a model for the world (Wolfram, 2010). The remainder of this chapter is for those who are intrigued by this possibility.

Making Math *More* Meaningful

Today's mathematics classrooms stress skills that few students will use while neglecting skills that employers really need.
— Arnold Packer, former U.S. assistant secretary of Labor

A Call for Change

As we saw earlier, more students struggle with and fail in mathematics than any other subject—at both the high school and college levels. This contributes significantly to high dropout rates (Singham, 2005; Steen, 2007). And so we might ask: to what extent does this academic pain translate into real-world gain—or success in STEM careers?

Answers are emerging. I've interviewed dozens of people who completed advanced mathematics in high school and college. This group includes nurses; doctors; tradespeople; scientists; and numerous mechanical, electrical, and aerospace engineers. They worked at nuclear power plants, laboratories, factories, hospitals, observatories, and engineering firms. All of them expended enormous amounts of time and energy completing the algebra-to-calculus course sequence that has predominated for more than a century (Furr, 1996). Yet nearly all of them were emphatic in telling me that they rarely used algebra-based mathematics in their work. Practical, applied arithmetic and statistics play a much larger role in their daily work—which conventional math coursework (as we've seen) doesn't emphasize.

What does this mean for math educators, especially at the secondary level? With a little probing, countless teachers have told me that they would love to tell their students how the required math standards apply to the real world—but they usually can't. As the late Lynn Steen (in Hacker, 2016) pointed out,

> mathematics teachers simply do not know much about how mathematics is used by people other than mathematicians. (p. 40)

Are textbooks helpful here? I recently examined the "application" portions of each unit for two popular high school algebra texts. The great majority were preposterously abstract and contrived. Despite the slick photos and catchy headings like "Music" or "Sports," none of the examples would apply to the actual work of any musician or athlete. As writer Nicholson Baker (2013) discovered, one of the most widely used Common Core algebra books is as abstract as its old-school predecessors—and almost devoid of real-world applications. This shouldn't surprise us: as we saw, the Common Core architects were wholly unsuccessful in reducing the sheer number of required standards at the high school level, which left less room for application (Heitin, 2016).

For these and similar reasons, a legion of mathematicians, scientists, math educators, economic experts, and working professionals have begun to call for changes to secondary and college-level mathematics. The case for such changes has expanded significantly since I wrote the first edition of this book.

A Math-Work Mismatch?

Andrew Hacker is a professor at New York University and a *New York Times* best-selling author. For his 2016 book, *The Math Myth*, Hacker interviewed multiple world-class scientists. E. O. Wilson, who is perhaps our greatest living biologist, told Hacker that he has never used algebra-based mathematics in his work. According to Wilson, "Many of the most successful scientists in the world today are mathematically no more than semiliterate." Darwin, he pointed out, "had no talent for mathematics" (Hacker, 2016, p. 54).

Avi Loeb chairs the astrophysics department at Harvard. He informed Hacker that numbers are enormously important in science—but that his field relies predominantly on arithmetic and statistics (Hacker, 2016, p. 55).

Stanford's Carl Wieman is a Nobel Prize–winning physicist. But scientists, he points out, "use more sophisticated mathematics less and less" (Hacker, 2016, p. 55). Hacker also interviewed the chief engineer on the Mars Rover project. He told Hacker that he flunked geometry twice; his teacher gave him an *F+* just to move him along

(p. 61). As we'll see, the link between engineering and advanced mathematics is more tenuous than many admit (Hacker, 2016, pp. 52–54).

Math professor David Edwards at the University of Georgia teaches advanced math courses required for a degree in computer science. When recruiters from a software company visited his campus, he sought them out to ask, "What mathematics do you actually use?" After a moment, they "sheepishly responded, 'None'" (Hacker, 2016, p. 50).

Hacker's book features dozens of similar interviews with people in the most representative STEM careers, whose training included the claim that they needed advanced, algebra-based math to succeed in their employment. But as he demonstrates, their work required little or no advanced math—though it did require a sophisticated facility with applied arithmetic and statistics.

We'll hear from numerous others whose work supports Hacker's general findings. But first, let's hear from his critics.

Hacker's Critics

Hacker has some prominent critics. But their criticisms are revelatory. For though they claim he is misguided, that he underestimates the importance of algebra-based mathematics, they appear to affirm his central contentions.

In *Scientific American,* mathematician Evelyn Lamb (2016) claims that Hacker's case against algebra is overblown. Yet she concedes that "Hacker's conclusions aren't entirely without merit" and concurs with him that math, as currently taught, "fails to show the relevance of mathematics to the real world." She even laments how high school and college math has evolved into "a straight line to calculus"—in which the primary objective is not how to use or apply math but merely how to pass these grueling, abstract courses. Her piece concludes with a strong recommendation against requiring algebra-based math for students entering professions in which they will not use it—which is the majority of STEM careers (Lamb, 2016).

From my reading, Lamb's conclusions precisely represent the essence of Hacker's argument.

A. K. Whitney, writing for *The Atlantic,* also disagrees with Hacker, describing the "joy later in life" of mastering algebra, of discovering how it "does apply" to our knowledge of compound interest, credit cards, and the dangers of variable-rate mortgages (Whitney, 2016). Fair enough: but Hacker himself explicitly advocates for teaching the algebra that truly applies to life and work. And even his harshest critics admit that it is seldom taught in this manner. This brings us to one of Hacker's most formidable critics.

Keith Devlin—Time for a "Major Makeover"

Stanford mathematician Keith Devlin is well known as National Public Radio's "math guy." He too believes Hacker—a nonmathematician—is out of his depth and misunderstands algebra. He mentions three examples of how he himself has applied algebra to real-world problems. But his examples are revealing: they are so exotic that only a small percentage of world-class experts—like Devlin himself—would ever have the opportunity to work on such tasks.

But the most interesting part of Devlin's (2016) comments is his concession that algebra-based mathematics instruction does not apply to the real world. His take on high school and college algebra instruction is scathing: it has become a "meaningless game with arbitrary rules that *does more harm than good.*" He writes that "the subject now taught in schools under the name of algebra is a travesty." He speaks of the "negative effect [high school math coursework] has had on generations of school students" and the "antipathy this has generated." For Devlin, no less than a "a major makeover of 'school algebra'" is in order. More radical still, this makeover would replace most of the "formulas and symbolic equations" with an unprecedented focus on real-world problems.

Most interesting of all: Devlin (2016) is convinced that there is "massive support" among the mathematics community for such a makeover.

You need not agree with Hacker's critique in its entirety. But if we acted on only the aspects of his work *on which he and his critics agree,* it would constitute a "major makeover" of math education in America. There appears to be a groundswell of support for this among mathematicians. The chancellor and administration of the California Community Colleges System—the largest in the United States—is now calling for an end to the requirement that non-STEM majors (*about 75 percent of its student body*) take college algebra. They want to replace the requirement with statistics or applied mathematics (Watanabe & Xia, 2017). The California State University system is now seriously considering the removal of this requirement for students wishing to transfer to four-year programs (Xia & Watanabe, 2017).

And for what it's worth: I recently spoke at the National Council of Supervisors of Mathematics conference. When asked about these issues, the great majority of the audience expressed a desire to significantly reorient math education toward authentic, applied mathematics.

Why? Because of the growing evidence of a mismatch between math education and the working world, which we've already touched on. Let's now look more closely at the case for what Devlin (2016) calls a "major makeover"—and hear from a larger sample of educators, mathematicians, and economists who are also calling for it. I don't think math education will change until enough of us have an encounter with this evidence.

The Case for a "Major Makeover"

In the first edition of this book, I cited Lynn Steen (2007), the former president of the Mathematics Association of America, who was among the first to question whether the "historic algebra-based mainstream" should be taught to all students. I also shared the findings of a lengthy *Education Week* report on the patent mismatch between high school math and the math that is needed in the workplace. Cavanagh (2007) found that 80 percent of the workforce, including those in the highest-paying, most prestigious careers, would *never use anything beyond addition, subtraction, multiplication, and division; that only 5 percent of the workforce* makes use of *any* math beyond Algebra II.

More recently, the Georgetown University Center on Education and the Workforce similarly affirmed that only about 5 percent of employees would ever use advanced mathematics in their careers (Hacker, 2016, p. 29). This is why Evelyn Lamb (2016) and others can't understand why algebra-based coursework is required to complete programs in medical, managerial, or actuarial professions.

Nor can Tara Holm, a Massachusetts Institute of Technology (MIT)–trained mathematics professor at Cornell. She writes, "It is time to re-evaluate the single-file death march that leads to calculus"—because the traditional regimen rarely allows students to learn how math applies to workplace problems and tasks (Holm, 2015).

Another Cornell mathematician, Steven Strogatz, would like to see the amount of math significantly diminished—to make *more room for application.* Echoing Keith Devlin, he is convinced that there is a "silent majority" of math educators who agree on the need for such changes (Baker, 2013).

This incongruity is present in even the most prestigious institutions. Kristen Wolfe, an MIT graduate, did her thesis on "Understanding the Careers of the Alumni of the MIT Mechanical Engineering Department." She studied 300 MIT graduates a full decade into their careers. Despite their having taken the full battery of "obscure mathematics," graduates felt that "almost no time at MIT" prepared them for the actual work they did (Wagner & Dintersmith, 2015, p. 167).

Mitzi Montoya was the dean of engineering at Arizona State University and is now dean of the Oregon State University College of Business. She told Hacker, "If you go out and look at what engineers use, it's not calculus or differential equations," even for the most sophisticated projects. So her department designed some practical, problem-based math courses that matched the work that engineers do in the real world. Unfortunately, the math department shut down the effort (Hacker, 2016, pp. 53–54).

What of other STEM professions? A panel of experts from five representative STEM careers recently reviewed what is tested in math on the National Assessment of Educational Progress (NAEP). They found that "there are hardly any test items in the pool at 12th grade that are applied" in STEM careers. It's all "theoretical stuff," according to Jeremy Kilpatrick, coauthor of the study and a mathematics education professor at University of Georgia. As the panelists told him, "This is not relevant to what we want" (Sparks, 2012). The panel's findings support the equally interesting discovery that advanced math proficiency doesn't even make the "top 10 list of the skills employers deem most important" (Wagner & Dintersmith in Hacker, 2016, p. 58). For reasons like these, Arnold Packer, a former U.S. assistant secretary of Labor, long ago called for the United States to abandon what he regards as a "failed [math] curriculum" that insists on advanced coursework but "relegates applications to an afterthought" (in Steen, 1997, pp. 138–139).

Such views no longer occupy the fringe; on the contrary, they appear to confirm Devlin's perception that there may be "massive support" among mathematicians and economists on the need to recast math education. This is not to advocate that we abandon algebra, geometry, and calculus. Rather, we should appreciably reduce the number of standards and operations we teach in these courses so that we can—for the first time—reorient math education toward problems and applications that students will encounter in life and in STEM careers.

And that will in turn require an acknowledgment that sophisticated applications of arithmetic and middle school mathematics are more integral to application and problem solving than are advanced mathematics.

Real-World Arithmetic

As Steen (2007) pointed out, life and work abound in challenging, complex problems that require "sophisticated thinking with elementary skills (for example, arithmetic, percentages, ratios)" (p. 13).

To equip students for the challenges they'll encounter in science, technology, and engineering, they need far more opportunities to apply "simple skills" as they tackle issues such as "global warming, college tuition and gas prices… data-rich topics that can also challenge them with surprising complications" (p. 13).

We sell arithmetic short. Henry Pollack was the director of the Mathematics and Statistics Research Center of AT&T Bell Labs. He also served as the chairman of the advisory board of the School Mathematics Study Group. In "Solving Problems in the Real World," he demonstrates that the predominant demands of current and future careers will require the ability to apply *basic* math—and arithmetic—to *complex* situations and problems (Steen, 1997).

For instance, career opportunities in finance are projected to be among the fastest-growing high-income occupations in the coming decade (Palmer, 2014). In their highly reputed guide to finance, *Financial Intelligence,* authors Karen Berman and Joe Knight (2013) address what keeps so many people from pursuing careers in this field: fear of math. "Well, join the club," they write:

> It might surprise you to know that, for the most part, finance involves addition and subtraction. When finance people get really fancy, they multiply and divide. … So have no fear. (p. 24)

And how about careers in medicine? Richard Kayne is a physician and dean of admissions at New York's Icahn School of Medicine at Mount Sinai. When he was shown some test items on the Medical College Admissions test, he admitted that he couldn't solve them—and saw no reason for them to be on the exam. He avers that "only arithmetic is needed in patient care" but adds that practitioners should be able to understand the statistics used in journal articles.

Professor Julia Gainsburg trains high school math teachers at California State University, Northridge. She spent several weeks observing and interviewing engineers to see what kind of math they used in their work. She too discovered that "virtually all they used was multiplication and division." This accords with what David Edwards, the University of Georgia mathematician, discovered: that the vast majority of working engineers use "only eighth-grade mathematics" (Hacker, 2016, pp. 52–53).

Marc Tucker is president of the National Center on Education and the Economy. He is aghast at the unquestioned devotion to typical school mathematics. He recommends a strong turn toward middle school math—and an end to the requirement for students to complete Algebra II to graduate. His organization demonstrated that even students who receive high grades in high school math courses are unable to apply middle school math and arithmetic to complex, real-world situations—because they spend almost all of their time in high school and college learning advanced algebraic equations and algorithms (Tucker, 2014).

At a minimum, we should agree that students need more opportunities to use arithmetic to solve real-world quantitative tasks, while using algebra-based mathematics wherever it can be usefully applied. Until we do, we will continue to inflict real damage on students and their learning.

And the Damage Done...

What is the negative effect of continuing to embrace the status quo in math education? First, there is the psychic damage. Wagner and Dintersmith (2015) write of the "soul crushing" consequences of current math education (p. 102). If this seems like overstatement, remember that failure rates are by far the highest in math; in some school districts, the rate is more than 80 percent—and that's not counting those who pass with a grade of D (Singham, 2005). And it should interest the K–12 teaching community that this is about the same as math failure rates in community colleges (Hacker, 2012). Overall, more than half of all college students receive a D or an F in college algebra (Shakerdge, 2016).

Many of us who struggled in math were made to feel that we simply weren't smart enough to attend college; our scores on college entrance exams, which give so much weight to math performance, confirmed this sense. Even if we performed well in history, English, music, or science, it was intimated that we might not be "college material" if we weren't good at math.

And what of the psychic damage to math teachers, who are seldom ready for what Harvard's David Perkins calls "that ballistic missile"—the recurring question "Why do we need to know this?" I think we underestimate the toll this takes on teachers, who don't know and have never been told how the math they teach is actually used in life or work (Hacker, 2016, p. 40; Hough, 2015).

An irony lurks at the center of this discussion: when abstraction trumps application, people receive high scores in mathematics courses but are poor at *real-world* math. I saw this in my own daughters' case; they always received high grades and scores in math but didn't know how to tackle complex real-world quantitative tasks. I had to teach them. Peter J. Denning, a world-class computer scientist and former chair of the computer science department at George Mason University, discovered that even after taking all of their algebra-based high school math courses, students did not know how to "practice mathematics." For all their coursework, they were functionally illiterate in math (Steen, 1997, p. 106).

Then there is the fact that math acts as a barrier to STEM careers. In a recent report, the Mathematical Association of America acknowledges that math is indeed "the most significant barrier" to completing a degree in both STEM and non-STEM fields (Shakerdge, 2016).

Mitzi Montoya, already mentioned, knew students who had completed exceptional science, engineering, and robotics projects in high school. They would have made outstanding engineers. But they never had the chance—because they couldn't pass college calculus. She wonders how many "incipient Edisons" we are losing because of these requirements (Hacker, 2016, p. 54). E. O. Wilson, also mentioned earlier in this chapter, is one of the world's most esteemed biologists. Like Montoya, he speculates that math requirements have unnecessarily "deprived science of an immeasurable amount of sorely needed talent" (Hacker, 2016, p. 55). Experts at Georgetown's Center on Education and the Workforce are similarly frustrated by "irrelevant job requirements that are denying entry to talented individuals who can become top performers" in STEM fields. Both individuals and the professions suffer when higher levels of "abstract mathematics are required for access to certain professions"—when such math is unnecessary "in the work of these professions" (Hacker, 2016, p. 49).

In Search of Lost Time

Ultimately, the damage is a function of lost time; because so much is devoted to computing and learning abstract operations, the most relevant skills are never learned and real-world problems are never tackled. A vivid case of this can be seen in the difference in enrollment between Advanced Placement (AP) Statistics and AP Calculus. Knowledge of statistics (properly taught) applies to innumerable real-world tasks and professional work. And yet *more students enroll in AP Calculus than in AP Statistics "by an order of magnitude"* (Wagner & Dintersmith, 2015, p. 98; emphasis added).

Something is amiss. Conrad Wolfram, one of Britain's foremost mathematicians and an astute observer of the relationship between school math and real-world numeracy (Wagner & Dintersmith, 2015, p. 94), finds it maddening that students spend the bulk of their time in high school computing complex algebraic algorithms by hand, even though this can now be done with calculators and computers. The most successful professionals do not (and usually cannot) complete these calculations. Wolfram (in Wagner & Dintersmith, 2015) makes the compelling point that when industry professionals stopped computing, productivity and profits didn't decline; they skyrocketed, as people could now apply their time and intelligence to innovation and problem solving. He recommends that we drastically reduce the time students spend computing so that they have more time to "take on harder and harder real-life problems" (Wagner & Dintersmith, 2015, pp. 94–95).

It's all about time: we will continue to deprive students of such opportunities until we reduce standards and reorient our curriculum toward application. As Lynn Steen (1992) put it, "Let's face it. For most students, the current school approach to algebra is an unmitigated disaster" (p. 258).

If Steen and the many experts cited here are *even half right,* then we are obligated to consider making serious changes to math education—now and in the future. Let me conclude with a look at possible actions that could allow us, in Conrad Wolfram's (2010) words, to "leapfrog the rest of the world" in our ability to teach and apply real-world mathematics.

Moving Forward

We should take advantage of this moment. Here are some possible ways we could move toward a more practical, meaningful math education. I'd be happy to see any combination of these efforts implemented, in whatever order makes the most sense.

• Stop requiring Algebra II for high school graduation. Very few people believe this is productive (Baker, 2013). At the very least, suspend the requirement until we have convincing evidence that it benefits students and industry.

• Carefully review math standards and curriculum from the highest-achieving countries and use these to accomplish what the Common Core failed to do: assemble *much-reduced* standards documents that are as clear and concise as those of the highest-achieving countries (Heitin, 2015; Hirsch, 2016).

• Use these much-reduced standards to

—Revise state assessments.

—Assemble and disseminate simple, minimalist, but *full-year* course curriculums—or pacing guides—that could be used or adapted by school districts to develop their own focused curriculum maps.

• Enlist national or regional entities (e.g., the U.S. Department of Education, the National Council of Teachers of Mathematics (NCTM), the U.S. Department of Commerce) to conduct a systematic study of which arithmetic and advanced mathematics are *actually needed* for employees to flourish in various professions, including STEM professions (e.g., manufacturing, medicine, science, technology, agriculture).

• Conduct similar initiatives at the state level. The Every Student Succeeds Act (ESSA) allows this and might promote healthy competition among states or consortia to demonstrate that their math curriculum and assessment system are *truly aligned with the mathematical needs of the economy.*

All of these efforts would facilitate the eventual publication of an exciting new generation of applied mathematical texts and online materials. These books would be less dominated (as Keith Devlin and others recommend) by equations and algorithms and more by authentic, engaging, math-based scenarios, tasks, and problems. This could create an explosion of interest in math and in various STEM professions.

Who knows? Such actions at the K–12 level might exert an influence on the way math is taught in college and on the disproportionate amount of weight given to math performance on college entrance exams—and admissions. For that reason, we should enjoin the college and university community as we embark on this worthy and consequential project.

I will end by reiterating that these seemingly radical changes are being called for by some of the best minds in mathematics, science, economics, and industry. If we take their advice, we could make math more practical and pleasurable than it has ever been for tens of millions of students. That's an exciting prospect.

• • •

Representative Math Learning Objectives

See also: literacy-based learning objectives in Chapter 4.

I can...

• Solve a multistep problem by using _____ (operation/algorithm/formula).

- Complete _____ problems by applying/using _____.
- Write/develop a plan/solution to _____ [in a complex/multi-step/word problem].
- Write an evaluation of three countries' health care systems, using comparative data on services and benefits, cost, mortality rates, and so forth.
- Demonstrate/model _____ by using _____.
- Create a (graph/chart/diagram) illustrating _____.
- Explain/demonstrate _____ with _____ [equations/graphs/diagrams].
- Design a home for a family of four, with 2,000 square feet, on graph paper—and explain the allotment of square footage.
- Explain why _____ makes sense in _____ [problem/situation].
- Write an argument for ____ [method/approach/solution].
- Make a model/graph to illustrate _____.
- Write an evaluation of three different representations of data [for accuracy, clarity, effectiveness].
- Create a tentative budget for _____ [a class party, operating a small business—possibly within budgetary constraints].

Conclusion: Why Wait?

The Current Opportunity: Commitment to the Best Evidence-Based Practices

The argument of this book is that the strategies and structures described in these chapters will allow virtually any school to make palpable progress toward equity and higher achievement—within one or two school years. The schools and districts described in these chapters attest to this. In each case, ordinary teachers made an extraordinary impact by turning their time and energy away from common or popular practices and toward the very best, most amply substantiated practices. In doing so, they took full advantage of the following supremely important facts about educational quality:

• *Even fairly decent, content-rich curriculum changes everything.* It accelerates students' ability to read fluently and with comprehension; it ensures consistency in what is taught to each and every child, regardless of which teacher they have; and it drastically reduces superfluous classroom activities, a reliance on worksheets, group work, and full-length movies, which now consume an inordinate portion of the time students spend in school. Common curriculum makes teachers exponentially more effective and is the central prerequisite to effective teacher collaboration. It lends coherence to the entire educational enterprise, perhaps more than any other factor.

• *Liberal amounts of fairly ordinary curriculum-embedded reading, discussion, and writing (and writing instruction) will transform the lives of students.* When students have more opportunities—far more than they currently have—to read and analyze and discuss the issues in fiction and nonfiction texts in all courses, learning in every subject improves by an order of magnitude.

• *Vastly more students will succeed—on daily, weekly, and annual assessments—the moment we begin to employ simple strategies for frequently monitoring student understanding and success during their lessons—and then reteach or adjust instruction whenever necessary (i.e., often).* Such strategies promote success on virtually any lesson and equip students to succeed on independent and project-based learning tasks. Their impact is both immediate and profound—and key to teachers' own ongoing improvement.

These are not tentative, speculative facts about education. They are, on the contrary, perhaps the most reliable, evidence-based practices we know. Because of this, we dare not postpone their deployment in schools. Every year that we do, we sacrifice millions of students on the altar of experimentation, distraction, and delay.

Bibliography

ACT, (2010). A first look at the Common Core. (Report). Iowa City, IA: ACT.

Adams, M. J. (2010/2011). Advancing our students' language and literacy: The challenge of complex tasks. *American Educator*. Retrieved from http://www.aft.org/pdfs/americaneducator/winter1011/Adams.pdf

Alberts, B. (2006–2007). Why I became a scientist. *Educational Leadership, 64*(4), 18.

Allington, R. L. (2001). *What really matters for struggling readers*. New York: Addison Wesley Longman.

Allington, R. L. (2011). What at-risk readers need. *Educational Leadership, 68*(6), 40–45.

Alter, C. (2014, Sept. 10). 10 questions with Sheryl Sandberg. *Time,* 84.

American Educator. (2010–2011). Common core curriculum: An idea whose time has come. *American Educator, 34*(4), 2.

Ancess, J. (2008). Small alone is not enough. *Educational Leadership, 65*(8), 48–49.

Anderson, J. (2012). States try to fix quirks in teacher evaluations. *The New York Times.* Retrieved from http://www.nytimes.com/2012/02/20/education/states-address-problems-with-teacher-evaluations.html

Anderson, R. C., Wilson, P. T. & Fielding, L. G. (1998). Growth in reading and how children spend their time outside of school. *Reading Research Quarterly, 2*(3), 285–303.

Archer, A. L., & Hughes, C. A. (2011). *Explicit instruction: Effective and efficient teaching*. New York: Guilford Press.

Azzam, A. (2008). Engaged and on track. *Educational Leadership, 65*(6), 93–94.

Baker, N. (2013). Wrong answer: The case against Algebra II. *Harper's Magazine.* Retrieved from https://harpers.org/archive/2013/09/wrong-answer/

Banner, J. (2009). Assessing the teaching of history. *Education Week, 28*(36), 24–25.

Barnwell, P. (2016). Students' broken moral compasses. *The Atlantic.* Retrieved from https://www.theatlantic.com/education/archive/2016/07/students-broken-moral-compasses/492866/

Bartlett, T. (2003). Why Johnny can't write, even though he went to Princeton. *Chronicle of Higher Education.* Retrieved from http://www.u.arizona.edu/~mwalker/Article030103Chronicle.htm

Barzun, J. (1991). *Begin here.* Chicago & London: University of Chicago Press.

Bauerlein, M. (2008). Online literacy is a lesser kind. *Chronicle of Higher Education.* Retrieved from http://chronicle.com/article/Online-Literacy-Is-a-Lesser/28307

Bauerlein, M. (2009). *The dumbest generation: How the digital age stupefies young Americans and jeopardizes our future.* New York: Jeremy P. Tarcher/Penguin.

Bay-Williams, J. (2016). Common Core math implementation: The good, the bad, and the ugly. *Common Core Watch*/Thomas B. Fordham Institute. Retrieved from https://edexcellence.net/articles/common-core-math-implementation-the-good-the-bad-and-the-ugly

Bennett, T. (2015). Group work for the good: Unpacking the research behind one popular classroom strategy. *American Educator.* Retrieved from http://www.aft.org/ae/spring2015/bennett

Berliner, D. (1984). The half-full glass: A review of research on teaching. In P. Hosford (Ed.), *Using what we know about teaching* (pp. 51–77). Alexandria, VA: ASCD.

Berliner, D., & Biddle, B. (1995). *The manufactured crisis: Myths, fraud, and the attack on America's public schools.* Cambridge, MA: Perseus Books.

Berliner, D. C., & Casanova, U. (1996). *Putting research to work in your school.* Thousand Oaks, CA: Corwin.

Berman, K., & Knight, J. (2013). *Financial intelligence.* Boston: Harvard Business Review Press.

Bermudez, C. (2016). We can't even write a complete sentence and here's why. *Education Post.* Retrieved from http://educationpost.org/we-cant-even-write-a-complete-sentence-and-heres-why/

Black, P., & Wiliam, D. (1998). Inside the black box. *Phi Delta Kappan, 80*(2), 139–144.

Boss, S. (2014). The Hattie effect: What's essential for effective PBL? *Edutopia.* Retrieved from https://www.edutopia.org/blog/hattie-effect-whats-essential-effective-pbl-suzie-boss

Bracey, G. (2004). Value-added assessment findings: Poor kids get poor teachers. *Phi Delta Kappan, 86*(4), 331–333.

Braselton, S., & Decker, B. C. (1994). Using graphic organizers to improve the reading of mathematics. *The Reading Teacher, 48*(3), 276–287.

Brookhart, S., & Moss, C. (2013). Leading by learning. *Phi Delta Kappan, 95(8),* 13–17.

Bryson, M., Maden, A., Mosty, L., & Schultz, S. (2010). Doing RTI right. *Educational Leadership, 68*(2). Retrieved from http://www.ascd.org/publications/educational-leadership/oct10/vol68/num02/Doing-RTI-Right.aspx

Buckingham, M. (2005). *The one thing you need to know: About great managing, great leading, and sustained individual success.* New York: Free Press.

Burns, M. (2004). Writing in math. *Educational Leadership, 62*(2), 30–33.

Burns, M. (2007). Nine ways to catch kids up. *Educational Leadership, 65*(3), 16–21.

Burnton, S. (2012). 50 stunning Olympic moments no 28: Dick Fosbury introduces 'the flop.' *The Guardian.* Retrieved from https://www.theguardian.com/sport/blog/2012/may/08/50-stunning-olympic-moments-dick-fosbury

BusinessWeek. (2000, Apr. 24). The pros and cons of globalization. Retrieved from https://www.bloomberg.com/news/articles/2000-04-24/the-pros-and-cons-of-globalization

Bybee, R., & Van Scotter, P. (2006–2007). Reinventing the science curriculum. *Educational Leadership, 64*(4), 43–47.

Campbell, A. (2015). Making failure harder work than passing. *Edutopia.* Retrieved from http://www.edutopia.org/blog/making-failure-harder-work-angela-campbell

Carmody, T. (2012). "What's wrong with education cannot be fixed with technology"— The other Steve Jobs. *Wired.* Retrieved from https://www.wired.com/2012/01/apple-education-jobs/

Cavanagh, S. (2007). What kind of math matters? Diplomas count: A report by *Education Week. Education Week, 26*(40), 21–23.

Cavazos, S. (2016). Bye-bye bubble sheets: New Hampshire's innovative approach to testing appeals to Indiana, other states. Retrieved from http://www.chalkbeat.org/posts/in/2016/05/17/bye-bye-bubble-sheets-new-hampshires-innovative-approach-to-testing-appeals-to-indiana-other-states/

Coleman, D., Pimentel, S., & Zimba, J. (2012). Three core shifts to deliver on the promise of the Common Core standards in literacy and math. *State Education Standard, 12*(2), 9–12.

Collins, J. (2001a). *Good to great.* New York: Harper Business.

Collins, J. (2001b). Good to great. *Fast Company, 51*(1), 90–104.

Collins, J. (2005). *Good to great and the social sectors.* Boulder, CO: Author.

Colvin, R., & Johnson, J. (2007). Know the game and cover the action. *Education Week, 27*(19), 36.

Common Core State Standards Initiative. (2010). English language arts standards. Retrieved from http://www.corestandards.org/ELA-Literacy/

Conley, D. (2005). *College knowledge: What it really takes for students to succeed and what we can do to get them ready*. San Francisco: Jossey-Bass.

Conley, D. (2007). The challenge of college readiness. *Educational Leadership, 64*(7), 23–29.

Cookson, P. (2009). Teaching for the 21st century. *Educational Leadership, 67*(1), 8–14.

Corcoran, T., Fuhrman, S. H., & Belcher, C. L. (2001). The district role in instructional improvement. *Phi Delta Kappan, 83*(1), 78–84.

Cunningham, P., & Allington, R. L. (2007). *Classrooms that work: They can all read and write*. Boston: Pearson.

Cushman, K. (1993). *How the national standards debate affects the essential school* [online article]. Retrieved from http://essentialschools.org/horace-issues/how-the-national-standards-debate-affects-the-essential-school/

Cushman, K. (2007). Facing the culture shock of college. *Educational Leadership, 64*(7), 44–47.

Danielson, C. (2015). Framing discussion about teaching. *Educational Leadership, 72*(7), 38–41.

Darling-Hammond, L. (2010). *The flat world of education*. New York & London: Teachers College Press.

Darling-Hammond, L. (2010–2011). Soaring systems. *American Educator, 34*(4), 20–23.

Denning, P. J. (1997). Quantitative practices. In L. Steen (Ed.), *Why numbers count* (pp. 106–117). New York: The College Board.

De Vise, D. (2006, Dec. 5). Local schools to study whether math – topics = better math education. *Washington Post,* A1.

Devlin, K. (2016). The math myth that permeates "The Math Myth" [blog post]. *Devlin's Angle*. Retrieved from http://devlinsangle.blogspot.com/2016/03/the-math-myth-that-permeates-math-myth.html

DeWitt, P. (2016a). The myth of walkthroughs: 8 unobserved practices in classrooms [blog post]. *Peter Dewitt's Finding Common Ground*. Retrieved from http://blogs.edweek.org/edweek/finding_common_ground/2016/04/the_myth_of_walkthroughs_8_unobserved_practices_in_classrooms.html

DeWitt, P. (2016b). Why ability grouping doesn't work [blog post]. *Peter DeWitt's Finding Common Ground*. Retrieved from http://blogs.edweek.org/edweek/finding_common_ground/2016/02/why_ability_grouping_doesnt_work.html

Dreilinger, D. (2013, May 25). Former Recovery School District superintendent Paul Vallas criticizes teacher evaluations. *New Orleans Times-Picayune.*

Retrieved from http://www.nola.com/education/index.ssf/2013/05/former_recovery_school_distric_1.html

DuFour, R. (2007). Clarity is the key to skillful leadership. *Journal of Staff Development, 28*(2), 69.

DuFour, R. (2015). *In praise of American educators.* Bloomington, IN: Solution Tree.

DuFour, R., DuFour, R., Eaker, R., & Many, T. (2006). *Learning by doing: A handbook for professional learning communities at work.* Bloomington, IN: Solution Tree.

DuFour, R., & Marzano, R. (2011). *Leaders and learning.* Bloomington, IN: Solution Tree.

Duke, N. (2010). R&D: The real-world reading and writing U.S. children need. *Phi Delta Kappan, 91*(5), 68–71.

Edmundson, M. (2004). *Why read?* New York: Bloomsbury.

Ehrenworth, M. (2017). Why argue? *Educational Leadership, 74*(5), 35–40.

Elmore, R. F. (2000). *Building a new structure for school leadership.* Washington, DC: The Albert Shanker Institute.

Engelmann, S., Haddox, P., & Bruner, E. (1983). *Teach your child to read in 100 easy lessons.* New York: Simon & Schuster.

Esquith, R. (2007). *Teach like your hair's on fire.* New York: Penguin Books.

FairTest Examiner. (2013). Common Core brings a new chapter of high-stakes test horrors. Retrieved from https://www.fairtest.org/Common-Core-Testing-Horror-Stories

Ferguson, R. (2016). Aiming higher together: Strategizing better educational outcomes for boys and young men of color. *Urban Institute.* Retrieved from: https://www.urban.org/research/publication/aiming-higher-together-strategizing-better-educational-outcomes-boys-and-young-men-color

Ferrandino, V. L., & Tirozzi, G. (2004). Wanted: A comprehensive literacy agenda preK–12. *Education Week, 23*(24), 29.

Finn, C. E., Jr. (2014). Is differentiated instruction a hollow promise? [blog post]. *Flypaper.* Retrieved from https://edexcellence.net/commentary/education-gadfly-daily/flypaper/is-differentiated-instruction-a-hollow-promise

Fisher, D., & Frey, N. (2007). *Checking for understanding.* Alexandria, VA: ASCD.

Fitzhugh, W. (2006). Bibliophobia. *Education Week.* Retrieved from http://www.edweek.org/ew/articles/2006/10/04/06fitzhugh.h26.html

Ford, M. P., & Opitz, M. F. (2002). Using centers to engage children during guided reading time: Intensifying learning experiences away from the teacher. *The Reading Teacher, 55*(8), 710–717.

Friedman, T. L. (2005). *The world is flat: A brief history of the 21st century*. New York: Farrar, Straus & Giroux.

Friedman, T. L. (2008). *Hot, flat and crowded*. New York: Farrar, Straus & Giroux.

Friedman, T. L., & Mandelbaum, M. (2011). *That used to be us*. New York: Farrar, Straus & Giroux.

Fuhrman, S. H., Resnick, L., & Shepard, L. (2009). Standards aren't enough. *Education Week, 9*(7), 28.

Fullan, M. (2010). *Motion leadership: The skinny on becoming change savvy*. Thousand Oaks, CA: Corwin.

Furr, J. (1996). A brief history of mathematics education in America. *University of Georgia*. Retrieved from http://jwilson.coe.uga.edu/EMAT7050/HistoryWeggener.html

Gallagher, K. (2009). *Readicide: How schools are killing reading and what you can do about it*. Portland, ME: Stenhouse Publishers.

Gallagher, K. (2017). The writing journey. *Educational Leadership, 74*(5), 24–29.

Gamerman, E. (2008, Feb. 29). What makes Finnish kids so smart? *The Wall Street Journal*. Retrieved from https://www.wsj.com/articles/SB120425355065601997

Gardner, H. (2009). Five minds for the future. *The School Administrator, 66*(2), 16–21.

Garnaut, J. (2007, May 21). Best teachers get top marks from study. *Sydney Morning Herald*. Retrieved from http://www.smh.com.au/news/national/best-teachers-get-top-marks-from-study/2007/05/20/1179601244341.html

Garner, D. (2010). Inferior national standards: English language arts. *EducationNews.org*. Retrieved from http://www.educationnews.org/commentaries/71559.html

Gatto, J. T. (2002). *Dumbing us down*. Gabriola Island, BC: New Society Publishers.

Gewertz, C. (2010a). How to move from standards to curricula? *Education Week, 29*(32), 1, 22.

Gewertz, C. (2010b). Little progress seen in student results on reading NAEP. *Education Week*. Retrieved from https://www.edweek.org/ew/articles/2010/03/31/27naep-2.h29.html?

Goldberg, M. (2001). An interview with Linda Darling-Hammond: Balanced optimism. *Phi Delta Kappan, 82*(9), 687–690.

Gomez, L. M., & Gomez, K. (2007). Reading for learning: Literacy supports for 21st century learning. *Phi Delta Kappan, 89*(3), 224–228.

Good, T. L., & Brophy, J. E. (1997). *Looking into classrooms* (7th ed.). New York: Longman.

Goodlad, J. I. (1984). *A place called school*. New York: McGraw-Hill.

Goodwin, B. (2015). *Simply better*. Alexandria, VA: ASCD; Aurora, CO: McREL.

Graff, G. (2003). *Clueless in academe*. New Haven, CT: Yale University Press.

Graff, G., & Birkenstein, C. (2007). *"They say, I say": The moves that matter in persuasive writing*. New York: W. W. Norton & Company.

Graff, G., & Birkenstein, C. (2015). *"They say, I say" with readings: High school edition*. New York: W. W. Norton & Company.

Green, E. (2014, Jul. 31). How to Build a better teacher. *Parade*, 6–9.

Greenstone, M., Patashnik, J., Looney, A., Li, K., Harris, M., & Hamilton Project. (2012). A dozen economic facts about K–12 education. *Policy Memo*. Retrieved from http://www.hamiltonproject.org/assets/legacy/files/downloads_and_links/THP_12EdFacts_2.pdf

Hacker, A. (2012, Jul 28). Is algebra necessary? *The New York Times*. Retrieved from http://www.nytimes.com/2012/07/29/opinion/sunday/is-algebra-necessary.html

Hacker A. (2016). *The math myth and other STEM delusions*. New York: New Press.

Hakim, J. (2007). *Freedom: A history of US* (3rd revised ed.). Oxford, UK: Oxford University Press.

Halberstam, D. (1993). *The fifties*. New York: Random House.

Hammond, B. (2009, Nov. 7). More Oregon students are getting math. *The Oregonian*. Retrieved from http://www.oregonlive.com/education/index.ssf/2009/11/more_oregon_students_are_getti.html

Hansel, L. (2013). The Common Core needs a common curriculum. *Education Week*. Retrieved from http://www.edweek.org/ew/articles/2013/05/22/32hansel_ep.h32.html

Hapgood, S., & Palincsar, A. S. (2006–2007). Where literacy and science intersect. *Educational Leadership, 64*(4), 56–61.

Harrop, F. (2010). Slobs and American civilization. *Projo.com*. Retrieved from https://www.realclearpolitics.com/articles/2010/02/11/slobs_and_american_civilization_100255.html

Hattie, J. (2009). *Visible learning*. New York: Routledge.

Hattie, J. (2015). High impact leadership. *Educational Leadership, 72*(5), 36–40.

Haycock, K. (2003). *Testimony of Kati Haycock, President, the Education Trust, before the U.S. House of Representatives Committee on Education and the Workforce Subcommittee on 21st Century Competitiveness*. Retrieved from https://edtrust.org/press_release/testimony-of-kati-haycock-president-the-education-trust-before-the-u-s-house-of-representatives-committee-on-education-and-the-workforce-subcommittee-on-21st-century-competitiveness/

Haycock, K. (2005). Improving academic achievement and closing gaps between groups in the middle grades [PowerPoint slides]. Retrieved from https://edtrust.org

Heitin, L. (2015). Math-modeling PD takes teachers beyond the common core. *Education Week*. Retrieved from https://www.edweek.org/ew/articles/2015/09/30/math-modeling-pd-takes-teachers-beyond-the-common.html

Heitin, L. (2016). *Cultural literacy* creator carries on campaign. *Education Week*. Retrieved from http://www.edweek.org/ew/articles/2016/10/12/cultural-literacy-creator-carries-on-campaign.html

Heitin-Loewus, L. (2016). Next Generation Science Standards group offers tips on "bundling" skills to teach [blog post]. *Education Week/Curriculum Matters*. Retrieved from http://blogs.edweek.org/edweek/curriculum/2016/08/next_generation_science_standards_bundles.html

Henig, R. M. (2009). A hospital how-to guide that Mother would love. *The New York Times*. Retrieved from http://www.nytimes.com/2009/12/24/books/24book.html

Hernandez, A., Kaplan, M. A., & Schwartz, R. (2006, October). For the sake of argument. *Educational Leadership, 64*(2), 48–52.

Hillocks, G. (1987). Synthesis of research on teaching writing. *Educational Leadership, 44*(8), 71–82.

Hirsch, E. D. (2008). An epoch-making report, but what about the early grades? *Education Week, 27*(34), 30–31, 40.

Hirsch, E. D. (2009). *The making of Americans*. New Haven, CT: Yale University Press.

Hirsch, E. D. (2010). First, do no harm. *Education Week, 29*(17), 30–31, 40.

Hirsch, E. D. (2016). *Why knowledge matters*. Cambridge, MA: Harvard Education Press.

Holm, T. (2015, Feb. 15). Teach fun side of math, not rote memorization. *Boston Globe*. Retrieved from https://www.highbeam.com/doc/1P2-37672093.html

Hough, L. (2015). What's worth learning in school? *Ed. Magazine,* 36–41 Retrieved from https://www.gse.harvard.edu/news/ed/15/01/whats-worth-learning-school

Hoven, J., & Garelick, B. (2007, November). Singapore math: Simple or complex? *Educational Leadership, 65*(3), 28–31.

Hurley, P. (2015). Communication named most sought-after skill set in corporate recruiter survey. *The Hurley Write Blog*. Retrieved from www.

hurleywrite.com/Blog/92444/Communication-Named-Most-Sought-After-Skill-Set-in-Corporate-Recruiter-Survey

Hyde, A. (2007). Mathematics and cognition. *Educational Leadership, 65*(3), 43–47.

Ivey, G., & Fisher, D. (2006). When thinking skills trump reading skills. *Educational Leadership, 64*(2), 16–21.

Jago, C. (2005). *Papers, papers, papers.* Portsmouth, NH: Heinemann.

Kalaidis, J. (2013). Bring back social studies. *The Atlantic.* Retrieved from https://www.theatlantic.com/education/archive/2013/09/bring-back-social-studies/279891/

Kalanithi, P. (2016). *When breath becomes air.* New York: Random House.

Killian, S. (2015). Top 10 evidence based strategies. *The Australian Society for Evidence Based Teaching.* Retrieved from http://www.evidencebasedteaching.org.au/evidence-based-teaching-strategies/

Killian, S. (2017). Top 10 evidence-based teaching strategies. *UNL Announce.* Retrieved from http://newsroom.unl.edu/announce/csmce/5272/29630

Kohn, A. (2010). Debunking the case for national standards. *Education Week, 29*(17), 28, 30.

Lamb, E. (2016). It doesn't add up. *Slate.* Retrieved from http://www.slate.com/articles/health_and_science/education/2016/03/andrew_hacker_s_the_math_myth_is_a_great_example_of_mathematics_illiteracy.html

Landsberg, M. (2008a, Mar. 9). In L.A., Singapore math has added value. *Los Angeles Times,* A2.

Landsberg, M. (2008b, Jun. 21). Teacher instills a love of words, but the lesson is about life. *Los Angeles Times.* Retrieved August 16, 2010, from http://beta.latimes.com/local/la-me-holmes21-2008jun21-story.html

Lasch, C. (1995). *Revolt of the elites.* New York: Norton.

Lee, J. & Wu, Y. (2017). Is the Common Core racing America to the top? Tracking changes in state standards, school practices, and student achievement. *Education Policy Archives, 25*(25). Retrieved from http://epaa.asu.edu/ojs/article/view/2834

Leinwand, S., & Ginsburg, A. L. (2007). Learning from Singapore math. *Educational Leadership, 65*(3), 32–36.

Lemov, D. (2015). *Teach like a champion 2.0.* San Francisco: Jossey-Bass.

Lemov, D. (2017). How knowledge powers reading. *Educational Leadership, 74*(5), 10–16.

Lin-Siegler, X., Ahn, J. N., Chen, J., Fang, F.-F. A., & Luna-Lucero, M. (2016). Even Einstein struggled: Effects of learning about great scientists' struggles on high school students' motivation to learn science. *Journal of Educational Psychology, 108*(3), 314–328. Retrieved from https://www.apa.org/pubs/journals/releases/edu-edu0000092.pdf

Lipson, M. Y., & Wixson, K. K. (2008). New IRA commission will address RTI issues. *Reading Today, 26*(1), 1, 5.

Loewen, J. (1995). *Lies my teacher told me.* New York: Touchstone.

Loewus, L. (2017). Next-generation science tests slowly take shape. *Education Week.* Retrieved from http://www.edweek.org/ew/articles/2017/05/24/next-generation-science-tests-slowly-take-shape.html

Lunsford, A. A., & Ruszkiewicz, J. J. (2009). *Everything's an argument.* New York: Bedford St. Martin's.

Maranto, R., Ritter, G., & Levine, A. (2010). The future of ed. schools. *Education Week, 29*(16), 25, 36.

Markowicz, K. (2017, Jan. 21). Why schools have stopped teaching American history. *New York Post.* Retrieved from http://nypost.com/2017/01/22/why-schools-have-stopped-teaching-american-history/

Marshall, K. (2003). A principal looks back: Standards matter. *Phi Delta Kappan, 85*(2), 105–113.

Marshall, T. (2015). *Prisoners of geography.* New York: Scribner.

Marshall Memo (2017). #700 [online newsletter]. Retrieved from https://marshallmemo.com

Marzano, R. J. (2003). *What works in schools: Translating research into action.* Alexandria, VA: ASCD.

Marzano, R. J. (2007). *The art and science of teaching.* Alexandria, VA: ASCD.

Marzano, R. (2009). Helping students process information. *Educational Leadership, 67*(2), 86–87.

Marzano, R. J. (2011a). Objectives that students understand. *Educational Leadership, 68*(8), 86–87.

Marzano, R. J. (2011b). The perils and promises of discovery learning. *Educational Leadership, 69*(1), 86–87.

Marzano, R., & Kendall, J. S. (1998). *Awash in a sea of standards.* Denver, CO: McREL.

Marzano, R. J., Kendall, J. S., & Gaddy, B. B. (1999). *Essential knowledge: The debate over what American students should know.* Parker, CO: McREL.

Marzano, R. J., Pickering, D. J., & Pollock, J. E. (2001). *Classroom instruction that works.* Alexandria, VA: ASCD.

Mathews, J. (2010, Feb. 21). Help pick non-fiction for schools. *The Washington Post.* Retrieved from http://voices.washingtonpost.com/class-struggle/2010/02/help_pick_non-fiction_for_scho.html

Mazur, E. (1997). *Peer instruction: A user's manual.* Upper Saddle River, NJ: Prentice-Hall.

McConachie, S., Hall, M., Resnick, L., Ravi, A. K., Bill, V. L., Bintz, J., et al. (2006, October). Task, text, and talk. *Educational Leadership, 64*(2), 8–14.

McDowell, M. (2017). *Rigorous PBL by design*. Thousand Oaks, CA: Corwin.

McKeown, M. G., Beck, I. L., & Blake, R. K. (2009). Rethinking reading comprehension instruction: A comparison of instruction for strategies and content approaches. *Reading Research Quarterly, 44*(3), 218–253.

Meier, D. (2010). Are national standards the right move? *Educational Leadership, 67*(7), 23.

Mortimore, P., & Sammons, P. (1987). New evidence on effective elementary schools. *Educational Leadership, 45*(1), 4–8.

Munson, L. (2011). What students *really* need to learn. *Educational Leadership, 68*(6), 10–14.

National Commission on Writing. (2003). *The neglected "r": The need for a writing revolution*. New York: The College Board.

Ness, M. (2007). Reading comprehension strategies in secondary content-area classrooms. *Phi Delta Kappan, 89*(3), 229–231.

Next Generation Science Standards. (2018). Retrieved from https://www.nextgenscience.org/standards/standards

Nuzzo, R. (2005). Profile of Bruce Alberts: The education president. *Proceedings of the National Academy of Sciences, 102*(26), 1. Retrieved from http://www.pnas.org/content/102/26/9109.full

Oakes, J. (1992). Can tracking research inform practice? *Educational Researcher, 21*(4), 12.

Odden, A. (2009). We know how to turn schools around—We just haven't done it. *Education Week, 29*(14), 22–23.

Odden, A., & Wallace, M. J. (2003). Leveraging teacher pay. *Education Week, 22*(43), 64.

Ohio State University. (2008). Students who use "clickers" score better on physics tests. *ScienceDaily*. Retrieved from http://www.sciencedaily.com/releases/2008/07/080717092033.htm

Olson, L. (2008). Skills for work, college readiness are found comparable. *Education Week, 25*(36), 1, 19.

Packer, A. (1997). Mathematical competencies that employers expect. In L. Steen (Ed.), *Why numbers count* (pp. 137–154). New York: The College Board.

Packer, A. (2007). Know what the real goals are. *Education Week*. Retrieved from http://www.edweek.org/ew/articles/2007/11/07/11packer.h27.html

Palmer, K. (2014). Why finance jobs are growing fast. *U.S. News and World Report*. Retrieved from http://money.usnews.com/money/blogs/alpha-consumer/2014/02/05/why-finance-jobs-are-growing-fast

Paulson, A. (2014). Report: Students read way below level that prepares them for college, careers. *The Christian Science Monitor*. Retrieved from https://www.

csmonitor.com/USA/Education/2014/1118/Report-Students-read-way-below-level-that-prepares-them-for-college-careers

Pearson, P. D., & Hiebert, E. H. (2010). National reports in literacy: Building a scientific base for practices and policy. *Educational Researcher, 39*(4), 286–294.

Perkins-Gough, D. (2006–2007). The status of the science lab. *Educational Leadership, 64*(4), 93–94.

Petrilli, M. J. (2015). The new ESEA will be "loose-loose" because Arne Duncan went overboard with "tight-tight" [blog post]. *Flypaper*. Retrieved from https://edexcellence.net/articles/the-new-esea-will-be-%E2%80%-9Cloose-loose%E2%80%9D-because-arne-duncan-went-overboard-with-%E2%80%9Ctight-tight%E2%80%9D

Petrilli, M. (2016). College readiness versus college completion: Variation by race [blog post]. *Edexcellence.net*. Retrieved from https://edexcellence.net/articles/college-readiness-versus-college-completion-variations-by-race

Pfeffer, P., & Sutton, R. (2000). *The knowing-doing gap*. Boston: Harvard Business School Press.

Phillips, V., & Wong, C. (2010). Tying together the common core of standards, instruction, and assessments. *Phi Delta Kappan, 91*(5), 37–42.

Pianta, R., Belsky, J., Houts, R., & Morrison, F. (2007). Teaching: Opportunities to learn in America's elementary classrooms. *Science, 315*(5820), 1795–1796.

Podhoretz, N. (1967). *Making it.* New York: Harper Colophon.

Pollack, H. (1997). Solving problems in the real world. In L. Steen (Ed.), *Why numbers count* (pp. 91–105). New York: The College Board.

Pondiscio, R. (2014a). A missed opportunity for Common Core. *Common Core Watch*. Retrieved from https://edexcellence.net/articles/a-missed-opportunity-for-common-core

Pondiscio, R. (2014b). It pays to increase your word power. *Education Gadfly, 14*(50). Retrieved from https://edexcellence.net/articles/it-pays-to-increase-your-word-power

Popham, W. J. (2008). *Transformative assessment*. Alexandria, VA: ASCD.

Pulakos, E. D., Mueller-Hanson, R. A., O'Leary, R. S., & Meyrowitz, M. M. (2012). *Building a high-performance culture: A fresh look at performance management*. Alexandria, VA: Society for Human Resource Management.

Ravitch, D. (2010). We've always had national standards. *Education Week, 29*(17), 28, 30.

Ravitch, D. (2013). Robert D. Shepherd: Beware the social engineer and his abstractions. Retrieved from http://dianeravitch.net/2013/06/12/robert-d-shepherd-beware-the-social-engineer-and-his-abstractions

Reeves, D. B. (2008). *Reframing teacher leadership to improve your school.* Alexandria, VA: ASCD.

Reisman, A. (2017). How to facilitate discussions in history. *Educational Leadership, 74*(5), 30–34.

Ripley, A. (2010). What makes a great teacher? *The Atlantic.* Retrieved from http://www.theatlantic.com/magazine/archive/2010/01/what-makes-a-great-teacher/7841/

Ripley, A. (2013). *The smartest kids in the world.* New York: Simon & Schuster.

Rose, M. (1989). *Lives on the boundary.* New York: Viking Penguin.

Roseman, J. E., Linn, M.C., & Koppal, M. (2008). Characterizing curriculum coherence. In Y. Kali, M.C. Linn, & J. E. Roseman (Eds.), *Designing coherent science education* (pp. 13–36). New York: Teachers College Press.

Rosenholtz, S. J. (1991). *Teacher's workplace: The social organization of schools.* New York: Teachers College Press.

Rosenshine, B. (2012). Principles of instruction: Research-based strategies that all teachers should know. *American Educator, 36*(1), 12–19, 39.

Roth, K., & Garnier, H. (2006–2007). What science teaching looks like: An international perspective. *Educational Leadership, 64*(4), 16–23.

Rotherham, A. J. (2008). 21st-century skills are not a new education trend but could be a fad. *U.S. News and World Report.* Retrieved from http://politics.usnews.com/opinion/articles/2008/12/15/21st-century-skills-are-not-a-new-education-trend-but-could-be-a-fad.html

Sahm, C. (2017). Why curriculum counts [blog post]. *Flypaper.* Retrieved from https://edexcellence.net/articles/why-curriculum-counts

Sanders, W. L., & Horn, S. P. (1994). The Tennessee value-added assessment system. *Journal of Personnel Evaluation in Education, 8*(3), 299–311.

Sawchuk, S. (2015). Study casts doubt on impact of teacher professional development. *Education Week.* Retrieved from http://www.edweek.org/ew/articles/2015/08/19/study-casts-doubt-on-impact-of-teacher.html

Schmidt, W. H. (2008). What's missing from math standards? Focus, rigor, and coherence. *American Educator, 32*(1), 22–24.

Schmoker, M. (2001). *The results fieldbook: Practical strategies from dramatically improved schools.* Alexandria, VA: ASCD.

Schmoker, M. (2006). *Results now: How we can achieve unprecedented improvements in teaching and learning.* Alexandria, VA: ASCD.

Schmoker, M. (2008–2009). Measuring what matters. *Educational Leadership, 66*(4), 70–74.

Schmoker, M. (2009). Do we really need a longer school year? *Education Week.* Retrieved from http://www.edweek.org/ew/articles/2009/07/07/36schmoker.h28.html

Schmoker, M. (2010). When pedagogic fads trump priorities. *Education Week.* Retrieved from http://www.edweek.org/ew/articles/2010/09/29/05schmoker.h30.html

Schmoker, M. (2016). *Leading with focus.* Alexandria, VA: ASCD.

Schmoker, M., & Graff, G. (2011). More argument, fewer standards. *Education Week.* Retrieved from http://www.edweek.org/ew/articles/2011/04/20/28schmoker.h30.html

Schmoker, M., & Jago, C. (2013). Simplifying the Common Core; demystifying curriculum. *Kappa Delta Pi Record, 49*(2).

Schmoker, M. & Marzano, R. (1999). Realizing the promise of standards-based education. *Educational Leadership, 56*(6), 17–21.

Schweikart, L., & Allen, M. (2014). *A patriot's history of the United States.* New York: Sentinel.

Shakerdge, K. (2016). High failure rates spur universities to overhaul math class. *Hechinger Report.* Retrieved from http://hechingerreport.org/high-failure-rates-spur-universities-to-overhaul-math-class/

Shanahan, T. (2011). Common Core standards versus guided reading, Part II [blog post]. *Shanahan on literacy.* Retrieved from http://shanahanonliteracy.com/blog/common-core-standards-versus-guided-reading-part-ii

Shanahan, T. (2014). How and how not to prepare students for the new tests. *The Reading Teacher, 68*(3), 184–188. Retrieved from https://www.scribd.com/document/265954704/How-and-How-Not-to-Prepare-Students-for-the-New-Tests-Shanahan-T

Shanahan, T., & Duffett, A. (2013). *Common Core in the schools: A first look at reading assignments.* Washington, DC: Thomas B. Fordham Institute. Retrieved from http://edexcellencemedia.net/publications/2013/20131023-Common-Core-in-the-Schools-a-First-Look-at-Reading-Assignments/20131023-Common-Core-in-the-Schools-a-First-Look-at-Reading-Assignments-FINAL.pdf

Shanahan, T., & Shanahan, C. (2008). Teaching disciplinary literacy to adolescents: Rethinking content-area literacy. *Harvard Educational Review, 78*(1), 40–59.

Shanahan, T., & Shanahan, C. (2017). Disciplinary literacy: Just the FAQs. *Educational Leadership, 74*(5), 18–22.

Silva, E. (2008). Measuring skills for the 21st century. *Education Sector.* Retrieved from http://elenamsilva.com/wp-content/uploads/2013/05/MeasuringSkills.pdf

Silver, H. F., Strong, R. W., & Perini, M. J. (2007). *The strategic teacher: Selecting the right research-based strategy for every lesson.* Alexandria, VA: ASCD.

Singham, M. (2005). *The achievement gap in U.S. education.* Lanham, MD: Rowman & Littlefield.

Sizer, T. (1992). *Horace's school*. Boston: Houghton-Mifflin.

Smith, F. (2006). *Reading without nonsense*. New York: Teachers College Press.

Sparks, D. (1998). Making assessment part of teacher learning. *Journal of Staff Development, 19*(4), 33–35.

Sparks, S. (2011). RTI: More popular than proven? *Education Week, 30*(22), S16.

Sparks, S. (2012). Can NAEP predict college readiness? *Education Week*. Retrieved from http://www.edweek.org/ew/articles/2012/09/12/03nagb. h32.html

Sparks, S. (2014). Word problems should be given at the start of lesson, studies say. *Education Week*, 3, 2014; 10–11, 13, 34.

Sparks, S. (2015). RTI practice falls short of promise, research finds. *Education Week, 35*(12), 1, 12.

Steen, L. A. (1992). Does everybody need to study algebra? *Mathematics Teacher, 85*(4), 258–260.

Steen, L. A. (1997). *Why numbers count*. New York: The College Board.

Steen, L. A. (2007). How mathematics counts. *Educational Leadership, 65*(3), 8–15.

Stiggins, R. (1994). *Student-centered classroom assessment*. New York: Merrill.

Stiggins, R. (2006). Assessment crisis: The absence of assessment *FOR* learning. *Phi Delta Kappan*. Retrieved from http://www.electronicportfolios. org/afl/Stiggins-AssessmentCrisis.pdf

Stiggins, R. (2017). *The perfect assessment system*. Alexandria, VA: ASCD.

Stigler, J. W., & Hiebert, J. (1999). *The teaching gap*. New York: Free Press.

St. Jarre, K. (2008). Reinventing social studies. *Phi Delta Kappan, 89*(9), 649–652.

Stoltzfus, K. (2017). Joyful schools: What one U.S. educator learned from teaching in Finland. *Education Week Teacher*. Retrieved from http://blogs. edweek.org/teachers/teaching_now/2017/04/joyful_schools_what_one_ us_educator_learned_from_teaching_in_finland.html

Stotsky, S. (1999). *Losing our language: How multicultural classroom instruction is undermining our children's ability to read, write and reason*. New York: Free Press.

Stuart, D. (2017). Quantity, then quality [blog post]. *Dave Stuart Jr.* Retrieved from http://www.davestuartjr.com/quantity-then-quality/

TNTP. (2009). *The widget effect*. New York: TNTP. Retrieved from https://tntp. org/publications/view/the-widget-effect-failure-to-act-on-differences-in-teacher-effectiveness

TNTP. (2013). *Fixing classroom observations*. New York: TNTP. Retrieved from https://tntp.org/publications/view/fixing-classroom-observations-how-common-core-will-change-teaching

Tomlinson, C. A. (1999). *The differentiated classroom.* Alexandria, VA: ASCD.

Traub, J. (1998). Multiple intelligence disorder. *The New Republic, 4*(371), 20–23.

Trefil, J. (2008). *Why science?* New York: Teachers College Press.

Tucker, M. (2014). Double take: What must they master—Really? *Educational Leadership, 71*(4), 8.

Tucker, M. (2017). Our students can't write very well—It's no mystery why [blog post]. *Education Week.* Retrieved from http://blogs.edweek.org/edweek/top_performers/2017/01/our_students_cant_write_very_wellits_no_mystery_why.html

Tyack, D., & Cuban, L. (2003). *Tinkering toward utopia.* Cambridge, MA: Harvard University Press.

Tyre, P. (2012). The writing revolution. *The Atlantic.* Retrieved from https://www.theatlantic.com/magazine/archive/2012/10/the-writing-revolution/309090/

University of Southern California Rossier School of Education. (2011). View Park Preparatory Accelerated Charter High School: Argumentative writing across the curriculum. *Center on Educational Governance.* Retrieved from http://www.uscrossier.org/ceg/products-and-services/promising-practices-compendium/education-programs-of-charter-schools/view-park-preparatory-accelerated-charter-high-school-argumentativewriting-across-the-curriculum/

Vanderheyden, A., Burns, M., Brown, R., & Tilley, D. (2016). RTI works (when it is implemented correctly). *Education Week, 35*(15), 25.

Varlas, L. (2016). Syllabus-ted: Preparing students for the rigors of college reading. *Education Update, 58*(7).

Vassilaros, D. (2008, Oct. 10). Columbus was a hero. *Pittsburgh Tribune-Review.* Retrieved from http://triblive.com/x/pittsburghtrib/opinion/columnists/vassilaros/s_592550.html

Wagner, T. (2008). Teaching and testing the skills that matter most. *Education Week, 28*(12), 30.

Wagner, T., & Dintersmith, T. (2015). *Most likely to succeed.* New York: Scribner.

Walker, T. (2014). The testing obsession and the disappearing curriculum. *NEA Today.* Retrieved from http://neatoday.org/2014/09/02/the-testing-obsession-and-the-disappearing-curriculum-2/

Watanabe, T., & Xia, R. (2017, Jul. 17). Drop algebra requirement for non-STEM majors, California community colleges chief says. *Los Angeles Times.* Retrieved from http://www.latimes.com/local/lanow/la-me-california-community-colleges-algebra-20170717-story.html

Wattenberg, R. (2016). A knowledge-rich curriculum is the best prep for Common Core reading tests. *Education Gadfly*. Retrieved from https://edexcellence.net/articles/a-knowledge-rich-curriculum-is-the-best-prep-for-common-core-reading-tests

Wenglinsky, H. (2004). Facts or critical thinking skills? What NAEP results say. *Educational Leadership, 62*(1), 32–35.

Wenglinsky, H., & Silverstein, S. C. (2006–2007). The science training teachers need. *Educational Leadership, 64*(4), 24–29.

Wheeler, G. F. (2006–2007). Strategies for science education reform. *Educational Leadership, 64*(4), 30–34.

Whitney, A. K. (2016). Debunking the myths behind "the math myth." *The Atlantic*. Retrieved from https://www.theatlantic.com/education/archive/2016/06/the-math-myth/485852/

Wiener, R., & Pimentel, S. (2017). Practice what you teach. *The Aspen Institute*. Retrieved from http://www.aspendrl.org/portal/browse/DocumentDetail?documentId=2969

Wiggins, G. (1998). *Educative assessment.* San Francisco: Jossey-Bass.

Wiggins, G. (2013). Mandating the mere posting of learning objectives, and other pointless ideas [blog post]. *Granted, and...* Retrieved from https://grantwiggins.wordpress.com/2013/12/05/mandating-the-daily-posting-of-objectives-and-other-dumb-ideas/

Wiliam, D. (2007). Content then process: Teacher learning communities in the service of formative assessment. In D. Reeves (Ed.), *Ahead of the curve: The power of assessment to transform teaching and learning* (pp. 182–204). Bloomington, IN: Solution Tree.

Will, M. (2016). Common Core poses logistical challenges in writing instruction. *Education Week, 35*(36), 6.

Willingham, D. T. (2005). Ask the cognitive scientist: Do visual, auditory, and kinesthetic learners need visual, auditory, and kinesthetic instruction? *American Educator*. Retrieved from https://www.aft.org/ae/summer2005/willingham

Willingham, D. (2008). Education for the 21st century: Balancing content knowledge with skills. *Encyclopedia Britannica Blog*. Retrieved from http://blogs.britannica.com/2008/12/schooling-for-the-21st-century-balancing-content-knowledge-with-skills

Willingham, D. (2009a). *Why don't students like school?* San Francisco: Jossey-Bass.

Willingham, D. (2009b, Sep. 28). Willingham: Reading is not a skill—And why this is a problem for the draft national standards. *Washington Post*. Retrieved from http://voices.washingtonpost.com/answer-sheet/daniel-willingham/willingham-reading-is-not-a-sk.html

Wineburg, S. (2001). *Historical thinking and other unnatural acts*. Philadelphia: Temple University Press.

Wineburg, S. (2013). Steering clear of the textbook. *Education Week, 33*(14), 36.

Wineburg, S., & Martin, D. (2004). Reading and rewriting history. *Educational Leadership, 62*(1), 42–45.

Wineburg, S., & McGrew, S. (2016). Why students can't Google their way to the truth. *Education Week*. Retrieved from http://www.edweek.org/ew/articles/2016/11/02/why-students-cant-google-their-way-to.html

Wolfram, C. (2010). Teaching kids real math with computers. *TED*. Retrieved from https://www.ted.com/talks/conrad_wolfram_teaching_kids_real_math_with_computers/transcript

Wolk, R. (2010). Education: The case for making it personal. *Educational Leadership, 67*(7), 16–21.

Wu, J. (2010). Grade 3 students lagging on reading. *Boston.com*. Retrieved from http://archive.boston.com/news/education/k_12/mcas/articles/2010/06/10/grade_3_students_lagging_on_reading/

Xia, R., & Watanabe, T. (2017, Jun. 30). The politics of math: Is algebra necessary to obtain a college degree? *Los Angeles Times*. Retrieved from http://www.latimes.com/local/education/la-me-intermediate-algebra-qa-20170630-htmlstory.html

Zinn, H. (2003). *A people's history of the United States*. New York: Harper Perennial Modern Classics.

Zinn, H. (2007/2009). *A young people's history of the United States* (R. Stefoff, Adapt.). New York: Seven Stories Press.

Zmach, C. C., Sanders, J., Patrick, J. D., Dedeoglu, H., Charbonnet, S., Henkel, M., et al. (2006–2007). Infusing reading into science learning. *Educational Leadership, 64*(4), 62–66.

Zollman, A. (2009). Students use graphic organizers to improve mathematical problem-solving communications. *Middle School Journal, 41*(2), 4–12.

Index

About the Author

 **Mike Schmoker, Ed.D**, is a former teacher, administrator, and coach. He is the author of several best-selling books, one of which was a finalist for "book of the year" by the Association of Education Publishers. He has authored dozens of articles for educational journals, newspapers, and *TIME* magazine. In an *Education Week* survey of national educational leaders, he was identified as among the best sources of practical "nuts and bolts... advice, wisdom and insight" on effective school improvement strategies. Dr. Schmoker is a recipient of the Distinguished Service Award by the National Association of Secondary School Principals for his publications and presentations. As a much sought-after presenter, Dr. Schmoker delivers keynotes and consults internationally including throughout the United States, Canada, Australia, China, and Jordan.

He now lives in Tempe, Arizona, with his wife Cheryl, and can be reached at schmoker@futureone.com or 480-219-4673.

Related ASCD Resources

At the time of publication, the following resources were available (ASCD stock numbers appear in parentheses):

Print Products

Leading with Focus: Elevating the Essentials for School and District Improvement by Mike Schmoker (#116024)

Results Now: How We Can Achieve Unprecedented Improvements in Teaching and Learning by Mike Schmoker (#106045)

Analytic Processes for School Leadership by Cynthia T. Richetti and Benjamin B. Tregoe (#101017)

Align the Design: A Blueprint for School Improvement by Nancy Mooney and Ann Mausbach (#118005)

The Art of School Leadership by Thomas R. Hoerr (#105037)

Balanced Leadership for Powerful Learning: Tools for Achieving Success in Your School by Bryan Goodwin and Greg Cameron, with Heather Hein (#112025)

Building Leadership Capacity in Schools by Linda Lambert (#198058)

Five Levers to Improve Learning: How to Prioritize for Powerful Results in Your School by Tony Frontier and James Rickabaugh (#114002)

Improving Student Learning One Principal at a Time by Jane E. Pollock and Sharon M. Ford (#109006)

For up-to-date information about ASCD resources, go to www.ascd.org. You can search the complete archives of *Educational Leadership* at www.ascd.org/el.

ASCD myTeachSource®

Download resources from a professional learning platform with hundreds of research-based best practices and tools for your classroom at http://myteachsource.ascd.org/.

For more information, send an e-mail to member@ascd.org; call 1-800-933-2723 or 703-578-9600; send a fax to 703-575-5400; or write to Information Services, ASCD, 1703 N. Beauregard St., Alexandria, VA 22311-1714 USA.